MEDIEVAL PERSIA 1040–1797

A History of the Near East
General Editor: Professor P. M. Holt

★ The Prophet and the Age of the Caliphates: the Islamic Near East from the sixth to the eleventh century
Hugh Kennedy

★ The Age of the Crusades: the Near East from the eleventh century to 1517
P. M. Holt

The Rise of the Ottoman Empire 1300–1574
C. Kafadar

The Decline of the Ottoman Empire 1574–1792
R. C. Repp and G. Piterberg

★ The Making of the Modern Near East 1792–1923
M. E. Yapp

★ The Near East since the First World War: A History to 1995
Second Edition
M. E. Yapp

★ Medieval Persia 1040–1797
David Morgan

★ *Already published*

Medieval Persia 1040–1797

David Morgan

Longman
London and New York

Addison Wesley Longman Limited
Edinburgh Gate,
Harlow, Essex CM20 2JE, England
and Associated Companies throughout the world.

Published in the United States of America
by Addison Wesley Longman, New York

First published 1988
Sixth impression 1998

British Library Cataloguing in Publication Data
Morgan, David, 1945 Apr. 29–
Medieval Persia 1040-1797. – (A History of the Near East).
1. Iran–History–Medieval and modern, 640-
I. Title II. Series
955 DS288

ISBN 0-582-49324-2 PPR
ISBN 0-582-01483-2 CSD

Library of Congress Cataloging-in-Publication Data
Morgan, David, 1945–
Medieval Persia, 1040–1797.

(A History of the Near East)
Bibliography: p.
Includes index.
1. Iran–History–640–1500. 2. Iran–History–16th-18th centuries. I. Title. II. Series.
DS288.M67 1988 955′.02 87-3763
ISBN 0-582-01483-2
ISBN 0-582-49324-2 (pbk.)

Set in 10/12pt Linotron 202 Bembo
Produced by Addison Wesley Longman Singapore Pte Ltd
Printed in Singapore

Contents

List of Genealogical Tables and Map

Note on Dates

The Muslim era opens with the *Hijra* (sometimes spelt Hegira), i.e. the Flight or Emigration of the Prophet Muḥammad from Mecca to Medina in AD 622. Muslim years are therefore indicated by the abbreviation AH (*Anno Hegirae*). The Muslim year consists of twelve lunar months and is therefore approximately eleven days shorter than the solar year of the Western (Julian or Gregorian) calendar. To find the Western (AD) equivalent to Muslim (AH) dates and vice versa, conversion tables are necessary. A useful compendium is G. S. P. Freeman-Grenville, *The Muslim and Christian Calendars*, London 1963. It should be noted that the Muslim day begins at sunset and thus straddles part of two Western days.

Other peoples who appear in this book had their own ways of calculating the date: e.g. the Mongols used a twelve-year cycle (borrowed from the Chinese) in which each year was named after an animal. Hence if we are told that Chingiz Khān was born in the Year of the Pig, this may refer either to AD 1155 or to AD 1167. In this book dates are usually given in both AH and AD forms, in that order, e.g. 656/1258. In some cases the AH date is inappropriate, and a single date is always an AD one. To avoid unnecessary clumsiness, decades (e.g. "the 1250s") and centuries (e.g. "the thirteenth century") are given only in AD form.

Preface

This book is designed to offer the reader a straightforward account of the history of Persia from the arrival of the Saljūq Turks in the eleventh century AD to the rise of the Qājār dynasty at the end of the eighteenth. Much of the history of Persia in early Islamic times, before the Saljūq conquest, is dealt with in Hugh Kennedy's volume in this series, *The Prophet and the Age of the Caliphates*, and the Qājār period and after form part of the brief of Malcolm Yapp's two volumes. But the intervening seven centuries constitute a gap which demands to be filled. This is a negative reason for the writing of *Medieval Persia*: but there is also a positive one. As a discrete unit of historical study, Persia in the early Islamic period makes little sense: it has to be considered as an integral part of the Muslim world. This is in some degree always true, but from Saljūq times it becomes more feasible to treat Persian history, if not by any means in isolation, at least as a legitimate sub-division of Middle Eastern history.

So much for political geography. There is also the question of periodization. All historical periodization is to a greater or lesser extent arbitrary. But it is nevertheless essential, and I shall argue that these seven centuries may appropriately be termed 'medieval', and that they possess, in a real sense, a unity which more than justifies their treatment in a single book. It is for the reader to judge whether or not I have made out a plausible case. I thought it unwise, however, to begin with the Saljūqs without at least sketching in the historical background to eleventh-century Persia. Hence the book commences, in Chapter 2, with a bird's-eye view – unavoidably that of a bird flying rather high and fast – of Persian history between the third and the eleventh centuries. I hope that this will prove helpful rather than confusing.

I have been fortunate in having access in advance of publication to three important works: the late J. F. Fletcher's 'Western Turkestan: the emergence of the Uzbeks', forthcoming in the *Cambridge History of Inner Asia*; A. K. S. Lambton's *Continuity and Change in Medieval Persia: Aspects of Administrative, Economic and Social History, 11th–14th Century*; and B. F. Manz's *The Rise and Rule of Tamerlane*. My indebtedness to these studies will be readily apparent to any who are able, in due course, to read them for themselves.

I am grateful to Professor P. M. Holt for his invitation to write this book, for his constant encouragement, and for his comments on the final draft. The whole of the penultimate draft was read and commented on by Professor A. K. S. Lambton and Mr A. H. Morton. Professors Holt and Lambton each corrected a set of proofs. Dr K. S. McLachlan gave me an expert geographer's view of Chapter 1, and Dr G. R. Hawting criticized, indeed demolished, an early draft of Chapter 2. To all these friends I offer my warm thanks. My debt to them is very great, and if I have not invariably taken their advice, the responsibility, as for all remaining errors, is mine.

DAVID MORGAN
January 1987

CHAPTER ONE

The Land and Peoples of Persia

The boundaries of the Persian state, although they have contracted very markedly – especially in the north-west and the east as a result of nineteenth-century Russian expansion and the emergence of Afghanistan as a political entity distinct from its neighbours – are essentially those established by the Ṣafawid shāhs in the sixteenth and seventeenth centuries AD. Historically, and certainly during the period covered by this book, the Persian cultural and even political sphere was much wider than the present national boundaries. We shall be concerned with lands that are now part of Turkey, Iraq, the Soviet Union and Afghanistan as well as with Persia proper.

The official name of the country is Iran, and in 1934 Reza Shah Pahlavi decreed that even foreigners should use that name when referring to his country. The term "Persia" derives from an ancient Hellenized form, Persis, of the name of one province in the south-west of the country. That province, Parsa, was the cradle of two of the greatest Persian dynasties, the Achaemenians (6th–4th centuries BC) and the Sasanians (3rd–7th centuries AD). After the Arab conquest in the seventh century AD the province became known, as it still is, as Fārs (for there is no "P" in the Arabic alphabet: the Persians had to invent a new letter when they adapted the Arabic script for the writing of their language). The major language of Persia is Fārsī, Persian: in linguistic terminology "Iranian" refers to a large family of languages of which Persian is only one, though by far the most widely spoken.

When the English talk about Persia, or the French about la Perse, then, they are – usually unconsciously, no doubt – using a Greek term for one Persian province, in much the same way as a form of the Latin provincial name Germania is used for the whole country of Deutschland. On this analogy there seems no strong reason why "Persia" should be replaced by "Iran", any more than the Persians ought to feel obliged to give up calling the United Kingdom "Englestan".

Persian itself is the official language of the country and the natural first language of perhaps two-thirds of the population. Structurally it is classified as Indo-European: it is quite different from Arabic, a Semitic language, even though it is written in the same script – with the addition of some extra letters – and has absorbed a large amount of Arabic vocabulary. In terms of language types, Persian is nearer to English than to Arabic, and English speakers generally find it easier to learn than the other major Middle Eastern languages. This is true at least in the early stages and after the initial barrier presented by the Arabic script has been surmounted. It is perhaps only after a few years' experience that the student realizes that the language is a good deal more difficult than it seemed at first.

Persian is not exclusive to Persia. A form of it, called Tājīk, is the official language of the Soviet Central Asian republic of Tajikistan, and the traveller in the neighbouring Turkish-speaking republic of Uzbekistan will find it useful, especially in the ancient city of Bukhārā. It is the most widely spoken language in Afghanistan, where it is known as Darī, though the official first language is Pashto, also a member of the Iranian family. It was for some centuries the language of the court and the administration in northern India.

Persian is a mellifluous language, heard at its best – if not its most readily comprehensible – in the recitation of poetry of which, at any rate until recent years, many Persians could without notice reproduce large quantities – a facility which has suffered as literacy has advanced. Edward Gibbon, who did not know the language but was evidently well informed, characterized it as "a smooth and elegant idiom, recommended by Mahomet to the use of paradise though it is branded with the epithets of savage and unmusical by the ignorance and presumption of Agathias" (a sixth-century Byzantine scholar and poet).[1] After the Arab conquest Sasanian Persian (Pahlavī) was replaced by Arabic as a written language, though it continued in oral use and eventually emerged as what is called New Persian (see Chapter 2), taking its place as the second literary language of Islam. It has since then shown a remarkable stability: the Persian of the tenth century AD presents no greater problem to a modern Persian than Shakespeare does to an Englishman of today.

The emergence of New Persian did not at all mean that Arabic disappeared from Persia. It retained, and retains, its prestige as the medium of writing on matters Islamic, for it was regarded (being the language of the Qur'ān) as the language of God: hence it was only fitting that those who wished to write on theology or (religious) law should use the same tongue. Even historical writing long continued, in the main, to be in Arabic: it was not until the thirteenth century that the bulk of our historical sources came to be written in Persian, though the language began to be used in state documents in the Ghaznawid period. The final dominance of Persian as a medium for historical writing coincided with the Mongol occupation of Persia, and the coincidence is unlikely to have been accidental. For the Mongols, pagans from the east, Arabic had no special status: indeed, it would have been incomprehensible to them whereas Persian, in time, became something of a lingua franca throughout the Mongols' Asiatic empire.

Mongolian itself did not succeed in establishing a permanent position among the languages of Persia, although at least in documents it did for a time survive the collapse of Mongol rule. Presumably it was spoken by too small a proportion of the population to make much of a mark. The Mongol invasions certainly involved the immigration into Persia of large numbers of people, but most of them probably spoke one form or another of Turkish. When these immigrants were added to the Turkish speakers whose ancestors had already settled in Persia during the Saljūq period (11th–12th centuries AD), they became the largest linguistic minority in the country. Turkish is still the first language of many Persian citizens, notably the people of the north-west, in Āẕarbāyjān (which adjoins Turkey), but also among the Turkomans of the north-east and a number of nomadic tribes, including some of those in the south of the country. These varieties of Turkish are not uniform and none of them is identical with the Turkish of Turkey, though the latter and Āẕarbāyjānī Turkish are mutually comprehensible.

Other languages are spoken in addition to Persian and Turkish: Arabic (especially in Khūzistān in the south-west – the province was formerly called ʿArabistān), Kurdish and Balūchī are among the most important. A linguistic map of Persia would be a complex document.

By European standards Persia is a very large country, even in the rather truncated form in which it emerged from the Russian territorial depredations of the nineteenth century. It covers some 636,000 square miles. This is roughly equivalent to the combined surface area of France, West Germany, Italy, Switzerland and Spain. From north-west to south-east is 1,400 miles, from north to south 875 miles. The population is large compared with most Middle Eastern countries: the census of 1976 produced a figure of 33.7 million, and an estimate in 1986 put it at 45 million. This population is distributed very unevenly around the country, roughly 70 per cent of which is desert and waste, supporting few people or none at all. The biggest areas of desert are in the centre and south, the Dasht-i Kavīr and the Dasht-i Lūṭ. So far as the rest of the country is concerned, 10.9 per cent of Persia's total surface area is forest or pasture and only 10 per cent is cultivated cropland. The residue is marginal land, perhaps cultivable in sufficiently favourable circumstances.

Much of the country is high plateau, four to five thousand feet above sea level, with much higher peaks rising from it. The exceptions to this are Khūzistān and the Persian Gulf littoral, which are at an altitude only slightly above sea level, and the narrow coastal strip to the south of the Caspian Sea, which is itself 90 feet below mean sea level. The plateau is ringed to the north, west and south by high mountain ranges: to the north, the Alborz; to the west and south, the Zagros. The plateau is lacking in large rivers: the country's biggest, the Kārūn, flows from the Zagros through Khūzistān and into the Gulf. Rivers on the plateau, such as the Zāyanda-rūd, the river of Iṣfahān, for the most part find no outlet, but ultimately lose themselves in sands or swamps.

The climate varies greatly from place to place. The mean monthly summer temperatures (in July) vary between 99 °F at Ābādān and 77 °F at Tabrīz. Absolute maximum temperatures at the two places in July are 127° and 104° respectively. This, however, is by no means as unpleasant as it may sound. Because of the height of the plateau the heat is very dry and thus, usually, perfectly tolerable even to natives of colder and wetter climes (this, of course, is not the case in the much more humid areas off the plateau). There can be extreme variations of temperature between day and night, and between seasons.

The people of Persia may be divided not only on a linguistic or ethnic basis – Persians, Turks, Arabs, Kurds, Lurs, Balūch and so on – but also in terms of their way of life. There are townspeople, agriculturalists, and nomads. Islam is essentially an urban faith, and despite the dependence of the cities on the agricultural base there was always a division, and indeed a lack of sympathy and understanding, between townspeople and peasants.

Some of the largest cities in Persia have become important only relatively recently. These include Ābādān, in the oil region of Khūzistān, and the capital, Tehran, now a vast metropolis far larger than any other city. It is sometimes said that Tehran was of no importance before the Qājār dynasty made the city its capital at the end of the eighteenth century. This is not strictly true: according to the Castilian ambassador Clavijo, who passed through on his way to Tamerlane's Samarqand at the beginning of the fifteenth century, it was already flourishing at that time. Nevertheless, until the Mongol invasion in the thirteenth century the great city of northern Persia was not Tehran but Rayy, a few miles to the south of the modern capital.

Other cities have remained important for many centuries. Iṣfahān, in central Persia, was one of the Saljūq capitals, and later became the capital again under Shāh ʿAbbās I in the late sixteenth century. Tabrīz, in the north-eastern province of Āẕarbāyjān, was a major city, often the capital, throughout much of the period covered by this book since it was situated in the part of Persia most favoured by many of the dynasties that ruled the country. Shīrāz became the capital under the Buyids and the Zands and was the provincial capital of Fārs during the whole of the Islamic period. Some lesser cities, such as Yazd on the edge of the central desert, derived their permanent significance from the fact that they were oasis towns.

The great eastern province of Khurāsān was historically much larger than the present province of that name and included territory that is now in Soviet Central Asia and Afghanistan. It was divided into four quarters, centred on the cities of Marv, Balkh, Harāt and Nīshāpūr. Only the last of these is now in Persia, and it has been superseded in importance by Mashhad because of the presence there of the tomb of the eighth Shīʿī *imām*: a crucial consideration when Shīʿism became the official faith in the sixteenth century.

But most of the population were not town-dwellers: they were peasants, living in villages. The village rather than the isolated farmstead is the characteristic feature of the Persian rural landscape, though the villages vary very greatly in size. For the most part the peasants were not proprietors but tenants, usually holding their land (divided into *jufts*, the area that could be cultivated by a yoke of oxen) under a crop-sharing agreement with the landlord. Landlords were often absentees, living in the towns for most or all of the year. Although there was clearly a dominant landowning class, no really hereditary landed aristocracy was formed in Islamic times: the prevailing political instability and the nature of Islamic inheritance law militated against any such development.

The low rainfall over much of the country meant that most cultivation of crops had to be by irrigation. There were parts of the country in which dry farming could be practised, notably in Āẕarbāyjān and parts of Khurāsān, but elsewhere the usual method was by means of a device called the *qanāt*. This was an underground water channel which brought the water, often many miles, to where it was needed. The building of *qanāts* was a highly skilled operation and they required constant, and equally skilled, maintenance. Consequently the agriculture of Persia was peculiarly subject to the political vicissitudes that affected the country. If peasants were killed or driven away – as happened most notably during the Mongol period – neglect of the proper maintenance of the *qanāts*, even if they were not actually destroyed, could quite quickly have disastrous results. The land would not necessarily remain cultivable if simply left to itself.

The third sector of the population was the nomadic and semi-nomadic, which still exists, though it is now by no means as large a proportion as it once was. Nomadism flourishes mainly in the foothills of the Zagros mountains, in the west and south of the country. Some tribal confederations, such as the Bakhtiyārī of the Zagros, are of Iranian origin; others, such as the Qashqā'ī of Fārs, are Turks. For most of the period considered here, the parts of the country preferred by the nomads were Khurāsān and Āẕarbāyjān, because of their extensive grasslands on which flocks and herds could be pastured. One of the most notable semi-nomadic groups at the present day, the Shāhsevan, lives in the north of Āẕarbāyjān.

Most of Persia's rulers from the Saljūqs in the eleventh century to the Qājārs in the nineteenth were of nomadic, tribal origin, or (as in the case of the Ṣafawids) came to power with such tribal support. This is to be explained largely in terms of the close compatibility between the nomadic life-style and efficiency in warfare: the mobility and skills in riding and archery which were required for a life of herding and hunting were easily adapted to fighting; and since almost the whole adult male population of these tribes would possess such skills, they were able to mobilize for warfare a formidably large proportion of their people, already fully armed and trained. It should not, however, be supposed that the relationship between the nomads and the settled people was purely predatory. This varied a good deal. It was probably the case that Mongol government benefited few but the rulers themselves but in other periods, such as Saljūq times, there was – or could be – a more mutually beneficial symbiotic relationship between the different sectors of the population.

In the light of this great variety – ethnic, linguistic, and so on – it may be thought surprising that an entity which we can call "Persia" continues to exist. Yet the country of today is still recognizably, in some sense, the same country that Cyrus the Great ruled in the sixth century BC. There is an element of continuity that all the changes in rulers, peoples, religions and political boundaries have not contrived to eradicate. In what does this consist? It is probably hazardous to attempt too specific a definition. Concepts of "nationalism" are best avoided as a largely irrelevant and comparatively recent Western importation. The average Persian of two centuries ago, say, would not have defined himself as a Persian with a pedigree stretching back to Cyrus and Darius, of whom he would never have heard. He would probably have thought of himself, first and foremost, as a Muslim. Yet he was not the same as a Syrian or an Egyptian Muslim, and the difference was not simply one between the adherents of Sunnism and those of Shīʿism.

No doubt the survival, despite all its transformations, of the Persian language can do something to help explain the phenomenon – though this may be more symptom than cause. There does, in fact, appear to be a sense of Persian consciousness, of identity – *īrāniyyat* – which runs right through the country's history: or so Western historians seem to suppose. This is a cultural, not a "national" identity, but it is none the less real for all that. Arabs, Turks, Mongols and Europeans might come and go, but Persia, somehow, is still Persia.

NOTE

1. E. Gibbon, *The History of the Decline and Fall of the Roman Empire*, ed. J. B. Bury, 7 vols, London 1905–6, vol. 4, 362.

CHAPTER TWO

Persia in the Early Islamic Centuries

THE SASANIAN PERIOD

The period of Sasanian rule forms an important part of the background to the history of Islamic Persia. The Sasanian house, the last of the major pre-Islamic dynasties, ruled Persia from the early third century AD until the 630s. It is hardly surprising that this long stretch of centuries – a little over four hundred years – should have left its mark on Persian history and society. The most enduring of Persia's subsequent dynasties, the Ṣafawids, survived for not much more than two centuries, and this was unusually long by the standards of the Islamic era.

The Persian tradition preserved a large body of legendary material, but the national memory in so far as it relates to actual historical events hardly reaches back much further than the Sasanian period. This may be seen from the national epic as it is preserved in the poetry of the *Shāh-nāma* of Firdawsī. There is some surviving memory of the Sasanians' predecessors, the Parthians, but the Persians had contrived to forget the very existence of the founders of Persian greatness, the Achaemenians, who had for two hundred years been the major power in the ancient world. Cyrus and Darius are not traceable in the Persian memory. There is only a vestigial recollection of Alexander the Great's adversary, Darius III, who appears in the *Shāh-nāma* as Dārā, and Alexander himself, who under the form Iskandar became the focus of an elaborate legendary epic which spread even to the Far East. The Persian perception of their history before the Sasanians is, then, of a world of myth and legend. Reconstruction of what had in reality happened in the previous thousand years had to await the attentions of modern Western scholars, using such sources as the Old Testament, ancient Greek historians (especially Herodotus), and, above all, the findings of archaeology.

The foundations of the Sasanian Empire were laid by Ardashir I, a local ruler in Fārs who overthrew the last of the Parthians. His reign is dated from AD 224. The most striking Sasanian remains may still be seen in Fārs. At Fīrūzābād is a Sasanian palace, of some architectural importance since its dome is borne by the earliest known squinches (supports for a round dome on a square base). More extensive ruins are at Bīshāpūr, and there too is a notable series of carved reliefs, a Sasanian speciality. Others are at Tāq-i Bustān, near Kirmānshāh in the west of the country, and at Naqsh-i Rustam, the site of the Achaemenian kings' tombs near Persepolis in Fārs. But if Fārs was, and remained, the Sasanian heartland, the imperial centre was at Ctesiphon, on the Tigris a few miles from where the ʿAbbasid caliphs would later build their capital, Baghdad. The *īwān*, the sixth-century audience hall of the greatest of the Sasanians, Khusraw I Anushirvan, survives in part at Ctesiphon, and its open frontal arch is still the largest brick vault known ever to have been erected. As the fact of the capital being in modern Iraq indicates, the Sasanian Empire covered a much more extensive area than the modern Persian state, extending into the territory of the Soviet Union, Afghanistan and Pakistan as well as Iraq – and for a time before its end it stretched, to the west, even further.

Sasanian history may, in a rough and ready manner, be divided into two unequal parts: before and after the late fifth century AD. For nearly three hundred years the empire was administered in a rather decentralized fashion, with much power resting in the hands of hereditary local rulers. The king was almost literally a *shāhanshāh*, a king of kings: he has been termed a "principle of equilibrium". Part of the explanation for this decentralization lies in the enormous size of the empire: travel to the capital from the more remote provinces took a very long time. The theory of society divided it into four classes below the shāh himself: priests, warriors, scribes and peasants. The highest officers in the state were the chief minister, the *vuzurg-framadar*; the commander-in-chief, the *Eran-spahbad*; and the chief priest, the *mobadan-mobad*. The chief priest headed the state church, which professed the locally evolved religion of Zoroaster. Orthodoxy was established and strictly enforced, a process which is particularly associated with the priest Kartir, who flourished in the reign of Shapur I (241–72) and after. The corpus of Zoroastrian scriptures was assembled: this is known as the *Zend-Avesta*. The *Avesta*, though put together in the Sasanian period, is in part much older; the *Zend* is the commentary on it.

Zoroastrianism is a dualist faith, holding that two co-eternal principles of good and evil exist. Good is personified by Ahura-Mazda (otherwise Ohrmazd), and evil by Ahriman. Fire was the principal symbol of purity and the fire-altar with its perpetual flame the centre of worship: hence Zoroastrianism is sometimes (incorrectly) called "fire-worship". The Zoroastrian pantheon found room for other divinities, notably Mithra and the water goddess Anahita. As well as officially enforced orthodoxy there was a variety of sects, such as those of Zurvan and, most interesting of all, Mazdak, whose ideas will be considered later.

Sasanian Zoroastrianism even helped give rise to a new religion, Manichaeism. The faith preached by Mani, a native of Sasanian Mesopotamia, was a potent dualist amalgam of elements from Zoroastrianism and other religions, especially Christianity. Mani, declaring himself "Apostle of Jesus Christ", preached his universal religion until he was executed in 276, at the instigation of Kartir, for having provoked apostasies from Zoroastrianism. Although Manichaeism was suppressed in Persia, it had a long career ahead of it both in the Far East and Central Asia, and in the West: St Augustine of Hippo was at one time a Manichee, and the medieval dualist Bogomils and Cathars may have owed a debt to Mani. There are still some practising Zoroastrians in Persia, and also a flourishing community, the Parsees of Bombay, descended from exiles who fled to India. But perhaps the most conspicuous and permanent legacy of the pre-Islamic era is the New Year festival, Nawrūz, to this day celebrated on 21 or 22 March by all Persians of any religious allegiance or none: but this has long since ceased to have any religious significance.

Zoroastrianism, for reasons to be discussed, did not for long prove able to retain the allegiance of the bulk of its devotees after the Arab conquest. When one considers that the Zoroastrian religion (though Zoroaster's own date is much disputed) was an indigenous Persian religion in some form at least as old as Persia – if one dates Persia from the Achaemenians – then its direct contribution to Islamic Persia was surprisingly small. Some have argued that there was a Zoroastrian religious "input" – for example, there is a suggestion that the five Muslim daily prayers may have been based on Zoroastrian ritual – but the more obvious Sasanian legacy is not in the religious sphere so much as in those of political ideas and administrative practice.

In its first centuries the Sasanian Empire's main external foe had been the Roman Empire. Among the Persians' greatest victories was Shapur I's defeat and capture of the Roman emperor Valerian in 260, which is illustrated in one of the reliefs at Naqsh-i Rustam. By the latter part of the fifth century, however, the real danger came from the east, in the shape of the Hephthalites or White Huns. (The Hephthalites appear not to have been related to the Mongoloid Huns of Attila, though they were also nomads: they are thought to have been of Indo-European stock). In 484, in the region of Gurgān in the north-east of Persia, King Firuz was catastrophically defeated by the Hephthalites. The shāh and large numbers of the nobility were killed, and the disaster was followed by a serious famine. The debacle was so total that it became clear that the old Sasanian order was at an end. Drastic measures would be necessary if the Persian state were to survive.

Different views were held over what might be the appropriate course of action. It was in this period that the reformer Mazdak became influential. He propounded a radical version of Zoroastrianism, thoroughly hostile to the privileges of the nobles and the priestly class. He advocated an egalitarian society, and seems to have opposed polygamy and harems. In the chaos of the time his form of (almost) proto-communism gained a sympathetic ear even from the then reigning shāh. It caused great alarm, however, among those who stood to lose by the implementation of its doctrines, and to the Zoroastrian clergy it appeared socially subversive. Indeed, even after its suppression it remained for many centuries – well into the Islamic period – the bugbear of the socially conservative, a class which included most of the authors of the sources on which we now rely for our knowledge of Persian history. Any radical teaching was open to the damning accusation of "Mazdakism". This may be seen in the *Siyāsat-nāma* of Niẓām al-Mulk (late eleventh century), who gives us perhaps the fullest extant account of Mazdak, some of the details of which may be true. The menace of Mazdakism even turns up in the works of Rashīd al-Dīn, as late as the fourteenth century. It may indeed be that in some form Mazdak's ideas did survive him, and went on to make their contribution to some of the heterodox movements that emerged in Islamic times.

Those who feared the consequences of Mazdakism found a powerful ally in the crown prince, who was able in the 520s to mount an effective counter-revolution. The Mazdakites, at least on the surface, were totally suppressed and indeed exterminated. The prince himself became shāh in 531, and reigned until 579 as Khusraw I Anushirvan. He has always been regarded as the greatest of the Sasanian monarchs, and his justice became legendary, though it may in reality be largely mythical. Anecdotes about the perfection of his judgements and the excellence of his government accumulated around his name. He became, even for Muslim writers in Persia, the ideal of a just and wise king.

This is vividly encapsulated in a maxim attributed to him which, in varying forms, is continually repeated in works of the Islamic period. In the *Qābūs-nāma*, a book of advice written by a petty Persian prince of the eleventh century for the instruction of his son, it reads: "Make it your constant endeavour to improve cultivation and to govern well; for understand this truth: the kingdom can be held by the army, and the army by gold; and gold is acquired through agricultural development; and agricultural development through justice and equity. Therefore be just and equitable."[1] It is perhaps appropriate that even until very recently all obviously pre-Islamic buildings tended, popularly, to be attributed to Khusraw I, as Islamic constructions were to the Ṣafawid Shāh ʿAbbās I.

Khusraw did not by any means attempt to restore the old order. That was no longer possible or perhaps, in his mind, desirable. Local autonomy was brought to an end. Centralized government was the order of the day. The empire was divided into four military regions – north, south, east and west – and there was no commander-in-chief other than the king. A reformed taxation system was introduced, apparently heavily influenced by the Roman system of the emperor Diocletian. It was based on a new survey and had fixed scales of payment. Locally the government was represented by *dihqāns*, whose principal function was the collection of taxes. *Dihqān* is a difficult term to translate. In modern Persian, by a not uncommon process of descent down the terminological social scale, a *dihqān* is a peasant. In the Sasanian period and after – for the conquering Arabs, too, found the *dihqāns* administratively useful – they were perhaps something like a country gentry, though certainly not a high hereditary nobility.

Khusraw found an effective ally in the Turks, who were then becoming the major power in central and eastern Asia to the west of China. With their aid he defeated the Hephthalites in around 560. The menace from the east having been dealt with, the Persians were able to turn their attention to the west and to their old enemies the Romans, now in the form of the Byzantine Empire. It was in connection with these campaigns that important military innovations were made, especially in cavalry warfare. While fighting in Central Asia, the Sasanian army developed a new type of heavily armed and armoured cavalryman, usually called the cataphract. Such a figure may be seen in one of the late Sasanian reliefs at Tāq-i Bustān. The mounted warrior, encased in armour and wielding a long lance, could easily be mistaken for a medieval western European knight, though he preceded the emergence of the knight by many centuries. The Tāq-i Bustān cataphract is often taken to be a representation of Khusraw II Parviz, who was Sasanian shāh at the end of the sixth century. In due time the notion of the cataphract was passed on to the Persians' principal enemy, for the Byzantines found it necessary to try to meet heavy cavalry in kind.

Khusraw II was, at least for a time, the greatest military conqueror of his dynasty. Under his command the empire experienced a last series of astonishing triumphs before catastrophe overwhelmed it. Khusraw came to the throne in 590, but it was not until the latter part of his long reign that the military victories began in earnest. Sasanian forces invaded Byzantine Syria, and took Antioch in 613. Egypt came next: Alexandria fell in 619. In 620 the Persian army was opposite Constantinople, and it might have seemed that the shāh was on the verge of re-establishing the frontiers of the Achaemenian Empire. Certainly these were campaigns of conquest, not mere plundering raids: the archaeology of the Persian invasion of Anatolia makes it perfectly clear that the Persians had come to stay. But it was not to be. The Byzantine emperor Heraclius mounted an effective counter-attack, bypassing the Persian army in Anatolia and striking deep into Sasanian territory in Iraq.

The war finally ended, after twenty-five years, with – it is commonly supposed, with hindsight of what subsequently happened – both the great Near Eastern empires in a state of exhaustion. Khusraw himself died in 628, and with him died Sasanian dynastic stability: there were no fewer than eight rulers in the four years after 628, until the accession of the tragic figure who was to prove the last of the Sasanians, Yazdigird III. He ascended the Persian throne in 632, which was also the year in which the Prophet Muḥammad died – a fact the significance of which no doubt passed Constantinople and Ctesiphon by. The events of the next few years would make it clear that both empires might profitably have taken rather more notice of what had been happening in the Arabian peninsula.

THE ARAB CONQUEST OF PERSIA

The Sasanian Empire fell quickly, and in its entirety, to the Arab Muslim armies. The question why so long-lived and vast an empire should have collapsed so easily has been much, if inconclusively, debated. The weakening effects of the long war with Byzantium have already been mentioned. It is perhaps possible that twenty-five years of incessant campaigning – during which much responsibility was in the hands of generals rather than of the shāh – may have eroded feelings of loyalty to the Sasanian house. Again, it has been suggested that the "new order" introduced by Khusraw I Anushirvan may not yet have had sufficient opportunity to become firmly established. Dissent from the establishment and the officially enforced religion was still rife and the reconstructed Sasanian polity not fully stable.

There is also the consideration that the area nearest to the Arabs and most vulnerable to their attacks was Iraq, which although it was not part of Persia "proper" was the administrative centre of the empire and also the source of something like two-fifths of the government's revenue. Hence, once Iraq had fallen to the invaders, it may have proved impossible to mount an effective resistance from the Persian plateau. The Persian defeats at Qādisiyya (probably 16/637) and Nihāwand (21/642) were therefore decisive. Although Yazdigird III survived until 651, dying like the last Achaemenian in Khurāsān in the east, the issue of the struggle had long since been decided.

The Arabs, then, ultimately swallowed Persia whole. But they soon discovered that it was in some ways an indigestible meal. The "Persian" identity and the Persian language survived to an extent not paralleled in the former Byzantine provinces, such as Egypt and Syria, that were added to the Arab empire at much the same time as Persia was conquered. Possibly this indigestibility was in part the result of the fact that the entire empire was absorbed into the Muslim realm: there was no remaining Persian state to which Persians under Muslim rule could look for help or sympathy. They were therefore thrown back on self-reliance, and perhaps made a greater effort to preserve elements of their past than they might otherwise have done.

Persia had been, comparatively speaking, a unified polity with a common and generally – though far from universally – accepted official religion and a sense of identity which, though not racially based, was certainly real. By contrast the Byzantine Empire, though truncated, still existed after the Arab conquests and indeed still had eight hundred years of history ahead of it. The parts of the Byzantine Empire that fell to Arab attack were provinces, not the centre. The empire was reduced and impoverished by their loss, but it remained perfectly viable. Furthermore, those provinces had been to a greater or lesser extent disaffected from Constantinople's rule, not least on religious grounds. The peoples of Egypt and Syria, though certainly Christian, did not for the most part take kindly to the official imposition of Greek Orthodoxy. The varieties of Christianity that had strong local support were rather different. Nor could it be said that there was an overwhelming sense of a Syrian or perhaps even of an Egyptian identity which might have enabled the conquered peoples to resist becoming "Arabs".

There are many other factors that may help us to explain the fact that something we can legitimately call Persia survived the Arab conquest. Conceivably the Indo-European structure of the Persian language made it more resistant to assimilation to Semitic Arabic than were the languages of the former Byzantine provinces, such as Syriac and Coptic.

Again, Arab settlement in Persia was probably fairly thinly distributed compared with Syria and Egypt. But for whatever reasons, the conquered ex-subjects of the Byzantine Empire were ultimately absorbed into the new Arab-Muslim civilization. Indeed, it would be more accurate to say that they were themselves among the components of that civilization as it was gradually formed. If they had a separate identity it was much weakened, whereas the Persians, though Muslims, never became "Arabs". They are still Persians, and they still speak Persian.

It is not easy to say how quickly Islam itself spread in conquered Persia. The probability – as elsewhere in the Muslim empire – is that conversion from the previously dominant religions was fairly slow at first, though the practical advantages of adopting the faith of the new rulers no doubt became obvious enough. But we do not really know: attempts to estimate rates of conversion from, for example, analysis of the incidence of recorded Muslim names seem to involve assumptions that are far from self-evident.

There was no systematic persecution of Zoroastrianism, though it is arguable that in strict Islamic terms there ought to have been. Islam granted toleration to the "People of the Book", essentially the Jews and the Christians, whose sacred scriptures were recognized by Islam as being divinely inspired – albeit corrupted by men – and whose revelations were regarded as preceding Islam. Judaism and Christianity were now superseded, but they were true enough as far as they went. This could hardly have been thought to be so in the case of Zoroastrianism, whose dualism was alien to Judaism, Christianity and Islam alike. Nevertheless, the Zoroastrians were granted *de facto* the status of People of the Book: they were not treated as idolaters, to be presented with the alternatives of Islam or the sword.

Quite what was the rationale behind this is not clear. Perhaps it was simply that the Arabs baulked at the prospect of having to impose Islam (or death) on the entire population of Persia other than the Christian and Jewish minorities. In the long run the policy of toleration (mixed with contempt and second-class status) was effective as well as expedient. Zoroastrianism did not prove to have the staying power of Judaism or Christianity. Possibly this may have been linked to the old faith's official position within the Sasanian Empire. They fell together because they were so closely connected: Zoroastrianism had been so inextricably bound up with the Sasanian polity that it could not survive, as a faith for the masses, without it. Judaism and Christianity, by contrast, had ample experience of persecution and official discrimination to draw on.

Ultimately most of the Persians, under pressure from Shāh Ismāʿīl I and his successors in the sixteenth and seventeenth centuries, opted for the minority form of Islam, Shīʿism, whereas most of the Islamic world adhered to the Sunnī version of the faith. It used to be argued that there was something specifically Persian about Shīʿism: that it was in fact a means by which the submerged Persian spirit could reassert itself against the alien invader. Such an argument would point out that the main matter thought to be at issue between Sunnīs and Shīʿīs, at least in origin, was the question of who should succeed Muḥammad as leader of the Muslim community and become his caliph (successor or representative). The Shīʿī view was the dynastic, legitimist one – the succession should be handed down in Muḥammad's family – and this, it was said, was easily compatible with the Persians' monarchically oriented way of looking at things. It was further pointed out that according to legend, one of the early Shīʿī *imāms* – those regarded by the Shīʿīs as rightful heads of the Islamic community – had married a princess of the Sasanian royal house.

This equation of Shīʿism with the Persian spirit is still sometimes encountered, but it has long been clear that it has no scholarly basis. Early Shīʿism was far from being a specially Persian movement, and there is little doubt that at the time when Persia did become officially Shīʿī the majority of the population was Sunnī. As everyone now knows, the Persians eventually became irrevocably attached to Shīʿism and their commitment has remained unshakable: to that we shall return.

THE RULE OF THE CALIPHS

For a century Persia was ruled by Arab governors who were responsible to the Umayyad caliph in Damascus. Like the Sasanians, the Arabs based their administration of Persia on Iraq. On the Persian plateau they tended to rely to a large extent on the Persian *dihqāns* to act as their local agents and tax-collectors. By the mid-eighth century trouble was brewing, and the religio-political rising that overthrew the Umayyads began in Persia, in the province of Khurāsān. This was the ʿAbbasid Revolution.

It would be a brave man who would attempt to explain that revolution in a few lines: there are almost as many explanations as there are publications on the subject. It has been thought a movement of Persians versus Arabs, and one of some Arab tribes against others, or as one of some Arabs plus some Persians against other Arabs. It has been argued that it was caused by the resentment of the *mawālī* (sing. *mawlā*). A *mawlā* in this context was a non-Arab who had accepted Islam, and who in order to secure his position in the Muslim community had to become a client (*mawlā*) of an Arab tribe. Perhaps some of the Persian *mawālī* were discontented with the treatment they were receiving as rather second-class Muslims. In this connection it is pointed out that the leader of the rising, Abū Muslim, was himself a Persian *mawlā* – though it has to be remembered that he was sent to Khurāsān from Iraq by his Arab ʿAbbasid superior.

Whatever the causes and character of the ʿAbbasid Revolution, it undeniably had momentous consequences in terms of the perpetuation of Persian traditions. First, the new dynasty of caliphs transferred the capital of the Islamic empire from Damascus in Syria to the newly founded city of Baghdad. Baghdad may have been new, but it was in Iraq and near Ctesiphon: the imperial centre was again where it had been in Sasanian times. Baghdad, the building of which was begun in 145/762 by the caliph al-Manṣūr, was planned as a round city, like Sasanian Fīrūzābād. It had a carefully isolated royal palace, its audience hall fronted by a Persian-style *īwān* 45 feet high and 30 feet across, and it was guarded by Khurāsānī troops.

Secondly, the position of the caliph himself became more influenced than it had been by Persian imperial precedent. The Umayyad caliphs, at least in their early days and in theory, had still to some extent been tribal chieftains, treated without excessive deference and always readily available to their subjects. The ʿAbbasid caliph was a remote, inaccessible figure, to be approached only with due (and elaborate) ceremony: a true Oriental monarch in the traditional style, an emperor.

It is important not to take this argument too far: the ʿAbbasid caliphs were not shāhs in a thin Islamic disguise. They had to try to establish their legitimacy in Islamic, not Persian terms, and they did not revive Sasanian titles or adopt other specifically backward-looking measures. Nor can suggestions that ʿAbbasid administration was merely that of the Sasanians come into its own again really stand up: it has been shown, for example, that the institution of the office of *wazīr*, the caliph's chief minister, did not derive directly from Sasanian precedent, as used to be supposed. Nevertheless there is a certain Persian flavour to the rule of the early ʿAbbasids, something which had been less apparent in the Umayyad period. The ancient Middle Eastern imperial tradition had in a sense been re-established in the Islamic city of Baghdad.

The ʿAbbasids had been brought to power, if not by Persians, at least by supporters from Persia; and the survival of the dynasty in its early years depended on the backing of the Khurasanian army in Iraq. Too much reliance on the Khurāsānīs was soon seen to be potentially dangerous. In 138/755 the caliph had the excessively influential Persian architect of the ʿAbbasid Revolution, Abū Muslim, murdered. Serious revolts promptly broke out in Khurāsān, and in later troubles rebel leaders sometimes claimed to be the "real" Abū Muslim. In the 830s the caliph al-Muʿtaṣim decided that radical measures were necessary, and that the whole basis of recruitment of the ʿAbbasid army should be changed.

The core of the army was now to be, not the traditional Khurāsānī supporters of the dynasty, but imported Turkish slaves. This was a momentous innovation: Turks were to form the military elite in the Islamic Middle East for a thousand years. They came by purchase or capture from the east as youths, were converted to Islam, and trained as soldiers. The theory (and at first the practice) was that as slaves of the caliph they would be unwavering in their loyalty, since they had no other focus for it, having been uprooted from their home environment. There was nothing dishonourable about this slavery: a Muslim military slave could rise to the highest ranks in the state or the army, without necessarily even having been manumitted by his master. Such a successful slave would in due course acquire slaves of his own. In the thirteenth century the military slave (*mamlūk*) system became the basis of two major Muslim polities, the Mamlūk sultanate in Egypt and Syria and the Delhi sultanate. In these states the rulers and the ruling (military) class were slaves or of slave origin.

The difficulty proved, however, to lie in maintaining a distinction between the military and the civil authority. The loyalty of the Turkish troops to the ʿAbbasid dynasty was steady enough, but it soon became evident, once the succession to the caliphate was in dispute, that no one member of that house could rely on it. Before long, caliphs were nominated, deposed and murdered by their Turkish *mamlūk* generals. After the mid-ninth century, real power in Iraq was in the hands of the Turkish commander-in-chief, not of the caliph himself. No one thought of abolishing the caliphate, or even of displacing the ʿAbbasid house: the caliphate was seen as necessary for the legitimation of political rule that was in reality in the hands of others. For a further four hundred years Muslim sovereigns continued to seek "appointment" by the caliph. Not until the Mongols forcibly suppressed the caliphate in 656/1258 did the Sunnī Muslim world discover, slightly to its surprise, that it could quite well do without a caliph at all.

THE "INDEPENDENT" DYNASTIES

General confusion at the centre, and the series of succession struggles between different *mamlūk* factions (supporting different caliphal candidates), meant that the grip of the central government began to slacken in the provinces of the Islamic empire. Local dynasties, to a greater or lesser extent enjoying *de facto* independence, emerged in North Africa, Egypt, Persia and Central Asia. Few of these rulers cared to place any theoretical emphasis on their lack of submission to Baghdad, and the line between a semi-autonomous governor and a genuinely independent ruler was often a fine one. Which side of the line a particular ruler fell on might well, in practice, become evident in his attitude towards a single issue: whether or not he would remit taxes to the caliph when they were demanded.

The first of the Persian "independent" dynasties is traditionally the Ṭahirids, four generations of whom ruled Khurāsān between 206/821 and 259/873. They were of Persian *dihqān* descent: at the time of the Arab conquest, the ancestor of the eponymous founder Ṭāhir had been a *mawlā* of an Arab governor of Sīstān, in south-east Persia. Ṭāhir's grandfather had been involved in the ʿAbbasid Revolution, and thereafter the family's rise to prominence was unchecked. In 194–5/810–11 Ṭāhir had been a leading general in the civil war between the rival brother caliphs al-Amīn and al-Ma'mūn: he had been on the winning side, and was rewarded with important offices in Iraq. In 206/821 he was made governor of all the lands east of Iraq. It is important to note that many later Ṭahirids also held office in Iraq – even the military governorship of Baghdad. While their possession of such offices no doubt strengthened their "independent" position in the east, the evidence seems to indicate that they were regarded – and regarded themselves – as loyal ʿAbbasid governors, not at all as rebels, let alone independent monarchs. They marked a step on the road to local Persian separatism, but they were not really a full-fledged example of it.

The next family to appear on the Persian political scene was a very different matter. This was the Ṣaffarid dynasty. They arose in the province of Sīstān, a turbulent area in which only the major cities such as Zarang and Bust (the sites of which are now both in Afghanistan) were effectively garrisoned by the central government or its local representatives. Much of the real power was in the hands of the Kharijites, a dissident Islamic grouping. In these circumstances the people of Sīstān were obliged for their own protection to resort to self-help, and bands of what were called *ʿayyārūn* were formed. An *ʿayyār* was perhaps somewhere between a vigilante and a straightforward bandit. Yaʿqūb the Coppersmith (*ṣaffār*) joined such a band, took it over, built up his power and drove out the representatives of the Ṭahirids, declaring himself *Amīr* in 247/861.

He incorporated the Kharijites into his forces on terms favourable to them, and then expanded his power both eastwards into modern Afghanistan and westwards into Persia. In 259/873 he ended Ṭahirid rule in Khurāsān. All this was without reference to the caliph, and indeed in 262/876 Yaʿqūb had advanced to within fifty miles of Baghdad when he was defeated. As a major state the Ṣaffarid empire was short-lived: Yaʿqūb's brother and successor ʿAmr lost control of Khurāsān in 287/900, and was executed in Baghdad two years later. His successors, however, retained possession of Sīstān for most of the next hundred years, and even after, members of the Ṣaffarid family were influential in Sīstān until well into the Ṣafawid period.

Although ʿAmr did at times enjoy caliphal recognition, and did acknowledge the caliph on his coins, the Ṣaffarid state was unmistakably not a slightly autonomous ʿAbbasid province. It was the creation of a genuinely independent local dynasty. What is more, the Ṣaffarids were consciously a dynasty of Persians. They made use of something approximating to Persian "national" feeling to make propaganda against the ʿAbbasids as Arabs, and despite their lowly origins they claimed to be descended from the Sasanian royal house. This presumably indicates that even two centuries after the Arab conquest there was still political capital to be made from such a claim. Possibly it helped the Ṣaffarids, rebels against the ʿAbbasid caliph, to achieve an alternative form of legitimacy in the eyes of their followers.

ʿAmr's disastrous defeat had been inflicted on him by the Samanids, who were next to take the centre of the Persian political stage. The base of their power was in Transoxania, especially the great cities of Bukhārā and Samarqand, where they had acted as local governors for the Ṭahirids. The fall of the Ṭahirids left them as virtually independent rulers in Transoxania, and Ismāʿīl Sāmānī's victory over ʿAmr gave them control over Khurāsān. Ismāʿīl's relations with the caliph were correct, unlike those of Yaʿqūb the Coppersmith, but they were fairly formal: he apparently sent no tribute to Baghdad. The Samanid empire began to lose its peripheral territories in the 970s, and in 389/999 the Qara-Khanid Turks from further east ended Samanid rule in their homeland of Transoxania. The Turkicization of Transoxania, formerly an Iranian-speaking land, began in the Samanid period.

Ismāʿīl Sāmānī's reputation among later writers for exemplary justice and equity may to some extent be compared to Khusraw Anushirvan's. It has often been held that the apparently very efficient Samanid administrative machine, a blend of Sasanian, Islamic and Central Asian elements, provided a model for later dynasties to follow. It was a model which may have influenced the Saljūqs and, through them, virtually all their successors until the nineteenth century, though in fact the Saljūqs probably took rather more notice of Ghaznawid practice and perhaps of the ʿAbbasid administration they encountered in Baghdad.

Although the Samanids did not labour their "Persian" identity in quite the Ṣaffarid style, they were of Persian origin and they did offer important encouragement to the now-emerging New Persian literary language. They patronized both poetry – for example the poet Rūdakī – and prose. Of prose works the most important was perhaps that of Balʿamī, who was *wazīr* to Ismāʿīl's grandson Naṣr. Around 352/963 Balʿamī produced what is usually described as an abridged Persian translation of the *Ta'rīkh* of Ṭabarī, the greatest work of Arabic historical writing up to that date. The book still awaits a modern critical edition, but it is becoming clear that to depict it as a mere translation of Ṭabarī is to do it less than justice. It is in fact Balʿamī's own historical work, based on Ṭabarī but containing much additional information, especially on events in Persia. Hence it ought to take its place as the first major history in Persian – something of a landmark. Persians had indeed played an important part earlier in the recording of Islamic history; but (as in the case of Ṭabarī, himself a Persian from the Caspian province of Ṭabaristān) they had written in Arabic.

THE GHAZNAWIDS AND THE BUYIDS

The principal rulers in Persia after the fall of the Samanids were in the east, the Ghaznawids and in the west, the Buyids. The Ghaznawids were the first major Islamic dynasty to have their centre in the territory of what is now Afghanistan, at that time and for long after on the very fringes of the Islamic world. Their capital was at Ghazna, to the south of Kābul. This was largely fortuitous: in 350/961 Alptegin, the Turkish commander-in-chief for the Samanids in Khurāsān, had been involved in a conspiracy (with the historian Balʿamī) to place his own candidate on the throne in Bukhārā. After the failure of the plot Alptegin judged it prudent to withdraw to Afghanistan, out of harm's way. There he was succeeded by his henchman Sebüktegin, who still had the formal status of a Samanid governor.

It was Sebüktegin's son Maḥmūd (reigned 388–421/998–1030) whose reign saw the apogee of Ghaznawid power. His empire eventually stretched from western Persia to Khwārazm in the north, and to the borderlands of India: for many years he mounted regular winter expeditions into India. The main practical result was enormous plunder in bullion and slaves, but since the Indians were heathen, religious credit also accrued to Maḥmūd's name, though little attempt was made at this stage to convert the Indians to Islam. The lengthy process of conversion which has made the Indian sub-continent one of the world's major concentrations of Muslims began rather later. But at least no one could doubt Maḥmūd's Muslim credentials; and since he was a fervent Sunnī in an age of Shīʿī successes, he became something of a favourite with the caliphs in Baghdad.

The administration of Maḥmūd's empire was based on that of the Samanids. Although the Ghaznawids were of Turkish origin, there seems to have been little that was identifiably Turkish about the way in which their empire was run, or indeed about the culture they patronized. We should, however, remember that our sources were written by Persian contemporaries, who might have been unlikely to lay much stress on the non-Persian (and ultimately non-Islamic) elements that may have been present. It was under Maḥmūd that Firdawsī wrote the *Shāh-nāma*, which epitomized the "Persian" character of the Persian tradition (even in Ghazna, on the borders of India) – though the story goes that Maḥmūd was a grudging patron. The Ghaznawid period also saw the writing of one of the finest of all Persian historical works, whether considered from a scholarly or a literary point of view: the *Ta'rīkh* of Bayhaqī. Only a small part of this great chronicle, on the history of the reign of Masʿūd (421–32/1030–41), has survived (hence it is known as the *Ta'rīkh-i Masʿūdī*): we would give much to have Bayhaqī's account of the empire at its height under Maḥmūd. But even as it is, to read Bayhaqī is to gain a direct insight into the day-to-day workings of a medieval Persian state that is hard to parallel.

The imperial phase of Ghaznawid history was short. Masʿūd had to face the problem of the advance of the Saljūqs into Persia: he failed to cope satisfactorily, and the Ghaznawids' defeat at the Saljūq's hands at Dandānqān in 431/1040 marked the end of their rule in Khurāsān. They managed, however, to retain their original territories in eastern Afghanistan and their conquests in northern India. In India they held on until as late as 582/1186, when they were displaced by the Ghurids, whose homeland in the inaccessible mountains of central Afghanistan had proved beyond the power even of Maḥmūd of Ghazna to bring to submission.

In western Persia and Iraq the major power contemporary with the Ghaznawids was the Buyid dynasty, which was to prove the last significant Persian dynasty of Persian ethnic origins and background until the Zands in the eighteenth century. They came from Daylam, in the Alborz mountains to the south-west of the Caspian Sea. Between 322/934 and 334/945 the three Buyid brothers established themselves in Shīrāz, Rayy and Baghdad. At its height in the later tenth century the Buyid empire included Iraq, central, northern and western Persia, Kirmān in eastern Persia, and even ʿUmān, across the Persian Gulf. Shīrāz was the capital. After the death of the supreme Buyid ruler ʿAḍud al-Dawla in 372/983, succession struggles ensued, outlying territories began to fall away, and the empire was never the same again. In the end, like the Ghaznawids, the Buyids had to yield to the Saljūqs. They lost control of Baghdad in 447/1055 and of Shīrāz in 454/1062.

The Caspian provinces had proved resistant to Islam: at the time when the Buyids advanced into Iraq and on to the Persian plateau, the Daylamites were still quite recent converts. They had been converted by missionaries of the Zaydī sect, a variety of Shīʿism. Consequently the Buyid occupation of Baghdad apparently resulted in the curious spectacle of political power in the capital of the Sunnī caliphate – if by this date it is legitimate to speak of Sunnism as a defined position – being in the hands of Shīʿīs. While the Buyid rulers tended to treat the caliphs in a somewhat cavalier fashion, they made no move to suppress the ʿAbbasid caliphate, as they presumably had the political power to do had they so wished. Indeed, they continued to allow the *khuṭba* (the sermon at Friday prayer) to be said in the name of the caliph, and his name also – with Buyid permission – appeared on the coinage. Both of these were regarded as essential indicators of whose authority was acknowledged in the state.

No doubt the Buyids were influenced by the fact that whatever their own religious convictions may have been – a matter requiring much clarification – most of their subjects were not Shīʿīs. Perhaps more important, the Buyid army consisted of two fairly clearly defined components: the Daylamites themselves, tribal forces of infantry and presumably Shīʿī; and the cavalry arm, Turkish in origin and likely to lean in the Sunnī direction. There was a good deal of dissension between these two groups, and it may well have seemed that to abolish the ʿAbbasid caliphate would serve only to exacerbate the situation further. In any case, a caliphate that was under close political control was possibly safer than no caliphate at all, or than the alternative available after 358/969: submission to the Shīʿī Fatimid caliphate in distant Egypt.

As might be expected from mention of the Caspian provinces' resistance to Islamization, the old pre-Islamic Persian traditions were unusually strong in that part of the country. Mardāwīj, a prince of Gīlān who was the three Buyid brothers' patron (and with whom they later quarrelled) had celebrated the Nawrūz festival, had had himself seated on a golden throne, and had worn a crown of the Sasanian type. Once the Buyids were established in power, the "Persian" element in their kingship came to the fore. In 351/962 Rukn al-Dawla issued a commemorative medal which showed him crowned and had on it a Pahlavī inscription, that is one written in both the language and the script of Sasanian times. This read: "May the glory of the *shāhanshāh* [king of kings] increase". By 369/980 a complete Sasanian genealogy had been fabricated for the Buyid family, and ʿAḍud al-Dawla was calling himself *shāhanshāh* on his coins. Although the Buyids were some kind of Muslim, and although ʿAḍud al-Dawla was invested as ruler by the ʿAbbasid caliph in 366/977, the Buyid period marks the most sustained attempt to set up a kingship in Persia that had direct and overt continuity with the Sasanian tradition.

It was also the last for a very long time. We do not see a similar archaizing tendency in any later Persian dynasty until the reign of Fatḥ ʿAlī Shāh Qājār at the beginning of the nineteenth century and, to a much more pronounced degree, during the period of Pahlavi rule in the twentieth century. By that time thirteen hundred years of Islam meant that to hark back nostalgically to a pre-Islamic past (with the implication that that past was in some sense superior to Islam) was extremely hazardous. The Buyids' immediate successors, the Saljūqs, certainly presided over a Persia whose dominant culture was Persian rather than Turkish or Arabic. But the Saljūqs did not see themselves primarily as Persian *shāhanshāhs*, although some of them included that title on their coins. They were granted by the caliph the title of *sulṭān*, an Arabic word originally meaning "power". Beyond any question, they were Islamic sovereigns first and foremost. Nevertheless, the Sasanian legacy – whether in language, culture, political thought or forms of administration – had remained in some sense alive and potent for four hundred years. It was to form a permanent part of the amalgam of influences which came together to form medieval and modern Persia.

NOTE

1. Kay Kā'ūs b. Iskandar, *Qābūs-nāma*, ed. R. Levy, London 1951, 125.

CHAPTER THREE

Turkish Rule in Persia: the Great Saljūq Sultanate at its Height (431–485/1040–1092)

The arrival of the Saljūq Turks marks a new era in Persian history. There had been Turks in the Islamic world before the eleventh century – the caliph's *mamlūks* in Baghdad, such dynasties as the Ghaznawids – but these were all, in origin, slaves who had been recruited as individuals. In so far as they had held power, they had acquired it by taking over a going concern from the inside. The Saljūqs were different. They conquered Persia, and other lands, from the borders of the Dār al-Islām; they were still nomads, and they were still organized tribally. Their conquest marked the beginning of Persia's period of Turkish rule, a period which lasted until the early sixteenth century and even, in some sense, until 1925.

THE ORIGINS OF THE SALJŪQS

The Saljūqs were a tribe of Ghuzz or Oghuz Turks, named after their leader, Saljūq (or, in a more Turkish spelling, Seljük). We first hear of them in the second half of the tenth century, when they were living on the lower reaches of the River Jaxartes in Central Asia, at the edge of the Dār al-Islām proper. At that time they were converted to Islam, apparently as a result of missionary work on the part of travelling *ṣūfīs*. Such *ṣūfīs* professed a personal and emotional mystical faith. At this stage they had only loose associations, though the Saljūq period saw the foundation of convents for them, and also of orders or systems of organization (*ṭarīqa*, "way"). Each of these had its own form of instruction, initiation and ritual, and each its hierarchy of teachers. Early Saljūq Islam was probably, then, of a popular kind likely to be viewed with suspicion by the orthodox Sunnī *ʿulamāʾ*. It may have included elements that were closer to the traditional beliefs of the Central Asian steppe than to "official" Islam; though it is noticeable that when the Saljūqs had established themselves in Persia and Iraq, the Islam they supported was of a very orthodox Sunnī type.

Around the end of the tenth century, the Saljūqs gained a foothold in the Islamic lands. They were hired as mercenaries, first by the Samanids and then by the Qara-Khanids, the Turkish dynasty which had established itself in the former Samanid territories in Transoxania. The Saljūqs settled in that area, the land between the Oxus and Jaxartes rivers. In 416/1025 Maḥmūd of Ghazna, who also hoped to find them useful, installed some of them in Khurāsān, to the south-west of their earlier home. But this group behaved in a disorderly fashion and was driven out.

The Ghaznawids, as we have seen, ran into difficulties after the death of Maḥmūd in 421/1030, and during the ensuing disorders the Saljūqs as a whole were able, in 426/1035, to move into Khurāsān, led by two brothers, Toghril Beg and Chaghri Beg. It would seem that Saljūq rule did not strike the population of Khurāsān as less acceptable than that of the Ghaznawids. At any rate, the province speedily submitted. Nīshāpūr was taken in 428/1037, and later became the first of the Saljūq capitals. Open warfare with the Ghaznawids culminated in the battle of Dandānqān in 431/1040, at which the forces of Masʿūd of Ghazna were routed. The Ghaznawids withdrew to their Afghan lands and, ultimately, to India. The Saljūqs were the new masters of Khurāsān.

TOGHRIL BEG: THE ESTABLISHMENT OF THE SALJŪQ EMPIRE

The two Saljūq brothers ruled together till the death of Chaghri Beg in 452/1060. This was in accordance with the Turkish conception of the nature of political sovereignty which they had brought with them from Central Asia. The Turks and Mongols of the steppe, organized as they were as nomadic tribes, saw sovereignty as the possession more of the ruling family as a whole than of any one individual member of that family. Hence, while the overall supremacy of Toghril was accepted, it was equally perfectly regular that when he headed to the west in order to extend Saljūq rule further into the Dār al-Islām, Chaghri should remain as ruler in Khurāsān. The division of power between the various members of the ruling family was later to be a cause of strife, but this initial arrangement between the brothers appears to have been amicable enough.

After the expulsion of the Ghaznawids from Khurāsān, the Buyids in western Persia and Iraq were the major enemy. They were soon eliminated, though they survived in some areas for a few more years as subject rulers to the Saljūqs. Toghril entered Baghdad in 447/1055, and the capital of the caliphate was at last restored to demonstrably Sunnī rule.

So far as the ʿAbbasid caliphs were concerned the change of secular ruler was distinctly for the better, though this did not mean that relations between them and the Saljūqs were always free of tensions and disagreements – even, at times, breaches in relations. The caliph al-Qā'im conferred on Toghril the title of *sulṭān*. There was, and is, much discussion as to quite what was meant by this. An older generation of scholars, accustomed to concepts deriving from European history, liked to suppose that Toghril had become emperor to the caliph's pope: that we see here a clear division between the spiritual and the secular power. More recent scholars have emphasized that the church/state distinction did not exist in medieval Islam, and moreover that the caliph, though certainly recognized as head of the Islamic community, had few of the powers of the pope: for example, he had no authority (at least in this period) in the matter of defining doctrine.

Muslim thinkers at the time, too, were aware of the difficulty. The leading intellectual of the day, al-Ghazālī, carefully formulated a theory that would accommodate the institution of the sultanate acceptably within the boundaries of Islamic thought. His approach was to argue that the sultanate was not separate from the caliphate, or imamate: it should be seen, he contended, as a part of the imamate. Thus the risk of positing an illegitimate division between spiritual and secular government and authority was, though possibly only notionally, avoided.

This was fair enough as far as it went, but it did, perhaps, come perilously close to envisaging the sultanate almost as a medieval papal propagandist might have wished to see the position of the Holy Roman Emperor: as the secular arm of the caliphate. Whatever the theory might say, and whatever the situation may have been in the early days of the caliphate, historians do seem to be to some extent arguing against the political realities if they deny that there was, in practice, a distinction of function in this period between caliph and sulṭān: a distinction which, at least up to a point, looks suspiciously like one between the ecclesiastical and the secular spheres.

It is also perhaps worth remarking that Islamic historians, in their wholly justifiable enthusiasm for discouraging misleading parallels between Islamic society and medieval Europe, have sometimes tended to exaggerate the extent to which medieval Christians drew a church/state distinction that was as sharp as in later centuries. In the central Middle Ages (to use, again, a European term of limited usefulness for the Islamic world), the relative positions of "church" and "state" in the two societies, though not identical, were more like each other than the experts on either side sometimes appear to imply.

By around 451/1059 Saljūq rule was established, reasonably securely, throughout Persia and Iraq, as far as the frontiers of Syria and of the Byzantine Empire in Anatolia. Toghril's capital was at Rayy, a few miles from modern Tehran (the capital was later transferred to Iṣfahān). Chaghri Beg's death in 452/1060 had left his brother as sole ruler, and when Toghril himself died in 455/1063, he could legitimately have claimed to have founded an empire. It was a remarkable feat for the chieftain of a tribe of Turkish nomads to have achieved in less than thirty years.

THE CONSOLIDATION OF THE SALJŪQ EMPIRE (455–485/1063–1092)

Toghril Beg left no sons. He was therefore succeeded by his nephew, Chaghri Beg's eldest son, Alp Arslan. This was not allowed to pass without opposition from other members of the family and their supporters, but Alp Arslan was the most experienced of the contenders; and, like his father, he had a formidable power base in Khurāsān.

Alp Arslan's reign was one in which the newly established Saljūq Empire was stabilized. Even at this quite early stage, it had become apparent that to base the state on the military support of the Ghuzz tribesmen who had originally brought Toghril Beg to power was potentially hazardous. They were certainly highly efficient cavalrymen but they did not, except in wartime, take kindly to discipline; and they were not in the least inclined to submit to the central government of an Islamic sultanate.

The tradition of the steppe was quite different. According to this, a tribal *khān* would be freely elected, or acknowledged, by his tribe; and if he were to secure acceptance, he would need to be a member of an appropriately noble family. Which member of such a family would be accepted as *khān* would often depend on the tribe's judgement of who was most suitable. A prospective *khān*'s suitability might well be determined by his efficiency in wiping out or otherwise neutralizing the other contenders. Once accepted, he could expect to be obeyed in war, but in peacetime, while he would occupy a position of honour, his interference in the affairs of his tribesmen would not be welcomed.

Such a system of extremely limited government worked well enough in the nomadic environment of the steppe, but it could hardly be appropriate to the very different demands of a sultanate which purported to rule the largely settled and heavily urbanized lands of Persia and Iraq. In these circumstances the state required a military force on which it could permanently rely. Alp Arslan therefore created a standing army, much of which was made up of slave (*mamlūk*, *ghulām*) troops, also of Turkish origin, after what had become the normal pattern in the central Islamic lands. This army was probably about 10,000–15,000 strong.

Such numbers may not seem very large, but it has to be remembered that a standing army, unlike a tribal levy, had to be paid, and paid all the time. For a Central Asian nomad, warfare was simply an aspect of normal life to which the techniques used in hunting were adapted, with little change. A steppe nomad would hope for plunder from battle, but he would not expect a salary; and even after the Saljūqs had established their standing army, the tribal levy could still be called on for an individual campaign if greater numbers of troops were needed.

It was not only in military affairs that the Saljūqs speedily found that what had served them adequately in a different environment would not suffice when they had become the rulers of a great settled state. They discovered that they could not do without the services of the existing Persian bureaucracy. Toghril Beg's administration had been headed by a Persian *wazīr* (chief minister), al-Kundurī. He had had the misfortune to back one of the unsuccessful candidates for the throne after the death of Toghril in 455/1063, and his fall from power duly followed. His successor, perhaps the major figure in Persian history in the whole of this period, was Niẓām al-Mulk, who remained *wazīr* until almost the end of the reign of Alp Arslan's son, Malikshāh. During Niẓām al-Mulk's time in office an administrative framework was set up on Persian lines (see Chapter 4). This was of lasting importance, for in its essentials Persian government for many centuries followed the pattern established before and during the Saljūq period.

Fortunately for the historian, much may be learned about Niẓām al-Mulk's approach to government from a treatise of his that has survived: the *Siyāsat-nāma*, the "Book of Government". This work has much in common with a notable genre of Islamic, and particularly Persian, political writing known as "Mirrors for Princes". It consists of advice to the ruler about how the government was, and should be, run, with a strong ethical emphasis on the necessity of justice and right religion in the ruler. The advice is illustrated by appropriate anecdotes from the Islamic and, in the case of Persia, the pre-Islamic past. Certain heroes who are remembered as paragons of good and just government make numerous appearances in these anecdotes. From the Islamic period, Maḥmūd of Ghazna is especially prominent as, for the pre-Islamic period, is the great Sasanian shāh Khusraw Anushirvan.

As illustrations of Niẓām al-Mulk's points, the anecdotes serve admirably: this, after all, was their intended purpose. The difficulty arises over whether or not it is possible to use them as historical evidence, not for the Saljūq period but for the periods to which the stories refer. The temptation, for example, to give some credence to Niẓām al-Mulk's account of Mazdak and his subversive heresy is a strong one, for we are given a good deal of fascinating detail, and sources actually deriving from the Sasanian period are very scant. Nevertheless, while some of the material may well be accurate, it is impossible to tell what, or how much. What we can say – and this is in itself of some interest – is that we have in the *Siyāsat-nāma*, among other things, an impression of what was known and believed about the past in educated Persian circles at the end of the eleventh century. A further point which the *Siyāsat-nāma*'s anecdotes serve to emphasize is the extent to which the approach to government typified by Niẓām al-Mulk and the Persian bureaucracy of his day was influenced not only by Islamic models, but also by what were thought to have been the administrative traditions of pre-Islamic Persia.

Alp Arslan's reign did not see any considerable further expansion of the territory under Saljūq control. The most notable military event occurred near the end of the reign, as the result of the unruly behaviour of the Ghuzz tribesmen. Groups of them, unwilling to submit to the authority of the central Saljūq government, had kept going in a westerly direction, beyond the sulṭān's jurisdiction. They had ultimately arrived on the eastern Anatolian borders of the Byzantine Empire, where they proceeded to raid and plunder in the traditional nomad way. To permit this to continue in an uncontrolled fashion was unacceptable to Alp Arslan, and he therefore marched west, in an attempt to bring an end to this manifestation of frontier private enterprise.

The result was unexpected, and quite unintended by the sulṭān. The Byzantine Emperor Romanus Diogenes chose to march east with his own forces into eastern Anatolia. In Alp Arslan's view this was a breach of truce, and he therefore proceeded north from Syria to meet the Byzantine threat. The two armies met, in 463/1071, at Manzikert. The Byzantines were soundly defeated, and Romanus Diogenes himself was captured. Although the Byzantine Empire survived in various forms for nearly another four centuries, it was never again able to put so formidable an army into the field.

This was because of what happened in the aftermath of the battle. Byzantine control of eastern and central Anatolia lapsed, the Ghuzz tribesmen poured across the frontier, and there they stayed. The area they occupied had been one of the Byzantine Empire's chief sources of revenue, and also its principal military recruiting ground. At the end of the century the Byzantines were able, as a result of the First Crusade, to regain possession of western Anatolia and the coastal strips. But the centre was lost for ever. In due course a new Turkish state, the Seljük sultanate of Rūm (i.e. "Rome") was formed in Anatolia, to be followed after many vicissitudes by the Ottoman Empire. "Turkey" was a consequence of the battle of Manzikert, even though nothing had been further from Alp Arslan's intentions than to attack the Byzantines or to occupy any of their territory.

Alp Arslan died in 465/1072. His son, Malikshāh, made good his claim to the throne, but as before the succession was not undisputed. This time the main rival was Malikshāh's uncle, Qavord, who in accordance with the Turkish principle of family sovereignty had been made semi-independent ruler of Kirmān, in the south-east of Persia. His claim was based on the contention that as Alp Arslan's brother he was the senior member of the family, and should therefore take precedence over the late sulṭān's son. He resorted to arms, and was defeated and executed. Malikshāh's position was assured, and his reign was characterized by an imperial unity that was never subsequently to be seen in Saljūq times.

There was some expansion of Saljūq territory during the reign: Malikshāh made his mark in northern and central Syria, where (again conforming to the notion of family sovereignty) a subject kingdom was set up by his brother Tutush. Niẓām al-Mulk remained at the head of the bureaucracy throughout the reign. Attempts were made by jealous rivals to unseat him, but he successfully (though not always easily) fought them off, and he seems to have retained Malikshāh's confidence almost to the end.

Niẓām al-Mulk owed the security of his position in part to the extent to which he installed his own sons in responsible posts. There was no civil service "esprit de corps" in medieval Persia. The way to the top was often that of discrediting – and bringing about the fall of – the current *wazīr*. Only by retaining the support of the ruler and by installing as many reliable people as possible at the lower levels could a *wazīr* hope to remain in office. It is not naive, however, to say that one way of keeping in the good graces of the ruler was, in fact, to be an efficient administrator, since efficiency made for stability and high receipts from taxation. Niẓām al-Mulk seems to have been efficient, and he was probably honest enough according to his lights and by the standards expected of the powerful in his day.

In 485/1092 Niẓām al-Mulk was, literally, assassinated: that is, he was murdered by a member of the Nizārī Ismāʿīlī sect, otherwise known, at least in Europe, as the Assassins. They had become firmly established in Persia only two years before, in 483/1090, and their history therefore belongs in a later chapter. Niẓām al-Mulk was one of their first and most illustrious victims, but he was very far from the last. Malikshāh himself died in the same year, not long after his great minister. His death marked the end of stability in the Saljūq empire, and the beginning of a gradual decline.

THE IMPACT OF THE SALJŪQ CONQUEST OF PERSIA

It is important to remember that the Saljūqs came to Persia not as barbarian destroyers, but as quite long-standing converts to Islam who were familiar with – and to an extent sympathetic to – Islamic civilization and urban life. Their arrival had more the character of a tribal migration than of an outright invasion and conquest: it has been said that they acquired a vast empire "almost by chance".[1] There is no reason to doubt that their incursion involved some destruction and dislocation, at least temporarily; but this seems to have been comparatively incidental, and was probably no greater than that caused earlier by the depredations of the Ghaznawid armies. In all this the Saljūqs were very different, as we shall see in a later chapter, from the Mongol conquerors of the thirteenth century.

This was inevitably linked to the numbers involved in the migration. They seem to have been fairly small. We should be thinking in terms of tens rather than hundreds of thousands. Alp Arslan's standing army of 10,000–15,000 was not untypical. Contemporary and later chroniclers normally put tribal hordes of the period in the bracket 700–10,000. Such numbers of Turks, bearing in mind the very large area involved, are perhaps unlikely to have done an excessive amount of damage.

The most important long-term effect of the Saljūq conquest was probably the change it initiated in the balance of the population of Persia. This had both ethnic and economic aspects. A large proportion of Persia's present-day population is composed of Turks, i.e. those whose first language is some form of Turkish and whose ethnic origins are perhaps also Turkish. The question therefore arises: did the ancestors of these Turks come to Persia in the Saljūq period?

Scholars who have studied the problem have come to widely different conclusions, but as far as it is possible to judge, it would seem that while the Saljūq period certainly saw the beginnings of the significant Turkicization of Persia, the bulk of the Turks first arrived in later centuries. Nevertheless there were major Turkish movements into, for example, Gurgān and Marv in the north-east and Āẕarbāyjān and upper Mesopotamia in the north-west; and lesser settlements were established elsewhere. It would appear that the Ghuzz tribes tended not to establish themselves very extensively where there was already a significant tribal or semi-nomadic population, as in Fārs, Luristān and Kurdistān.

As we have seen, many of the Ghuzz took ill to the new Saljūq polity, and kept going to the west, to Syria as well as to Anatolia. But while this may have been in some ways a considerable relief to the central government, the difficulties did not go away. For the Ghuzz hordes were continually augmented, throughout the Saljūq period, by further immigration from Central Asia into the eastern parts of the empire, especially the province of Khurāsān. There, in the twelfth century, they presented Sanjar, the last of the Great Saljūq sulṭāns in Persia, with his most serious problem.

A further factor of great importance was that the newcomers were not only Turks: they were nomads. It is clear, then, that there was at least a limited shift of the balance of the population, not only ethnically but also away from the settled and towards the nomadic sector. It does not, however, seem that this necessarily resulted in a reduction in the amount of land cultivated, as certainly happened as a result of the Mongol invasions. There is good reason for supposing that, for the most part, the nomads probably occupied land that had previously been unexploited. Indeed, it would even be reasonable to suggest that the new nomadic settlements were beneficial to the country, in that they played an important part in the economy as a whole through their provision of meat and milk products, wool, and skins to the towns.

Overall, then, a verdict on, at any rate, the first half-century of the Saljūq period is likely to be a fairly positive one. The Saljūqs were not, by the standards of the region, destructive conquerors. The ethnic changes that occurred were not on an excessive scale. Economically the rule of the Saljūqs was probably, on balance, of advantage to the country. Administratively their achievement, or the achievement of the Persians they employed, was creative and lasting.

NOTE

1. A. K. S. Lambton, "IRAN v. – History", *Encyclopaedia of Islam*, 2nd edn, vol. 4, 25.

CHAPTER FOUR

Institutions of Saljūq Government: Steppe and Sedentary Traditions

DIVISIONS OF THE EMPIRE

The Saljūq empire may be divided into those areas that were administered directly by the sulṭān and those that were governed indirectly. Direct administration of cities and agricultural land was perhaps something that did not come altogether naturally to the Saljūqs, with their Central Asian nomadic background. Such areas as were ruled directly tended, for obvious reasons of administrative convenience, to be concentrated near the various Saljūq capitals. The first capital was Nīshāpūr, in the east. As Toghril Beg's forces proceeded westwards, Nīshāpūr was replaced by Rayy, to the south of modern Tehran. Later the main governmental centre was at Iṣfahān, though during Sanjar's long reign in the twelfth century he made Marv, in the far east of Khurāsān, his capital.

The greater part of the empire was governed indirectly. In the early years of Saljūq rule many of these areas were allowed to remain in the hands of the local families which had ruled them before the arrival of Toghril Beg. Such dynasties included a number in the region of the Caspian Sea, though it is possible that this was a matter of making a virtue out of necessity. The Caspian provinces had been, since before the rise of Islam, by far the most difficult area of Persia for the central government to bring under effective control. Even the Mongols, not a people to tolerate unnecessarily manifestations of local independence, did not succeed in conquering Gīlān until near the end of the Ilkhanate. The terrain, with its hot, damp, impenetrable forests and high, inaccessible mountains, was a forbidding proposition to any invading army. Other areas administered indirectly included Arab lands in Iraq and, for a time, territories under the control of members of the Buyid family whose rule over Persia and Iraq had been terminated by the Saljūq invasion.

This was the situation while Saljūq central power was at its strongest, until the deaths of Malikshāh and Niẓām al-Mulk. Thereafter, much land that had previously been ruled by local families was handed out as assignments, *iqṭā*ʿ*s* – an institution of great importance, to be discussed later – to powerful Turkish *amīrs*. Such assignments were not at that point by any means an innovation, but after 485/1092 they, and their allocation and reallocation, became decreasingly subject to the real authority of the central government.

The third kind of indirectly administered land was that occupied and governed by tribes, which were allowed a considerable degree of internal autonomy. These were to be found especially in Gurgān, in the north-east, in Āẕarbāyjān, in the north-west, in Khūzistān, in the south, and in Iraq. These, too, became a source of political fragmentation when the control exercised by the central Saljūq government became weaker.

THE CENTRAL ADMINISTRATION

The steppe tradition which the Saljūqs brought with them to Persia found its chief expression in one of the two halves of the administrative machine: the *Dargāh*, the court. Although the Saljūq empire, as we have seen, possessed a series of fixed capitals, the court itself was essentially itinerant. It might be possible to argue that this is evidence that the old nomadic way of life still had its appeal, even at the level of the court. It should, however, be pointed out that many monarchs in western Europe who were contemporary with the Saljūqs – Henry II of England, for example – lived a life that was no less itinerant than that of their Turkish counterparts; and no one has yet accused the Angevins of harking back to nomadic origins.

The fact of the matter is that a great royal court was an expensive institution, and in European conditions the costs of its maintenance, given the limits imposed on communications by medieval conditions, had to be spread more or less evenly about the king's possessions. It was no less important that the ruler should appear personally in the various parts of his dominions, if he were to maintain any degree of real control over his kingdom and ensure that the more powerful of his subjects were kept in check: in Persia this seems to have been the principal reason for the court's itinerancy.

The *Dargāh* was military in character. The sulṭān was still, in the last analysis, a commander-in-chief before he was anything else. He might have acquired legitimacy in Islamic terms through his acceptance as the ʿAbbasid caliph's "secular arm", but this legitimacy would avail him little if he were to be overthrown by some new invader. The maintenance of Saljūq power depended above all else on the retention of their military supremacy over all rivals: they had come to power as the result of military conquest, and their rule could be brought to an end by the same means.

It was not only the itinerancy of the court that made it an effective check on the power of local potentates. The *Dargāh*'s permanent population included not only the military establishment, the great *amīrs* of the Saljūq world, but also members of the families of the semi-autonomous rulers, kept honourably, but nevertheless kept, as hostages against good behaviour in the regions that were less under the immediate eye of the sulṭān and his administration.

The *Dargāh* acted too as a court in the judicial sense. The sulṭān was the ultimate judge short of God, and the *Dargāh* the final court of appeal. The subject had the right of audience with the sulṭān, whether or not he was able in practice to exercise that right. Niẓām al-Mulk portrays this as deriving from Islamic and pre-Islamic practice, though there may have been in it a residual element of the custom of the steppe; for a tribal *khān*, as we have seen, was expected to rule more by consultation, except in conditions of war, than as an autocrat in the Persian tradition. The law according to which the sulṭān gave his judgements was not the *sharīʿa*, the law of Islam, which was available in the courts of the *qāḍīs*, but *ʿurf*, customary law. His court was known as a *maẓālim* (court for the redress of grievances) rather than a *sharʿī* court.

The other half of the central administration was the *Dīwān*, which was staffed by members of the Persian bureaucracy. Parts of this were sometimes stationary, remaining in the capital rather than following the sulṭān about the empire. Its most important function by far was the collection of taxes.

The head of the *Dīwān*, and thus the official who was ultimately responsible for the collection of the state's revenue, was the *wazīr*. Hence he occupied a position which might be characterized as that of "Prime Minister and First Lord of the Treasury". His attendance on the sulṭān was expected, and he therefore usually travelled with the court. The power vested in the wazirate varied a good deal according to conditions prevailing at any particular time, and also depended to a considerable extent on the personality of, and the influence exerted by, the individual holder of the office. Niẓām al-Mulk, who was *wazīr* throughout the reigns of Alp Arslan and Malikshāh, was enormously powerful, and was effectively in charge of the whole administration of the empire. He even maintained his own private military force.

But Niẓām al-Mulk was exceptional. As the strength of the central government gradually drained away, so did the power of the *wazīr*. No *wazīr* after Niẓām al-Mulk was as influential as he had been, even though members of his family continued to hold high office for many years after his death. Once Malikshāh and Niẓām al-Mulk had passed from the scene, the power of the *wazīr* steadily declined as that of the Turkish *amīrs* increased.

The bureaucracy had four main departments. The *Dīwān al-inshā' wa'l-ṭughrā* was the Chancery, and was headed by the *ṭughrā'ī*. The *Dīwān al-zamām wa'l-istīfā'* was the accounts department, headed by the *mustawfī al-mamālik*, the chief *mustawfī* of the empire: he had under him, as well as the central staff of his department, a *mustawfī* for each tax district. The *Dīwān-i ishrāf-i mamālik* was the audit department, headed by the *mushrif-i mamālik*, with *mushrifs* operating in each district. The *Dīwān-i 'arḍ*, headed by the *'āriḍ*, was the military department. In later Saljūq times the *'āriḍ* was usually a Turkish *amīr* rather than a Persian bureaucrat, an indication of the increasing dominance of the military over the government. The department kept the records of the grant of *iqṭā's* and the military registers, though this did not mean that it actually ran the army.

This was the basic pattern of central government in Saljūq times. It owed much to what the Saljūqs had inherited from earlier regimes in the eastern Islamic world, such as the 'Abbasid caliphate, the Samanids and the Ghaznawids – especially the latter, as the details of the Ghaznawid administrative system to be found in Bayhaqī's history show. Under the first three Saljūq sulṭāns, the pattern became fixed in a way that proved remarkably durable. Despite countless wars, invasions, conquests and changes of dynasty, the administrative system which was institutionalized in the time of Niẓām al-Mulk was broadly, with variations in detail and terminology, the means by which Persia was governed until the nineteenth century. Apart from the machinery of the central administration, the most important single institution of Saljūq government, which also had a singularly long life ahead of it, was the *iqṭā'*. It must therefore be given special attention.

THE *IQṬĀ'*

The origins of the institution of *iqṭā'* lay far back in Islamic history: this was not something that in any sense came with the Saljūqs from the

Central Asian steppe. But as an instrument of government it gained prominence under the Saljūqs' immediate predecessors, the Buyids, and above all during the Saljūq period, when it became the most important administrative device available to the government. It may be defined, very broadly, as an assignment of land or its revenue; but there were several different types of *iqṭāʿ* even in Saljūq times, and the institution continued to evolve after their fall.

In theory, and in the early decades of Saljūq rule in practice as well, all *iqṭāʿs* were held at the will of the sulṭān and were revocable at his pleasure. Under no circumstances was an *iqṭāʿ* regarded as a hereditary grant – again in theory. But a powerful Turkish *amīr* who held an *iqṭāʿ* (a *muqṭaʿ*) could not, in periods when the authority of the central government was weak, be removed except by the threat or the actual use of force.

Later Saljūq sulṭāns were on occasion obliged to resort to desperate expedients in an attempt to control over-mighty *muqṭaʿs*. They would appoint an *amīr* to an *iqṭāʿ* that was already held by another *amīr*: the new grantee would be able to gain possession only if he was prepared to evict his predecessor by force. Worse, two *amīrs* might be given simultaneous grants of the same *iqṭāʿ*: the winner would occupy the *iqṭāʿ* and the sulṭān would at least be rid, with luck permanently, of one of two excessively powerful *amīrs*.

This was a period in which the collection of revenue, the payment of salaries and the administration of outlying provinces presented great problems to the central government. Resources and trained manpower were limited and communications difficult and uncertain. The *iqṭāʿ* proved itself a most useful way of coping with some of these governmental handicaps, and its use by no means necessarily implied a reduction in the authority of government, so long as that government was strong. But built into the system was the potential that, as the central government's power weakened, the abuse of the *iqṭāʿ* institution could contribute to the disintegration of the empire.

There seem during the Saljūq period to have been four main types of *iqṭāʿ*. There was, first, the grant by the sulṭān of a private estate, a pension or an allowance to an individual; secondly, a grant made to a member of the Saljūq family for his or her proper maintenance; thirdly, a grant of land or the revenue of land to an *amīr* in lieu of salary or in return for specified military service (the "military" *iqṭāʿ*); fourthly, a grant which was in effect equivalent to appointment as a provincial governor (the "administrative" *iqṭāʿ*).

Of these the two last were certainly the most significant. It was especially the administrative *iqṭāʿ* that enabled the Saljūqs both to solve the problem of effectively governing their vast empire and to satisfy the aspirations of their powerful *amīrs*. The holder of such a provincial governorship could be left to get on with the administration of his *iqṭāʿ* without the central government having to involve itself in the difficulties of direct supervision from the capital.

The *muqṭaʿ* would expect, and be expected, to profit from his appointment: he would retain much, if not all, of the taxation receipts for local expenses and for his own use. If he showed signs of undue independence he would, at least during the first half century of Saljūq rule, be dismissed from office. In the twelfth century, as we have seen, this might well be easier said than done; and an administrative *iqṭāʿ* could develop into a semi-independent hereditary principality. Khwārazm, an *iqṭāʿ* which ultimately became, under the descendants of its Saljūq *muqṭaʿ*, the nucleus of the empire of the Khwārazm-shāhs, is a conspicuous example of this tendency.

Parallels have often been drawn between the *iqṭāʿ* and western European feudalism. The two institutions were at their height in the same period, and there do seem at first sight to be strong similarities. The military *iqṭāʿ* is the variety that appears to offer the closest parallel. This kind of *iqṭāʿ*, like a European fief, was often granted in return for military services to the crown. It provided a means whereby the ruler could raise a military force of substantial size without the unacceptable expense of maintaining a large standing army.

So far the similarities, considered functionally, are real enough. But the differences between the *iqṭāʿ* and the fief are probably more striking, and remind one that the *iqṭāʿ* was in essence simply a bureaucratic device: it was in no sense basic to the whole structure of society. The eastern Islamic world was a society whose rulers used the *iqṭāʿ* as a matter of administrative convenience or, in periods of weak government, of inconvenience. It is another matter entirely to call such a society "feudal".

Feudalism arose in western Europe at a time when central government was weak, and it seems to have developed out of the need for protection – a protection which a local magnate might be able to provide, even if the king was unable to do so. Hence there was a relationship of mutual obligation between lord and vassal. The vassal received lands and powerful patronage from his lord; in return he contributed his agreed contingent (e.g. of knights or men-at-arms) for the lord's military requirements. He swore fealty to his lord, and he could expect that – other things being equal and after appropriate payment – his son would in due course succeed him as holder of his fief.

Little of this was true of the *iqṭāʿ* as an institution. It was utilized, initially, by a strong government, not created because of the absence of such a government. There was no element of protection or dependence involved. An *iqṭāʿ*, as we have seen, was not granted on the understanding that it should be hereditary. There was no relationship of mutual obligation between sulṭān and *muqṭaʿ*, and no real oath of fealty on the European pattern. An *iqṭāʿ* was simply a grant, made or withdrawn entirely at the will of the sulṭān. This was not feudalism: it was a by and large effective means for dealing with some of the administrative and financial problems of the Saljūq government. Like feudalism, the *iqṭāʿ* could, in certain circumstances, lead to the fragmentation of a kingdom into smaller units. But this ought not to blind us to its quite different origins, purpose and function in the state.

The precise character of the *iqṭāʿ* varied a good deal in later centuries. So did the terminology used. Variations on the *iqṭāʿ* were sometimes called *suyūrghāl*, a word of Mongolian derivation originally meaning "favour" or "reward"; the most enduring term, lasting into the Qājār period, was *tiyūl*. The Īlkhān Ghazan Khān used the term *iqṭāʿ* for his method of paying his troops, but he meant by it something dissimilar from anything that had prevailed in the Saljūq period. Nevertheless, whatever changes might occur in terminology or exact function, the *iqṭāʿ*, like the structure of the central administration, proved to be a lasting legacy of the Saljūqs to the subsequent history of government and society in Persia.

CHAPTER FIVE

The Later Saljūq Period and its Aftermath: Ismāʿīlīs, Qara-Khitais and Khwārazm-Shāhs (485–617/1092–1220)

THE DECLINE OF THE SALJŪQ SULTANATE

The unity of the Great Saljūq empire had always been, at least potentially, a precarious thing, for submission to the sulṭān was not easy to hold in tension with Turkish notions of the collective family nature of political sovereignty. Stability had endured for a full half century during the reigns of three formidable sulṭāns: Toghril Beg, Alp Arslan and Malikshāh. But it had not been an unchallenged stability, and both Alp Arslan and Malikshāh had had to fight for the throne against other members of the Saljūq family.

Stability died with Malikshāh – and, it would perhaps only be just to add, with his great minister, Niẓām al-Mulk. Saljūq rule lasted for a further century in one form or another, and for very much longer still in Rūm. But the great days were over. Succession struggles followed Malikshāh's death in 485/1092 and set the pattern for the future. A degree of central control was re-established during the reigns of Berk-yaruq (487–98/1094–1105) and Muḥammad (498–511/1105–1118), but this was to prove exceptional.

This gloomy picture is true at least for the western half of the empire. For many years, however, the eastern half, essentially Persia, was much more fortunate. For in 490/1097 the young Saljūq prince Sanjar became governor of Khurāsān; and there he stayed until his death, sixty years later. After 511/1118 he was generally recognized as Great Saljūq sulṭān, but he concerned himself mainly with the territories under his own immediate control. The eastern provinces therefore enjoyed several decades of governmental continuity which must have been the envy of the more turbulent western regions.

The capital of the Saljūq empire during Sanjar's reign was at Marv, where his tomb survives to this day. His choice of capital is a significant indication of Saljūq political priorities in the first half of the twelfth century. The establishment of the crusader states in Syria and Palestine, and the period of their greatest efflorescence, are contemporary with Sanjar's rule as governor of Khurāsān and then Great Saljūq sulṭān. Europeans sometimes like to imagine that the crusaders were a serious menace to the Islamic world; and perhaps Muslim rulers in Cairo or Damascus would have agreed. But so far as Sanjar was concerned, the real danger lay in the east.

Hence the significance of his remaining in Marv, a city that is so far to the east that it is not even within the borders of twentieth-century Persia at all: it is in Soviet Central Asia. If the Islamic world was not critically endangered by the founding of a few small states along the Syrian coastline, the eastern frontier with Central Asia was to prove a different matter. The Saljūqs had come to power at the head of nomadic Turkish Ghuzz tribesmen. In some respects, once the tribal leader had become an Islamic sulṭān, the Ghuzz, as we saw in Chapter 3, became an embarrassment. But they continued to filter in from Central Asia throughout the Saljūq period, and it was to meeting the danger to the state they posed that Sanjar devoted much of his energy over so many years.

There was no possibility of driving the Ghuzz out. They had to be kept in check, and if possible kept happy. Sanjar administered them through an official appointed for the purpose, known as the *shaḥna*. Until almost the end of his life, Sanjar managed to hold the line. But in 548/1153 he was himself captured by the Ghuzz, and held prisoner for several years. He was ultimately released but died shortly after, in 552/1157. He had no effective successors in the east. Saljūq power collapsed, and into the vacuum, in due course, stepped the Khwārazm-shāhs.

The western half of the Saljūq empire had a much less tolerable fate than the eastern half, even though Saljūq rule in the west, at least nominally, long outlasted the death of Sanjar. Between 511/1118 and 590/1194 there were no fewer than nine Saljūq sulṭāns. The last, Toghril III, was killed in battle with the Khwārazm-shāh. Central government had for the most part ceased to be effective during these nine reigns.

This had two important results. The first was the increasing importance of the institution of the atabegate. An *atabeg* (Turkish for "father of the prince") was a Turkish commander appointed to act as guardian and tutor to a young Saljūq prince who had been given a city or province to rule, and to exercise political power on his behalf until he was of age. The relationship was often cemented by a marriage between the *atabeg* and the prince's mother. The atabegate was a sensible enough arrangement when Saljūq power was strong, but it was open to serious abuse when this ceased to be so. In the twelfth century, any Saljūq prince who was under the guardianship of an *atabeg* stood a considerable risk of not in fact succeeding to his inheritance. In due course, dynasties of *atabegs* established themselves. Of these the most notable was founded by Zangī, *atabeg* of Mosul (reigned 521–41/1127–46), who is remembered especially for his conquest of Edessa from the crusaders in 539/1144, which marked the beginning of the Muslim counter-attack against the invaders from the west.

The other consequence of the decline of Saljūq control was the re-emergence of the ʿAbbasid caliphate as a political force. Although the caliphate had been maintained in Baghdad – even by the presumably Shīʿī Buyids – as an institution necessary for the proper organization of Islamic society, the caliphs themselves had not for several centuries exercised much real political power, even in Iraq. This now changed. In 547/1152 the caliph al-Muqtafī expelled the Saljūq officials from Baghdad, indicating that he proposed to rule himself, in fact as well as in name. The caliph al-Nāṣir (reigned 575–622/1180–1225) in his long reign became the leading local "secular" ruler in Iraq, and was a major political figure in the Islamic world. Under his headship the ʿAbbasid caliphate enjoyed a last period of power and influence: it was destroyed for ever by the Mongols a little over thirty years after his death.

THE ISMĀʿĪLĪS

From the point of view of the ʿAbbasid caliphate, the great virtue of the Saljūqs, when they arrived in Baghdad in 447/1055, had been that they were not only Muslims but also Sunnīs. Before their appearance on the scene it might well have appeared that Shīʿism was triumphant in most of the Islamic world. The rival Fatimid caliphate, a Shīʿī institution, had been established in Egypt since 368/969, and even Iraq was under some kind of Shīʿī government while the Buyids were in power. It is true that Maḥmūd of Ghazna had been fervently Sunnī, but his activities were concerned mainly with the eastern fringes of the Dār al-Islām and beyond.

Indeed, the Saljūqs have often been credited with initiating a "Sunnī revival". That there was such a revival in the eleventh century seems clear enough, but this is not to say that the Saljūqs were directly and consciously responsible for it: apparently the revival had in fact begun before their arrival in Baghdad. Nevertheless, there can be no doubt that the establishment of an avowedly Sunnī government, and the enhanced prestige that that brought to the ʿAbbasid caliphate, provided an environment favourable to the revival's continuation and success. Some of the most notable Sunnī intellectuals, above all al-Ghazālī, flourished under Saljūq rule; and if the Sunnī resurgence was to survive and spread, such developments as the encouragement of the foundation of *madrasas* (religious colleges) by Niẓām al-Mulk were no doubt of importance.

But while the Shīʿī threat had been dealt a severe blow by the success of the Saljūqs, it had by no means been eradicated. The Fatimid caliphate still existed in Cairo, where it survived until its abolition by the Sunnī Saladin in 567/1171. Its power gradually became weaker, but a more dangerous variety of Shīʿism was closer at hand from the last decade of the eleventh century.

In 487/1094 a dispute arose in Egypt over the succession to the Fatimid caliphate. Of the two candidates of the Ismāʿīlī house, al-Mustaʿlī was successful and his elder brother Nizār defeated. But many of Nizār's partisans refused to accept the political *fait accompli*, and the result was a permanent schism. Among the dissenters was Ḥasan-i Ṣabbāḥ, who had been acting as chief Fatimid agent, or Ismāʿīlī missionary, in Persia.

In 483/1090 he had succeeded, by trickery, in seizing the inaccessible castle of Alamūt, in the Alborz mountains south of the Caspian Sea, not far from the city of Qazwīn. This became the headquarters of the Fatimid cause in Persia, and after 487/1094 the nerve-centre of an independent Ismāʿīlī sect, the Nizārīs. Nizār himself had died in 488/1095. Ḥasan-i Ṣabbāḥ claimed to represent him and his successors, no more. Later chiefs of Alamūt declared themselves actually to be descended from Nizār and hence constituted themselves as the line of rightful Ismāʿīlī *imāms*, in contradistinction to the – as they saw them – usurper Fatimids of Cairo.

The capture of Alamūt foreshadowed the pattern of future Nizārī expansion. Ḥasan-i Ṣabbāḥ and his followers normally concentrated their efforts on the occupation of castles in remote mountain areas, where they would be at least comparatively safe from attack by the forces of Sunnism. Hence in Persia, apart from Alamūt and other castles in the Alborz, their other main centre was in Qūhistān ("land of mountains") in the east of the country. They later established a branch in Syria, based also, from the 1130s, in mountain castles. A famous head of this branch, Rashīd al-Dīn Sinān (died 589/1193), became well known to the crusaders as "the Old Man of the Mountain" (perhaps deriving from the Arabic *Shaykh al-jabal*).

The Nizārī Ismāʿīlīs were not, then, a great territorial power. But the challenge they presented to the established Sunnī order in society was out of all proportion to their numbers or the area they directly controlled. This was in large part the consequence of their idiosyncratic approach to warfare. They did not seek to meet their enemy in battle: instead they sent against him a single emissary, or a small group, whose aim was solely the destruction of that enemy. This they accomplished almost always with a dagger.

It was not easy to design an adequate defence against an adversary who showed no interest in slaughtering his opponent's rank-and-file troops but wished only to kill the leader; and whose devotees made no calculation about the prospects of escape – indeed, such Ismāʿīlīs rarely made any attempt to get away, so convinced were they that on execution they would go straight to paradise. Such single-minded fanaticism gave rise to stories, especially in Europe, that the Ismāʿīlīs were persuaded to do their dark deeds through the influence of the drug hashish: hence their alternative designation, "Assassins", a word which remains as a legacy of the Ismāʿīlīs in several European languages, though most scholars doubt the truth of the drug story itself.

In an age in which so much in the political arena depended on the individual who headed the state, the Assassins' way of waging war by going straight to the top with a dagger could well prove remarkably effective. Even when they were not actively so engaged, the threat always remained in the minds of Sunnī rulers. This, then, was in fact a form of state-sponsored terrorism, though not usually of an indiscriminate character. Attempts were indeed made to take Alamūt and to extirpate the Assassins. None succeeded, until the Nizārīs aroused the antagonism of an enemy against whom even they could not hope to stand: the Mongols.

Ismāʿīlī belief is a subject of immense and perhaps almost impenetrable complexity. It was held that as well as the apparent, open meaning of Islam there was an esoteric interpretation, the *bāṭin*, which could be known only to a few select initiates. Since many of our sources on the Nizārīs are the work of hostile Sunnī writers, by definition not among the initiated, it is not easy to say quite what the *bāṭin* amounted to. We do know that the Ismāʿīlīs held to a cyclical view of history very different from the linear view characteristic of orthodox Islam (and indeed of Judaism and Christianity). They believed that history was marked by an incessant cycle of *imāms* sent from God, beginning with Adam. First there would be a manifest *imām*, whose role was open and knowable; then a hidden *imām*; then another manifest *imām*; and so on.

Ismāʿīlī doctrine as taught at Alamūt went through some very curious vicissitudes. In 559/1164 the then Nizārī *imām* announced that the *qiyāma*, the Resurrection, had arrived. In practical terms this meant that true Muslims – that is, the Nizārīs – need no longer observe the constraints of Islamic law. For example, they could disregard normal Muslim practice with respect to prayer, permitted and forbidden foods and the fast of Ramaḍān. Nothing could have been better calculated to arouse the hostility and disgust of respectable Muslims, Sunnī and Shīʿī alike.

Yet in 607/1210, by as total a volte-face as could be imagined, the head of the order declared that from henceforth the Nizārīs would in fact become Sunnīs. It is hardly a matter for surprise that this apparent bid for religious acceptability met with a sceptical reception. Many Sunnīs will have recalled the doctrine, dear to the Shīʿīs, of *taqiyya*, tactical dissimulation of one's real religious views when it might be dangerous to avow them openly. Widespread suspicion that the Nizārīs' alleged conversion to Sunnism was no more than an example of *taqiyya* may well have been justified.

As we shall see in a later chapter, the suppression of the Ismāʿīlīs in Persia was the first of the Mongol Hülegü's commitments when he mounted his great expedition in the 1250s. Although the Mongols dealt a fatal blow to the Persian Nizārīs as a power in Persia and as a menace to society (an achievement for which Hülegü was praised by Muslim historians who had little other reason to be grateful to him), they were not totally extirpated. They continued in existence as a sect until in the nineteenth century their leader, the direct descendant of the *imāms* of Alamūt, fled to India, having clashed with the Qājār rulers of Persia. His present-day successor, the Aga Khan, is still the revered head of the sect. The Syrian branch survived its Persian parent by some years, eventually falling victim, in the 1270s, to the Mamlūk sulṭān Baybars. He, like Hülegü in Persia, effectively eliminated the power of the Nizārīs, but he retained some Assassins in his service for his own purposes.

THE QARA-KHITAI AND THE KHWĀRAZM-SHĀHS

To understand the history of the eastern Islamic world in the decades after the death of Sanjar we have to look further east, and go back some years in time. In 1125 the Liao Dynasty, the royal family of the Khitan people which had ruled Mongolia and north China since 907, was overthrown by the Jürchen of Manchuria, who set up a new dynasty in north China, the Chin. One Khitan prince, Yeh-lü Ta-shih, refused to submit to the new rulers and headed towards Central Asia with his followers. There, taking the title of Gūr-khān, he established an empire in the territories which today constitute, roughly, the Soviet Central Asian republics and the Chinese Central Asian autonomous regions. This is known to history as Qara-Khitai, which might be translated as "Black Cathay" (for the Khitans contributed the word "Cathay" to European languages). Yeh-lü Ta-shih's dynasty was regarded as still Chinese by the Chinese themselves: they gave it the dynastic title *Hsi Liao*, "Western Liao".

It may well be that the establishment of this strong new state contributed to Sanjar's troubles in that it would have been unwelcome to the Ghuzz tribesmen of the region, with their notorious distaste for submission to central governments of any kind: hence the arrival of the Qara-Khitai was an additional encouragement to them to head west and become a problem for Sanjar. But the impact of Qara-Khitai power on Sanjar was more direct than this. Transoxania, long an integral part of the Dār al-Islām, was subjected to Qara-Khitai rule, and a clash with the Great Saljūq sulṭān could hardly have been avoided. It came in 536/1141, on the Qaṭwān steppe near Samarqand.

Sanjar was defeated, and it has often been alleged that in this battle we have the origin of the legend of Prester John, the great Christian priest-king of remotest Asia who was thought to be hastening to the rescue of the crusaders in the Holy Land. The misunderstanding would have been comprehensible enough. Sanjar, after all, was the greatest Muslim sovereign of his day, and the Qara-Khitai ruler was his enemy. True, he was not in fact a Christian, but it was hard for twelfth-century Christendom to imagine that a great potentate who was opposed to Islam could be anything other than Christian. So there may be something in the theory that this encounter lay somewhere near the bottom of the Prester John Legend, though to believe so is essentially to apply the "no smoke without fire" principle, a dubious methodological tool when it comes to providing a historical explanation of legends.

As we have seen, Sanjar remained on the throne for a further sixteen years after the battle on the Qaṭwān steppe. But Transoxania fell to the pagan Qara-Khitai. They continued to hold it until, in the early thirteenth century, they were ousted by the Khwārazm-shāh. Yet Transoxania's fate under Qara-Khitai rule was not an insupportable one. The Qara-Khitai rulers were tolerant in matters of religion, and theirs was a decentralized polity in which large areas, including Transoxania, were allowed to enjoy a considerable degree of autonomy under their own local (and in Transoxania, Muslim) rulers.

Administratively the Qara-Khitai empire was a curious blend of Chinese and Central Asian elements. As befitted a sub-Chinese realm, the Chinese language retained its official status, and all coins were inscribed in it. But Persian and the east Asian Uighur variety of Turkish were also used. The Qara-Khitai army, too, combined aspects of Chinese military thinking (the use of infantry and a siege train, for example) with traditional steppe approaches to warfare (for the Khitans were in origin steppe cavalrymen, like their more formidable successors the Mongols). In time the army became more and more a force of steppe cavalry archers, organized decimally in the traditional nomad fashion that was to be inherited by Chingiz Khān.

Among those who were obliged to make their submission to the Gūr-khān of the Qara-Khitai was the Khwārazm-shāh. Khwārazm is the very fertile area where the River Oxus flows into the Aral Sea; it was therefore a close neighbour of the Qara-Khitai empire. Ultimately the rulers of Khwārazm, who adopted the ancient local title of Khwārazm-shāh, were to become the principal successors to the Saljūqs in Persia, and at the very end were able to throw off their subjection to the Qara-Khitai.

The Khwārazm-shāhs were not by any means an old-established royal house. They were merely the descendants of the Turkish *amīr* whom Malikshāh, in the late eleventh century, had appointed to govern Khwārazm. Their later fortunes are a vivid example of the abuses to which, as we saw in Chapter 4, the *iqṭāʿ* system was subject when the grasp of central government slackened.

Their rise to more than purely provincial power began under Atsiz, a contemporary of Sanjar who died in 551/1156. It continued under Il Arslan (died 568/1172), and most conspicuously in the reign of Tekesh (died 596/1200). They reached, though briefly, their greatest territorial expansion under Tekesh's successor ʿAlāʾ al-Dīn Muḥammad II. By the end of his reign he, in some sense, held most of central and eastern Persia; he occupied Transoxania in 606/1210, and in 612/1215 he conquered a large part of what is now Afghanistan from the Ghurid sulṭāns who had ruled from the central Afghan mountains. The Ghurid forces were obliged to withdraw to their lands in northern India, where some of their generals proceeded to set up a new and lasting state, the Delhi sultanate.

But as events were soon to show, a glance at a map of the Khwārazm-shāh's dominions would have given a quite illusory impression of the real strength of his position. His vast empire was riven with weaknesses both personal and structural. When the great test came with the invasion of Chingiz Khān in 616–20/1219–23, the Khwārazm-shāh's empire was to be found wanting. Indeed, it proved to be perhaps the least formidable of all the enemies the Mongols met in their long career of conquest.

Part of the problem was no doubt the very size of the empire. The most considerable additions to its territory had been made during the last few years of ʿAlāʾ al-Dīn Muḥammad's reign. There was simply insufficient time for the empire to be brought together into a coherent whole before its ruler had to attempt to cope with the challenge of the Mongols. Had the Khwārazm-shāh been granted some years' breathing space, it is possible that he would have managed to draw the threads together. It is possible but not, perhaps, probable. For the disparate nature and the recent acquisition of so large a part of his dominions were far from being the only, or the most disabling, difficulties he was confronted with.

Even the authority exercised by ʿAlāʾ al-Dīn Muḥammad as head of the state was itself tenuous. He was on very poor terms with his mother, Terken Khatun, who had wished another of her sons to succeed to the throne after Tekesh's death. In Khwārazm itself it is clear that she exercised more real power than did her son. Possibly more serious than this were the doubts that existed about the loyalty of the Khwārazm-shāh's army. Terken Khatun was in origin a princess of the Qipchaq or Qangli Turks, from the steppes to the north of Khwārazm. The bulk of the army, too, was composed of Qipchaq and Qangli mercenaries, and it was by no means clear that if an armed conflict broke out between mother and son, the son could rely on his army to fight for him rather than for his mother.

To add to these difficulties, there was also a Persian element in the Khwārazm-shāh's army, and serious tensions existed between them and the Turks. In these circumstances the Khwārazm-shāh would face an insoluble dilemma should he find himself having to deal with a military crisis. For if he concentrated his forces so as to defend his empire against an invader, there was a substantial risk that the army's first act would be his own deposition.

Nor were ʿAlāʾ al-Dīn Muḥammad's relations with the Islamic religious classes any better. The expansion of his empire coincided with the second half of the reign of al-Nāṣir, the most formidable and ambitious of the later ʿAbbasid caliphs. Affairs even degenerated to the extent that open armed conflict broke out between the forces of Khwārazm and Baghdad. The Khwārazm-shāh was not much more successful when it came to keeping on amicable terms with the Sunnī religious establishment within his own empire; and he exacerbated an already dangerous situation by having a noted and popular *shaykh* murdered. This was a serious matter, for a Sunnī ruler who wished to be accepted as legitimate could not easily do without at least the acquiescence of the caliph and his own religious classes. ʿAlāʾ al-Dīn Muḥammad tried, not with a great deal of success, to cope with this by leaning towards Shīʿism, presumably in the hope that he might in this way find an alternative basis of religious support, or at least bring pressure to bear on the Sunnī establishment to make its peace with him.

The Khwārazm-shāh could not rely, then, on the loyalty of his family, his army, or the religious officials of his empire. What, finally, of the attitudes of the vast unconsulted mass of the people? From the point of view of the ordinary subject, the regime would undoubtedly have been seen as predatory and oppressive. There was no question, then, of falling back on the residual loyalty of the population. No such sentiment existed. Few, if any, of ʿAlāʾ al-Dīn Muḥammad's subjects would regret the passing of his empire; and the people could not know that, when the Mongols came to destroy the empire and incorporate Persia into their own world state, the land would exchange a bad master for an immeasurably worse one.

CHAPTER SIX

The Mongols and their Coming to Persia

In the thirteenth century Persia became, and remained for more than a hundred years, part of the most extensive continuous land empire that has ever existed: that of the Mongols. The destruction and slaughter which the establishment of that empire involved were immense, on a scale unparalleled in the previous history of Asia. Persia itself had to endure many Mongol incursions as well as two major invasions, those of Chingiz Khān in the years after 1219 and his grandson Hülegü in the 1250s. From Hülegü's time until the 1330s, Persia itself constituted the major part of a Mongol kingdom, the Ilkhanate; and this was a kingdom whose rulers for its first forty years were not even Muslims. Mongol rule proved to be a grim experience, though it may not have been in every respect an entirely negative one, at least for those Persians who managed to survive.

"What event or occurrence", asked the greatest Persian historian of the Mongol period, Rashīd al-Dīn, "has been more notable than the beginning of the government of Chingiz Khān, that it should be considered a new era?"[1] It was the greatest upheaval Persia had suffered since the Arab invasions of the seventh century. Persia's earlier period of rule by nomads from the Central Asiatic steppe, in the shape of the Saljūqs, can have done little to prepare the land for the Mongol onslaught. For the Saljūqs, as we have seen, came in comparatively small numbers, indulged in little wanton destruction, and were already Muslims, needing no persuasion of the merits of Islamic civilization. None of this was true of the Mongols.

We cannot easily trace the Mongol people back beyond the period of the rule in Mongolia and north China of the Khitan Liao Dynasty (10th–12th centuries). There appears to have been a relationship of some sort between the two peoples, and the only partly understood Khitan language seems to be a form of what would later be called

Mongolian. The Khitans had garrisoned the oases of the Orkhon River in central Mongolia, and an identifiable Mongol people emerged in eastern Mongolia, behind the Khitan defensive screen. With the collapse of Khitan power before the attacks of the Chin from Manchuria in the early twelfth century, direct Chinese control of Mongolia lapsed. Among those who sought to fill the vacuum were the Mongols, and their leaders included the ancestors of Chingiz Khān.

The Mongols' way of life was in no way different from that of the other tribes of the central and eastern Asiatic steppe: indeed, it had much in common with that of the Ghuzz Turks before their entry into the Dār al-Islām. The Mongols were nomads, living at the north-eastern end of the territory which now forms the Mongolian People's Republic. Their flocks and herds were mainly of sheep and horses, though they also used camels and oxen. They migrated seasonally across their part of the vast belt of steppe grassland which stretched from Mongolia to the plain of Hungary.

They did not live in ignorance of the lands of settled civilization to the south, especially China. Indeed, they depended on the Chinese for some of the necessities of life such as metals for their weapons, as well as for luxury goods. The Chinese took some of the products of nomadism in exchange (though they were officially deemed to be tribute) and as a means of keeping the tribes quiet. This last was not always an easy task: the basic nomad attitude towards China was a predatory one, and every tribal *khān*'s dream was to be able to invade and occupy north China, that land of fabulous riches. Control of the tribes was therefore a matter of major importance for the rulers of north China. The traditional approach, which the Chin Dynasty adopted, did not involve attempting to rule the steppeland directly. The Chinese would watch for dangerous concentrations of power and would then back, with subsidies and titles, some other nomad chief whose function was to cut the over-powerful *khān* down to size. If their protégé in his turn became too powerful, the process would be repeated. This system's success rate was high, though it conspicuously failed to prevent the rise of Chingiz Khān.

The Mongols were not by any means the largest or the most important of the steppe tribes in the late twelfth century. A whole mosaic of tribes existed, some speaking Turkish, others Mongolian. The tribes – though generally claiming that their members possessed a common blood relationship, even descent from a common ancestor – were, in fact, more open in their membership than this would suggest. Tribes could, in fact, be joined. There were two institutionalized forms of relationship that had nothing necessarily to do with blood. A man could become the *anda*, the sworn brother, of another – a relationship of equality or near-equality – or he could become another's *nöker*, his comrade or follower, abandoning his allegiance to his own clan or tribe. In this way a young tribal leader who might have more personal charisma or military ability than actual wealth or social position could acquire a following and build up his power.

At the time of their arrival in Persia, and for long after, the Mongols continued to adhere to the traditional religion of the steppe peoples, Shamanism. In this rather amorphous complex of beliefs there was a supreme deity, Tengri, identified with the eternal blue heaven. Hence high places such as the tops of mountains, from where there was uninterrupted access to Tengri, were regarded as sacred. But of more practical importance was the lower level, the world of spirits. The shaman was the essential intermediary between men and this mysterious world, with which he communicated in trance. He acted also as exorcist and prophet, determining the future by examining the cracks on the charred shoulder-blades of sheep.

But Shamanism was neither a highly structured nor an exclusive faith. It sat rather lightly on the Mongols, who were known for their tolerance of – even their indifference to – all religions. It is perhaps not surprising that in due course the Mongols in their various Asiatic kingdoms adopted one of the locally dominant religions, Islam or Buddhism. Even Christianity, in its (from the standpoint of Rome) heretical Nestorian form, claimed a good many adherents among the people of the steppe. Adoption of one of the great world religions did not, however, necessarily mean that all traces of Shamanism withered away.

When the Mongols first conquered parts of the Dār al-Islām, they were a new phenomenon. The Saljūqs had had something in common with the Germanic barbarians who had invaded the western Roman Empire in the fifth century AD. Like most of the Germans, the Saljūqs came having already been converted to a form of the local religion. They respected Islamic society, shared many of its assumptions, and asked for nothing better than to be accepted: they did not come to destroy. Not so the Mongols, who knew themselves and their way of life to be superior to anything they would meet among the despised city-dwellers and agriculturalists of Persia. For many decades, the Mongols' new sedentary subjects were deemed to exist solely in order to be exploited. Such an attitude determined the character both of the Mongol invasions and of their subsequent rule. Not until the reigns of Ghazan in Persia (694–703/1295–1304) and, rather earlier, Qubilai in China, were signs of a more enlightened approach to be seen.

THE CAREER OF CHINGIZ KHĀN

The founder of the Mongol Empire was born, it is generally thought, in 1167, the Year of the Pig in the twelve-year animal cycle which the Mongols used for dating purposes. He was of noble blood, and his father, Yesügei, was a chieftain of some note, though not of the first rank. But Yesügei was murdered by the Tatars, the Mongols' hereditary enemies, when his son was only a child, and the young Chingiz's life, if we are to believe the Mongol sources, was a hard one in which he triumphed over many disadvantages before he was able to establish his power. He was evidently – and there can be no reason to doubt this – a young man of military ability, with qualities of leadership. In due course other young men attached themselves to him, becoming his *nökers*. He acquired, too, the support of one of the major steppe *khāns*, Toghril of the Kerait tribe, who had once been *anda* to Yesügei.

The basic Mongol source for the life of Chingiz Khān, the *Secret History of the Mongols*, seeks to give the impression that his rise to power occurred in spite of the enmity of some *khāns* and the treachery of others. It seems clear enough, however, that Chingiz was adept at making use of alliances for just as long as they served his purpose. He had little compunction in discarding those who had – no doubt for their own purposes – assisted him once he had no further use for them. In the years before 1206 he gradually, through military and diplomatic means, achieved supremacy over all the Turkish and Mongol tribes of the Mongolian steppe. Some tribes, notably the Tatars, were virtually wiped out. But most lost only their leaders: the rank and file, trained cavalrymen of great value, were incorporated into the Mongol military machine.

It was this formidable army that was to prove the essential instrument of Mongol world conquest and rule. It was organized decimally, in the traditional steppe fashion. The essential units were the thousand (*hazāra* in the Persian sources) and the *tümen* of, at least in theory, 10,000 men. Some tribes which had been loyal to Chingiz from the beginning of his rise to power were organized into military units formed out of their own warriors, but the defeated tribes, certainly the majority of the available manpower, were divided up among the new *tümens*. Hence Chingiz went some way towards averting any risk of revolt on the part of other tribes; and indeed it is possible to see the Mongol army as the creation of a kind of artificial tribal structure, in which the warrior's loyalty would be to his military commander and through him to Chingiz himself, rather than to the tribe into which he had been born.

The Mongol army was, at least initially, an exclusively cavalry force in which the principal weapon was the compound bow, made of layers of horn and sinew on a wooden frame. Although this army was virtually invincible in the field, it proved to have its limitations when the Mongols were fighting in sedentary areas, for cities cannot easily be taken by a cavalry charge. So in due course siege engineers were recruited, from both China and the Islamic lands. If our Persian sources are to be accepted, Mongol armies were colossal. There is a strong probability of exaggeration here, and it may well be that the unexampled manoeuvrability of the Mongol forces gave observers the impression of much larger numbers than were in fact present at any actual battle. Logistical considerations, too, cannot be ignored. All Mongol troopers travelled with several horses, perhaps as many as five or more. Hence, if the Persian chronicler Jūzjānī is right in his claim that the Mongol army which attacked the Khwārazm-shāh in 616/1219 was 800,000 strong, we have to ask ourselves how some 4 million or more horses could have been fed on the march towards Khurāsān.

On the other hand, it is clear that the Mongols were able to mobilize a far greater proportion of their manpower as active soldiers than would have been possible in any of the sedentary states with which they had to deal. In theory, and perhaps at times even in practice, the whole adult male population was available to serve in the army. Mongols learned to ride before they could walk, and fighting was regarded as no more than a variation on the ordinary daily life of the steppe nomad. The annual hunt, the *nerge*, an encircling operation designed to acquire stocks of meat for the winter, was organized on a vast scale and used techniques that were applied to warfare with little or no adaptation.

In 1206 the conclusion of the process of forcible tribal unification was marked by a *quriltai*, an assembly of notables. Here Chingiz Khān was "elected" as supreme ruler. This was the kind of election, familiar enough in the twentieth century, in which there was only one candidate: acclamation would perhaps be a more accurate word for the proceedings. At the *quriltai* the foundations were laid for the administration of the new polity, and Chingiz's most faithful followers received their due reward. A notable example was Chingiz's adopted brother, the Tatar Shigi-Qutuqu, who was made chief judge (*yarghuchi*) of the empire. This has generally been seen as the occasion of the laying down of Chingiz Khān's code of laws, the "Great *Yāsā*". While unwritten law and custom were of undoubted importance, however, there seems, in fact, no reason to suppose that a written code of Mongol law was instituted either in 1206 or later.

By the time of the 1206 *quriltai* Chingiz's Imperial Guard was, it is said, 10,000 strong. It was from the ranks of this Guard that the first generation of imperial administrators was recruited. As time went on, however, Chingiz relied to an increasing extent on experienced non-Mongol administrators, especially Uighur Turks and Khitans, to provide the necessary personnel and institutional machinery for the running of his empire. Later Mongol government in the conquered sedentary areas, especially China and Persia, tended to follow the previously existing patterns in those lands.

As in the case of the Arabs after their unification under the banner of Islam, there was little hope of maintaining the newly won tribal unity unless congenial and profitable warlike employment was promptly found for the army. The Mongol state therefore began to expand. The initial attacks were inevitably made on China. First the sub-Chinese kingdom of Hsi-Hsia, situated in north-west China across the main east–west trade routes, was brought to submission. Then the Chin Empire was attacked in a series of plundering raids that eventually became a systematic conquest. The Chin northern capital, near modern Peking, was taken in 1215; but the final defeat of the Chin was deferred until 1234, some years after Chingiz Khān's death. The much larger and richer – though possibly militarily weaker – Sung Empire in the south held out until 1279, when Chingiz's grandson Qubilai finally completed its subjugation.

The conquest of China was undoubtedly the most important Mongol political objective. But while Chingiz was still engaged against the Chin, his attention was diverted to the west. An old enemy, Küchlüg of the Naiman tribe, had fled to the Qara-Khitai after his defeat at Mongol hands. There he was received honourably, but this did not deter him from seizing the throne. Indeed, he went further. He had been brought up as a Nestorian Christian, but he now declared himself a convert to Buddhism and proceeded, in strikingly un-Buddhist fashion, to persecute those of his subjects who did not share his new faith. Many of these were Muslims, and they found their mosques closed by government decree. In 1218 Chingiz despatched a comparatively small force, commanded by his old *nöker* Jebei Noyon, into the Qara-Khitai lands. The Mongols were well informed about conditions there, for the ruler of the Uighurs, a subject of the Qara-Khitai, had already submitted. Jebei declared the religious persecution to be at an end, and the population lost no time in rising against Küchlüg. The great Central Asian realm was therefore added to the Mongol Empire, it would seem, by the desire of its inhabitants: an event unique in Mongol history.

THE FIRST MONGOL INVASION OF PERSIA

With the acquisition of the Qara-Khitai empire, Chingiz's territory bordered on that of the Khwārazm-shāh ʿAlāʾ al-Dīn Muḥammad. It is not clear whether at this stage the Mongols intended to attack him, though conflict would no doubt have occurred sooner or later. Chingiz had declared a wish to live in peace with the Khwārazm-shāh, though in the same message he had referred to ʿAlāʾ al-Dīn Muḥammad as his son, an assumption of superiority which was certainly provocative. But the Khwārazm-shāh himself made war inevitable. The governor of his frontier town of Utrār seized a caravan of merchants from Mongolia and executed almost all of them, on the (probably justified) ground that they were spies. One of the Mongol ambassadors sent to remonstrate was also executed. In Mongol eyes the person of an ambassador was sacred, and this act created a state of war.

We have already seen (in Chapter 5) that the Khwārazm-shāh was exceedingly ill-equipped for fighting a war against so formidable an opponent, and it is not easy to make sense of his actions. In fact he made no attempt to meet the Mongols in the field. Instead, perhaps fearing that his own forces were as much of a danger to him as the Mongols were, he divided them up as garrisons in the great cities of his empire. In 616/1219 the Mongols invaded Transoxania in a carefully co-ordinated three-pronged attack. The Khwārazm-shāh fled before them, to be pursued until he eventually found refuge on an island in the Caspian Sea, where he died.

There was massacre and destruction in Transoxania, but this was comparatively mild compared with the fate that was to befall the eastern Persian province of Khurāsān during the succeeding few years. Chingiz Khān put his youngest son Tolui in command of the operations that were to reduce Khurāsān to submission. This was done deliberately and with great brutality. As every city was summoned to surrender, it was warned that any resistance would be met with the total extermination of the population. This was in many cases literally done, except that craftsmen who might prove useful were spared so as to be shipped off to Mongolia. The great cities of Khurāsān such as Balkh, Harāt and Nīshāpūr were, we are told, razed to the ground. Millions, according to the contemporary and later chroniclers, were killed. The message soon spread that the Mongols meant what they said, for they usually kept their word and refrained from exterminating the people of any city that surrendered on demand.

Tolui's reign of terror continued until 620/1223. One can only speculate about why the Mongols chose to behave in so atrocious a fashion. No doubt they felt that they were punishing the misdeeds of the Khwārazm-shāh, though the punishment can hardly be said to have fitted the crime. Probably more important, they were removing permanently any possibility there might have been of a centre of power existing in Persia that could have rivalled Chingiz Khān himself. Lastly it may well be that, in the Mongols' steppe-oriented minds, the destruction of cities and agriculture was still a matter of little or no real consequence.

Chingiz Khān left the Dār al-Islām in 620/1223 to return to Mongolia. His last military campaign was against Hsi-Hsia, whose ruler had failed to contribute his due quota of troops for the expedition to the west. In 1227, probably aged about sixty, he died after a career of conquest which has few parallels in recorded history. But Chingiz was no mere military conqueror. He thought too in terms of organization and imperial structure. He left to his successors more than piles of plunder and corpses, though of both there was certainly a plentiful supply. He had laid the institutional foundations for an empire which could and did survive the death of its founder and indeed continued to expand.

Persia was not at this stage high on the Mongols' list of priorities. 'Alā' al-Dīn Muḥammad's son and successor, Jalāl al-Dīn Khwārazm-shāh, headed the resistance to the Mongols and was at first able, in the absence of the main Mongol army, to acquit himself fairly creditably. Unfortunately he chose to dissipate his energies in fighting a variety of other enemies as well, and ultimately his efforts had no effect on Mongol supremacy. For the three decades after Chingiz Khān's withdrawal, parts of Persia, especially the steppe-like grasslands in the north of the country, were under the rule of Mongol viceroys. Some major campaigns were mounted, notably the invasion of Anatolia by Baiju Noyon which culminated in the battle of Köse Dagh in 641/1243 and the submission of the Seljük sultanate of Rūm to the Mongols. But no sustained attempt was made to incorporate Persia fully into the Mongol Empire. With Hülegü's invasion in the 1250s a new situation was created.

HÜLEGÜ AND THE FOUNDATION OF THE ILKHANATE

The conception of political sovereignty as a family rather than a personal possession was found among the Mongols as it had been among the Turks. Hence on the death of Chingiz Khān his sons all received their due share. One son, the third, Ögedei, was recognized as Great Khān, as Chingiz had wished. But in other respects steppe precedent was followed. The youngest son, Tolui, received the original homeland in Mongolia; the eldest, Jochi, was given the most remote pastures, the lands that were later to form the Golden Horde in Russia and eastern Europe. As Jochi died shortly before his father, his share fell to his son Batu. The two middle sons of Chingiz Khān, Chaghatai and Ögedei, shared Central Asia between them.

This arrangement took account only of the steppelands. Chingiz Khān seems to have made no allocation of the sedentary territories he had conquered in Persia and China. But in any case his division of the empire was not long to endure. Ögedei died in 1241, his death precipitating a political crisis which among other things helped bring to an end Batu's great invasion of Europe (1237–42). Not until 1246 did Ögedei's son Güyük achieve recognition as Great Khān. This was in the teeth of Batu's disapproval, and only Güyük's death in 1248 averted the outbreak of open conflict between them. An alliance was then made between Batu and the sons of the now dead Tolui. In 1251 a *coup d'état* took place against the families of Ögedei and Chaghatai. With the support of Batu (whose virtual independence in his own territories was the price of his help), Tolui's eldest son Möngke became Great Khān.

Möngke had three brothers: Qubilai, Arigh-böke, and Hülegü. Qubilai was entrusted with the conquest of the Sung Empire in south China, while Arigh-böke remained in Mongolia. Hülegü was despatched to the west, to deal principally with two enemies: the Assassins and the ʿAbbasid caliphate.

So much, at least, we can state with reasonable certainty. It seems unlikely that at the beginning of their career of conquest the Mongols had seen themselves as having a divine commission to conquer the world. But they certainly came to hold that view when they found that they were in fact establishing a world empire. In this context Alamūt and Baghdad were alternative centres of power and loyalty which could not indefinitely be permitted to survive. What is not as clear is the exact nature of Hülegü's commission beyond the reduction of these two enemies. In particular, a question arises over whether or not Möngke intended that – as in fact happened – Hülegü should establish a kingdom in Persia for himself and his descendants.

There is some indication in the sources that the establishment of the Ilkhanate did indeed involve some irregularity, and that Möngke's original intention had been that Hülegü should return to Mongolia after he had completed his task in the Middle East. But as affairs turned out, such considerations became academic. For in 1259, while Hülegü was still campaigning in Syria, Möngke died, and civil war broke out over the succession to the Great Khanate between Qubilai and Arigh-böke, in which Qubilai was, by 1264, the victor. In these circumstances neither of the contenders was likely to suggest that a potentially valuable ally like Hülegü should give up his conquests.

Hülegü had set out from Central Asia with his army in 651/1253, proceeding very slowly towards Persia, where in 654/1256 he first of all attacked the Assassin castles, in both Qūhistān and the Alborz mountains. In some cases resistance was prolonged, though the head of the order surrendered quickly. He was later put to death, but not before he had made himself useful by ordering the commanders in his castles to submit to the Mongols. The end of real Ismāʿīlī power in Persia came swiftly and to all intents and purposes totally.

Baghdad was besieged in 656/1258 and the caliph, under the influence of an allegedly treacherous Shīʿī *wazīr*, refused to surrender. Baghdad was taken and sacked, and much of the population massacred. According to a later Persian historian, Ḥamd Allāh Mustawfī Qazwīnī, the death toll was as high as 800,000. Hülegü himself, in a letter of 1262 to King Louis IX of France, put it at more than 200,000. The caliph was executed and the ʿAbbasid caliphate brought to an end, though members of the family were maintained as at least nominal caliphs by the Mamlūk rulers in Cairo for a further two and a half centuries.

Syria was now invaded and the principal Ayyubid descendant of Saladin, al-Nāṣir Yūsuf, displaced. Aleppo and Damascus were taken, and Mongol forces penetrated deep into Palestine. It was at this point that Hülegü heard of the death of Möngke in China. Whether for this reason or (as he claimed when writing to King Louis) because of shortage of fodder and grazing in Syria, Hülegü withdrew with the bulk of his forces towards north-west Persia. He left behind a small force commanded by his general Kit-buqa.

In 648/1250 the Ayyubid regime in Egypt had been overthrown by its own slave soldiery, who set up the Mamlūk sultanate. The reigning sulṭān in 658/1260, Quṭuz, determined to resist the Mongol advance. Marching into Palestine with the assurance of the benevolent neutrality of the crusader states on the coast, he met and defeated Kit-buqa at ʿAyn Jālūt. A further defeat later in the same year made it clear that the Mamlūk regime was to survive and that Syria was to be part of its empire and not a Mongol province.

In the meantime Hülegü had to contend with the enmity of the Khān of the Golden Horde, Batu's brother Berke: indeed, fear of an attack by Berke in the Caucasus may well have been among Hülegü's reasons for withdrawing from Syria. Berke had become a Muslim, and it is reasonable to suppose that he was less than enthusiastic about the fate of the last ʿAbbasid caliph. But a more enduring cause of enmity between the khanates derived from disputes over whether the rich grazing lands of the Caucasus and Āẕarbāyjān should be under Golden Horde or Ilkhanid rule. Warfare in that region broke out in 659/1261 or 660/1262, and thereafter continued intermittently. Berke allied himself with the Mamlūks against the Ilkhanate, an alliance which was cemented by the practical consideration that the lands of the Golden Horde were the principal recruiting ground for fresh supplies of *mamlūk* soldiers. Mongols were now united with non-Mongols against other Mongols, and the inevitable result was that Mongol expansion in western Asia virtually ceased after 658/1260.

Nevertheless, Hülegü's achievement had not been negligible. Persia and Iraq, together with much of Anatolia, were brought definitively under Mongol control. Hülegü set up his capital at Marāgha in Āẕarbāyjān and the kingdom of the Īlkhāns was duly established, to be ruled by Hülegü and his descendants for the next seventy years.

NOTE

1. Rashīd al-Dīn, *Histoire des Mongols de la Perse*, ed. and trans. E. Quatremère, Paris 1836, 60–2.

CHAPTER SEVEN

The Early Mongol Rulers: Persia under Infidel Government (663–694/1265–1295)

Hülegü, conqueror of Persia and Iraq and founder of the Ilkhanate, died in 663/1265 – five years after the Mamlūks, by driving the Mongol forces out of Syria, had put a term to the expansion of the Mongol Empire in the Middle East. Hülegü was the first and last Īlkhān to be buried in the fully traditional Mongol fashion, with his funeral featuring human sacrifices. His remains were interred on an island in Lake Urmiyya, not far from Marāgha, the city in the north-west Persian province of Āẕarbāyjān which he had made his capital.

FOREIGN RELATIONS OF THE ILKHANATE

Hülegü was succeeded, without difficulty, by his son Abaqa, who asked for and obtained recognition as Īlkhān from the Great Khān Qubilai in China. Throughout the thirty years of the pagan Ilkhanate, relations with Qubilai remained close. Though there was never any question of the Great Khān actually nominating a new Īlkhān, his authentication of the arrangements made for the succession was thought to be necessary, and was more than a formality. Īlkhāns tended to defer their enthronement until Qubilai's approval arrived.

The selection process within the Ilkhanate was by no means always a peaceful one. It would seem that two, if not three, principles of succession were in conflict. One, a principle of steppe origin, was that the throne should pass to the senior member of the royal family, who might well be the late ruler's brother. Another, a practice more characteristic of Persian Islamic society, was that the throne should pass to the ruler's son. Overshadowing these was the consideration that the Īlkhān should be proved by his actions to be fitted for his position: incompetence, as so often in nomadic society, could result in *de facto* disqualification or deposition. It is a curious fact that throughout the period of the Ilkhanate – with the exception of the few months' reign of Baidu in 1295 – the succession passed according to the pattern son–brother–son–brother (see Genealogical Table 2).

The dynasty of Hülegü took its position as a subject realm to the Great Khanate seriously, and a permanent Mongol ambassador appointed by Qubilai resided in Persia. Qubilai's prestige, as the Great Khān who had finally conquered China and had been Hülegü's brother, was immense, and the connection between China and Persia remained strong until his death in 1294. There were sound practical reasons for maintaining the link, for Mongol unity was never re-established after the crisis of the 1260s. The Īlkhāns needed a powerful ally in the Mongol world.

Hostility to the Mamlūks in Egypt and Syria continued to be the basic feature of Ilkhanid foreign policy, with one brief and unsuccessful attempt at a *rapprochement* in the 1280s. This enmity resulted in a series of Mongol invasions of Syria. It is perhaps doubtful that the Īlkhāns seriously hoped or intended to incorporate Syria into their empire after the failure of 658/1260; and indeed, while some of their raids were successful, in other cases the advantage certainly lay with the Mamlūks. It may well be that the available grazing in Syria, as Hülegü had apparently found in 1260, was simply inadequate for the permanent needs of a Mongol army of occupation. But raids into Syria kept the Mamlūks busy and such expeditions, with the plunder they might yield, were perhaps a necessary precaution for the Īlkhāns. They needed to give their forces something useful and profitable to do if they were to avoid the dangers of faction and civil war in a period in which Mongol territory had ceased to expand.

The Īlkhāns could no doubt have coped much more effectively with the Mamlūk menace had Egypt been the only external enemy Persia had to face. But this was far from being the case. An even more powerful and nearer adversary was the Khanate of the Golden Horde to the north; and the Golden Horde–Mamlūk alliance against the Ilkhanate forged by Berke and the Mamlūk sulṭān Baybars in the 1260s proved enduring. Nor was this all. On their eastern frontier the Īlkhāns had to face not only incursions by the Chaghatai Khāns but also the implacable enmity of Qaidu, a member of the displaced house of Ögedei who established himself as the most powerful ruler in Central Asia and remained until his death in 1303 a serious menace to both the Ilkhanate and the Great Khanate in China and Mongolia.

It was in these worrying circumstances that the Īlkhāns began to consider the possibility of an anti-Mamlūk alliance with the once despised European powers. From the early 1260s envoys passed to and fro. At the time of Hülegü's invasion of Syria in 658/1260 the rulers of the crusading states, with the exception of the prince of Antioch and Tripoli, had felt that the Mongols were a greater danger to them than were the Mamlūks. In the light of previous experience of Mongol activities and behaviour this was a reasonable view, but the situation was now different. Mamlūk fortunes were thriving, and the reconquest of the Christian states was evidently among their aims. The now less formidable Mongols of Persia were the obvious potential allies.

Attempts were therefore made, in good faith on both sides, to form an alliance and to mount joint expeditions in Syria. The understanding was that in return for aid from the Christians, the Mongols would restore Jerusalem to them. Nothing, in fact, ever came of these efforts. The problems of distance and the difficulties of synchronization proved, in thirteenth-century conditions, to be insuperable. The crusaders' capital, Acre, fell to the Mamlūks in 690/1291, and apart from a brief moment in 699/1300 Syria remained within the Mamlūk, not the Mongol, sphere.

RELIGIOUS POLICY IN THE ILKHANATE

Attempts at alliance with Christendom were not interrupted by the conversion of the Ilkhanid Mongols to Islam in 694/1295: this was a development the Īlkhāns did not go out of their way to bring to the attention of the Christian powers. The popes, in particular, had always hoped that the Mongols in general and those of Persia in particular would become converted to Christianity, and there were a number of false alarms which seemed to suggest that this was indeed likely to occur. The Mongols were thought to have shown marked favour towards the Christians during their invasion of Syria, though in fact they were doing little more than acting in their traditional even-handed way. Nestorian Christians were known to be influential in the Ilkhanate, and were sometimes used as Mongol ambassadors to Europe.

The most conspicuous example of this practice was Rabban Ṣaumā, who travelled to Europe as envoy of the Īlkhān Arghun in the 1280s. He made a considerable impression, if his remarkable travel diary is to be believed, and he assured the assembled cardinals in Rome that many Mongols had become Christians. He had himself journeyed from the Far East with a disciple, Mark, who subsequently under the name Yaballāhā III became Catholicus – supreme head – of all the Nestorian churches of Asia, his seat being within Ilkhanid territory. Yaballāhā exercised considerable influence particularly at the court of Arghun, who had his son (later the Muslim Īlkhān Öljeitü) baptized and named Nicholas after the pope with whom Rabban Ṣaumā had negotiated.

But neither Arghun nor any other Īlkhān (with the possible exception of the ephemeral Baidu) ever in fact became a Christian. Islam triumphed in the end; but this took several decades, and in the meantime Buddhism enjoyed a brief period of official favour. Hülegü is said to have inclined towards it, though the circumstances of his funeral perhaps suggest that this did not go very deep. Under his successors, however, Buddhism was taken much more seriously, especially by Arghun. The preferred form of that faith, as in Mongol China, was a variety of the Lamaistic Buddhism of Tibet, in which magical practices dear to the hearts of the Mongols took a prominent part. This was a kind of Buddhism that was quite easily reconciled with the Mongols' ancestral Shamanism, which there is little reason to suppose was necessarily displaced by the Buddhism of the court.

Material evidence of Mongol Buddhism in Persia is very scant, for Buddhist structures were destroyed or converted to Islamic use after 694/1295. What has remained is what proved difficult to demolish. Outside Marāgha, Hülegü had had an astronomical observatory erected for the Shīʿī polymath Naṣīr al-Dīn Ṭūsī, who was high in his counsels. The observatory was on the top of a hill. Beneath it are a series of caves which, it has been shown, were in all probability constructed as a Buddhist religious complex. Other apparently Buddhist ruins exist near Marāgha which, as it was the first Ilkhanid capital, is where one would most expect to find them.

Despite residual Shamanism, the favour shown to Nestorian and other varieties (e.g. the Jacobite) of Christianity, and the Īlkhāns' dabbling with Buddhism, it was the indigenous religion, Islam, that the Mongols of the Ilkhanate ultimately adopted. The third Īlkhān, Tegüder, had taken the Muslim name of Aḥmad and announced his conversion. But no more was heard of this after his deposition and death in 683/1284. It was left to Ghazan, eleven years later, to take the definitive step and to carry his Mongol subjects with him.

THE ADMINISTRATION OF THE ILKHANATE

The fact that the first Īlkhāns did not greatly favour their Persian subjects' religion did not prevent the Mongols from drawing on Persian expertise in matters of government, administration and finance. The period saw the re-establishment of the Persian bureaucracy in its position of dominance over the day-to-day running of the country, apart from its military affairs. The only major exception to this rule occurred at the beginning of Arghun's reign, when Buqa, a Mongol *amīr* who had played a significant role in the deposition of Tegüder Aḥmad and his replacement by Arghun, became *wazīr* for several years.

But this was most unusual. In general it seems to have been felt that the nuts and bolts of administration were best left in the hands of those who understood the system as it had been inherited by the Mongols from previous regimes. This inevitably meant the Persians, though not necessarily always Muslim Persians: Buqa's successor as *wazīr* was Saʿd al-Dawla, a Jew.

The dominant figures until the mid-1280s were the Juwaynī brothers. The historian ʿAṭā' Malik had attached himself to Hülegü during the invasion of Persia, and ultimately died in office, in 682/1283, as governor of Baghdad and Iraq. His death came just in time to save him from execution. His brother Shams al-Dīn held the position of chief minister, with the title of *ṣāḥib-dīwān*, and retained it until his fall and execution in 683/1284. By that time members of the Juwaynī family had held high governmental positions almost uninterruptedly for some eighty years, serving Khwārazm-shāhs and Mongols in turn.

The position of chief minister was always precarious, and its holder was entirely dependent on the monarch's favour. This he could sometimes manage to retain against the intrigues of his rivals; but he might still have to face the difficulty of surviving a change of ruler, an event which occurred with some frequency, as the Īlkhāns tended to drink themselves to death at an early age. *Wazīrs* were in a position to accumulate great personal wealth, which in itself could increase their vulnerability: the dismissal of a minister and the expropriation of his property could easily be represented as a convenient way of solving temporarily a governmental cash crisis. Only one chief minister during the entire period of the Ilkhanate died a natural death, a statistic which does not seem to have deterred aspirants to the office.

The basic function of the Mongols' Persian ministers was a straightforward one: the extraction of as much revenue as possible from the Persian taxpayers, for the benefit of the Mongol ruling class. Hülegü's invasion had not, except in the case of the sack of Baghdad, been destructive to the extent of Chingiz Khān's. Presumably Hülegü knew well enough that he and his followers were coming to stay: there was little point in destroying their own potential property. But this did not mean that there was anything at all benevolent about subsequent Ilkhanid rule in Persia. The three decades that followed Hülegü's death were characterized by vigorous and oppressive short-term exploitation. The acceptability to the Mongols of a Persian *wazīr* would be measured before all else by the revenue receipts.

This, at least, is the impression deliberately given by our principal contemporary authority, the Persian historian Rashīd al-Dīn. Now Rashīd al-Dīn was chief minister to Ghazan, who on his accession in 694/1295 instituted reforms which were intended to rectify the abuses of the previous reigns. Hence Rashīd al-Dīn cannot be regarded as an unbiased source on those reigns. Nevertheless, his account in its essentials rings true enough. The Persian peasants, especially, had to endure a grim time under Ilkhanid rule.

The main instrument of this oppression was the taxation system, if system it can be called. The old pre-Mongol taxes, such as *kharāj*, continued to be levied, though the tax on non-Muslims, *jizya*, was in abeyance in a period of infidel government. But on top of these familiar taxes the Mongols imposed a series of their own exactions. These were many and various, but three in particular appear to have been the most important.

The most resented were *qūbchūr* and *qalān*. *Qūbchūr* had originally been a one per cent levy made on the Mongol and Turkish nomads' flocks and herds, but from the 1250s a tax of the same name was imposed on the sedentary subject population. Possibly following a precedent set by the Uighurs of Central Asia, it took the form of a poll-tax, its incidence determined by a census. The precise nature of *qalān* still remains obscure. In all probability it was a term used to cover a series of *ad hoc* exactions of a specifically "Mongol" character. The third of these taxes, *tamghā*, was a levy on commercial transactions: for all the difficulty the Mongols may have experienced in grasping the point of agriculture, they were always alive to the importance and profitability of trade.

Rashīd al-Dīn tells us – though we are not obliged to take this literally – that things reached such a pass that *qūbchūr* was being levied thirty or more times a year. The result, he says, was that the peasants left their land in droves. Inevitably this had its effect on the taxability of the agricultural sector, and ultimately led to government bankruptcy. Exploitation had been carried so far that the goose which laid the golden eggs was as good as dead. It was left to Ghazan, ably assisted by Rashīd al-Dīn, to try to retrieve something from the wreckage.

THE REIGNS OF THE ĪLKHĀNS

So much, then, for the general characteristics of the period between the death of Hülegü and the accession of Ghazan. We must now turn to look in more detail at the events of the individual reigns.

Abaqa (reigned 663–80/1265–82) made the most serious attack on the Mamlūk position in Syria since his father's expedition. It was not a success: the Ilkhanid army was defeated at Ḥimṣ in 680/1281. Abaqa did not long survive. He died in the following year – apparently of delirium tremens, to judge from Rashīd al-Dīn's account of his death. He expired at midnight after a drinking bout in his tent, gibbering about a non-existent black bird, possibly the Mongol equivalent of a pink elephant.

He had moved the capital of the Ilkhanate from Marāgha to Tabrīz, also in Āẕarbāyjān. There it stayed until Öljeitü (reigned 703–16/1304–16) moved it south-east to Sulṭāniyya. Tabrīz speedily developed into a great metropolis, situated as it was on one of the major east–west trade routes.

The Īlkhāns themselves, though they found it administratively and commercially convenient to possess a capital city, did not abandon their traditional ways. Unlike the Saljūqs, who were accustomed to living in cities, the Īlkhāns resided outside. They did not surrender their preference for living in tents, though the royal tent was no doubt of vast proportions and fitted with every conceivable luxury. From the nomad's point of view, Āẕarbāyjān was the most favoured province of Persia since it had the best pasturelands in the country: it was inevitable that the Ilkhanid capital should be situated there, even though it was perhaps dangerously close to the territory of the hostile Golden Horde.

Abaqa's death was followed by a succession dispute. A majority of the influential *amīrs* took the view that his brother Tegüder (reigned 681–3/1282–4) should become Īlkhān, rather than Abaqa's son Arghun. They were soon to regret their decision. It is perhaps unlikely that Tegüder's conversion to Islam and taking of the name Aḥmad in itself caused his downfall. Religious belief was not of overriding importance to the Mongols, and if Tegüder had simply wished, in his personal capacity, to be a Muslim it is unlikely that anyone would have objected. Berke of the Golden Horde had done precisely this without endangering his position, and his immediate successors did not feel it necessary to follow his example and accept Islam.

But Tegüder's conversion had consequences that were less acceptable. He wished to make peace with his new co-religionists, the Mamlūks of Egypt, and despatched two embassies to Cairo to try to bring this about. He was doubly unsuccessful. Sulṭān Qalāwūn viewed these Mongol overtures without enthusiasm, indeed with deep suspicion, and refused to have anything to do with Tegüder; and the Mongols of the Ilkhanate were aghast at the proposal to end for ever the long-standing and, to them, highly agreeable state of war with Egypt. The time was not yet ripe for the Ilkhanate to take its place among the Muslim powers of the Middle East.

In addition to this, Tegüder had not proved an able ruler; and he had shown unwise mercy towards his enemies when he had defeated the rival faction after Abaqa's death. The opposition and its figurehead, Arghun, were therefore still alive. They rose against the Īlkhān, whose half-hearted supporters melted away. He was defeated and captured. Arghun did not repeat his uncle's mistake: Tegüder was promptly executed.

Arghun reigned from 683/1284 to 690/1291. There was an immediate reversion to the more normal anti-Mamlūk policy, and it is even possible to argue that Arghun, an apparently sincere Buddhist who also favoured Christians, was more positively anti-Islamic than the Īlkhāns usually were.

During his first years the government was to a large extent in the hands of the Mongol *wazīr* Buqa. It is perhaps not a matter for surprise that the curious experiment of placing a Mongol at the head of the Persian bureaucracy was not a success. Buqa lost the Īlkhān's favour and is alleged to have conspired against him. He fell from power and was executed in late 687/early 1289, leaving the administration in need of a firm and competent hand.

Such a man was available in the shape of the Jew Saʿd al-Dawla, who lost no time in bringing in measures designed to reform the administration of government. He had earlier demonstrated his efficiency to the Īlkhān's satisfaction by greatly increasing the amount of taxation received from Baghdad – his methods, according to Rashīd al-Dīn, including the use of the bastinado and torture. There can be no doubt that Saʿd al-Dawla was an efficient and effective finance minister. All our sources, hostile to him though they are, are obliged to concede that he successfully reformed the administration and balanced the books.

But to those at court, this was a mixed blessing. His reforms had had the result of reducing the income of the leading Mongols and he had hostility to face, too, from both Muslims and Christians because of their objection to being at the beck and call of a Jew. He had unwisely behaved with great arrogance, perhaps forgetting how totally his position was bound up with the Īlkhān's favour or, even if he retained that, with his master's survival. He had accumulated a formidable number of enemies. Advantage was taken of Arghun's terminal illness in 690/1291 to seize and execute the most efficient chief minister since Shams al-Dīn Juwaynī. His death was followed by anti-Jewish pogroms in Tabrīz and Baghdad.

Arghun was killed not by alcohol but by his own curiosity about pseudosciences: he took a course of medicine which an Indian yogi asserted to be the elixir of life. Unfortunately it turned out to be poisonous. He was succeeded by his brother Geikhatu (reigned 690–4/1291–5), an amiable if dissolute individual who, like Tegüder Aḥmad, was to lose both throne and life essentially because he had also lost the confidence of the leading Mongols in his competence as a ruler.

Under Geikhatu the Ilkhanate's financial state reached a low point even by the standards set in his predecessors' reigns. By 693/1294 court extravagance and governmental inefficiency and corruption, coupled with the effects of a devastating cattle plague, had reduced the state to bankruptcy. Geikhatu's minister Ṣadr al-Dīn Zanjānī produced an attractive remedy. He proposed that paper currency, after the Chinese model, should be introduced into Persia.

The theory was that – the use of metal currency being forbidden on pain of the most fearsome penalties – all business would have to be transacted using the new paper money. This would be issued in exchange for coinage. Consequently all precious metal would fall into the hands of the government, whose economic problems, according to this rather crude variation on monetarist theory, would thus speedily be solved.

The system had worked well enough in China, though even there the economic troubles at the end of Mongol rule in the 1360s prompted an excessive reliance on issues of paper currency and caused a disastrous inflation. The currency certificates issued in Persia followed Chinese models very closely, and were given the name *chʿao*, a Chinese term. A *chʿao* note was oblong and had words in Chinese near the edge; but perhaps as a (rather ineffective) gesture towards local sentiment, it also had the Muslim confession of faith on both sides.

Whatever might have been the case in China, the whole idea was too utterly unfamiliar to be acceptable to the Persians. All commerce stopped dead, and the *chʿao* had to be withdrawn. Arghun's son Ghazan, who was acting as governor of Khurāsān, refused to have anything to do with the paper currency.

Perhaps surprisingly, Ṣadr al-Dīn survived the failure of the expedient with which he had been so closely associated. Not until 697/1298 was he executed by Ghazan for alleged embezzlement. Geikhatu himself, however, soon fell from power. He had grossly insulted his cousin

Baidu, and like Tegüder he had acted with injudicious clemency towards other enemies. In 694/1295 a faction headed by Baidu overthrew and killed him.

Baidu himself is a slightly enigmatic figure. Rashīd al-Dīn seems to have regarded his brief reign as in effect an interregnum between those of Geikhatu and his own patron Ghazan, for he ignores it entirely in his *Jāmiʿ al-tawārīkh*. Later in 694/1295 Ghazan was able to defeat and kill Baidu. The lesson about the dangers of excessive mercy had been learned only too well. In the first few years of his reign Ghazan executed numerous members of the house of Hülegü. The result was certainly, at least for a time, dynastic stability: Ghazan and his two successors held the throne without effective challenge until 736/1335. It was now to be possible to take serious steps towards putting the government of the Ilkhanate on to a more secure, efficient and equitable footing.

CHAPTER EIGHT

The Barbarians Civilized? Ghazan and his Successors (694–736/1295–1335)

CONVERSION TO ISLAM

While he was in Khurāsān during the reigns of Geikhatu and Baidu, Prince Ghazan had come under the influence of Nawrūz, a turbulent Mongol *amīr* whose family held considerable local power there. He was the son of Arghun Aqa, an Oirat Mongol who had been one of the most important early Mongol administrators in Persia. Nawrūz had long since been converted to Islam, and did his best to persuade Ghazan of the merits of such a course of action.

He was successful. Ghazan declared his conversion at the outset of his campaign against Baidu. Hence he became Īlkhān in 694/1295 as a Muslim. His *amīrs* followed his example in a body, and the Mongols of Persia as a whole duly conformed, at least in name. Ghazan ordered that Buddhists, if they did not wish to become Muslims, should leave the Ilkhanate and that their temples should be destroyed; though he later relaxed this severity slightly. Christians and Jews lost the status of equality which they had enjoyed under the tolerance of the pagan or Buddhist Īlkhāns. They reverted to their previous position, that of protected but second-class citizens. In due course their distinctive poll-tax, the *jizya*, was imposed on them once again.

Ghazan's motives for becoming a Muslim have been often, though inconclusively, discussed. Was he a sincere convert, as Rashīd al-Dīn predictably insists? Did he believe that Tabrīz was worth a *shahāda* (the Muslim profession of faith)? In the nature of the case we can never know. What is certain is that many of Ghazan's other actions were calculated to erode the alienation that existed between the Mongols and their Persian subjects. Conversion of the Mongols to the majority faith of Persia can only have helped in this process. The fact that the Mongols were infidels was by no means the only point of difference between them and the Persians; but it may well have been seen as the most conspicuous and unacceptable.

So far as the bulk of the Mongols of the Ilkhanate were concerned, their conversion was no doubt a fairly superficial affair, at least initially. As in the conversion of the Anglo-Saxon kingdoms to Christianity, it was the decision of the king that counted. If he held his kingdom with a sufficiently strong hand, it could be assumed that his subjects would conform to their monarch's faith. With the passage of time the new religion would establish itself genuinely as well as nominally.

But this did not happen overnight. During the reign of Öljeitü, according to his historian Qāshānī, the Mongol commander-in-chief Qutlugh-shāh, losing patience with a dispute at court between the adherents of two of the schools of Sunnī Islamic law, the Ḥanafīs and the Shāfiʿīs, expressed the view that Islam should be abandoned and that the Mongols should return to the good old ways of Chingiz Khān. Indeed, Qāshānī tells us that Öljeitü did in fact so revert, for a brief time. It is clear from Qutlugh-shāh's remarks, as reported, that he had an exceedingly weird conception of the actual tenets of the Muslim faith. This was after a number of years of "official" Islam; and Qutlugh-shāh was one of the most eminent Mongols in the Ilkhanate. We do not know whether he was typical, but his case should at least give us pause for thought.

Like other peoples of steppe origin, the Mongols as Muslims showed a marked preference for Islam in its mystical, *ṣūfī*, form. *Ṣūfī* masters like Shaykh Ṣafī al-Dīn Ardabīlī, founder of the Ṣafawid order and ancestor of the Ṣafawid dynasty (died 735/1334) were often treated with respect and favour by the Īlkhāns. The usual explanation for this, which may have an element of truth in it, is that a charismatic, perhaps wonder-working religious figure would most appeal to a nomad whose principal previous contact with men of religion had been with the shamans.

Ghazan's conversion to Islam did not by any means imply, as it had in the case of Tegüder Aḥmad, that attempts would be made to put relations with the Mamlūks on to a more friendly footing. Nor did Ghazan cease from trying to organize an anti-Mamlūk alliance with the Christian powers of Europe. Hostilities in Syria continued much after the customary pattern, and with a variable degree of success. On one occasion, however, Ghazan achieved a remarkable if ephemeral triumph. In 699/1300 he invaded Syria and drove all the Mamlūk forces back into Egypt. For a moment, more of Syria was in Mongol hands even than at the height of Hülegü's invasion forty years earlier.

The news, or garbled reports based on it, caused a sensation in

Europe. Pope Boniface VIII had declared 1300 a Year of Jubilee, and expectations of astonishing events were high. The story went that the Mongols had not only captured Jerusalem but had handed it back to the Christians.

The euphoria was short-lived. The Ilkhanid forces – perhaps faced with the usual difficulties over pasture; certainly suffering from the fact that a large proportion of the army's horses had died – soon withdrew from Syria. Ghazan in any case had to return home to deal with an invasion of his territory from the Chaghatai khanate of Central Asia. But the Īlkhān's hostile attitude towards his fellow-Muslims in Egypt remained constant throughout the reign. He may or may not have adopted Islam for reasons of internal political convenience, but it was certain enough that he would not allow the fact of his conversion to determine the shape of his foreign policy.

GHAZAN'S REFORMS

Despite his brief triumph in Syria, Ghazan was not markedly more successful in foreign affairs than his predecessors on the throne of the Ilkhanate. He concentrated his attention on domestic affairs, and in this sphere his achievements, or at least his good intentions, were remarkable.

He decided to institute a comprehensive series of administrative reforms, calculated to repair the damage caused by seventy years of Mongol misgovernment in Persia. His motives, according to a speech which his *wazīr* and historian Rashīd al-Dīn says he gave to the leading Mongol *amīrs*, were twofold.

Ghazan was concerned first of all about the short-sightedness of the conventional Mongol attitude towards conquered sedentary lands. Exploitation had been so merciless and unbridled that it had become self-defeating. If the peasants were taxed out of their livelihood they would have nothing left, and the yield from taxation would completely dry up. This, then, was an appeal to simple common sense which some of the more intelligent Mongols were perhaps capable of appreciating.

Secondly, however, he went further, pointing out that the Persians were in fact human beings, a consideration which the Mongols would do well to bear in mind when they were beating and torturing their subjects' wives and children. Here it may be reasonable to detect the humanitarian influence of Islam on the new convert. But we do not, of course, know whether the Mongol *amīrs* were impressed by this perhaps, to them, dangerously soft-hearted argument. Nor can we be certain that Ghazan ever really delivered such a speech. It may very well have been put into his mouth by Rashīd al-Dīn and have reflected as much the *wazīr*'s as his master's philosophy of government.

Rashīd al-Dīn preserves in his *Jāmi' al-tawārīkh* the texts of many of Ghazan's reforming edicts (*yarlīghs*). In this respect his history almost compensates for the fact that no archives have survived for this period of Persian history. This is by no means an unusual difficulty, being broadly true of the whole of Islamic history before the Ottoman period. Historians of the Muslim world are unavoidably more dependent on chronicle evidence than they would like. But at least it is something that one of our chroniclers should have elected to reproduce *in extenso* so large and important a body of documentary evidence.

The main areas chosen for reform were as follows. The rates and the methods and frequency of payment of taxation were regulated. All village property was to be properly registered for the assessment of taxation. The postal courier system, the *Yām*, was reorganized and measures taken to restrain the disorderly behaviour of *īlchīs*, travelling envoys who used and abused the *Yām* facilities. Attempts were made to improve security in the countryside and on the roads. The issue of drafts (*barāt*) payable on the revenue from the land was prohibited. Questions of disputed landownership were to be cleared up, and no claim dating back more than thirty years was to be entertained. Tax incentives were offered to any who would undertake the cultivation of the large areas of land that had fallen out of cultivation. The activities and payment of Islamic judges, *qāḍīs*, were regulated. The coinage was reformed, and weights and measures were standardized. The vexed problem of the payment of the army was tackled.

This last was a difficult matter: now that the Ilkhanate was no longer expanding and the supply of plunder could not be relied on, the soldiers needed to have an assured income if their loyalty and efficiency were to be maintained. Various methods had been attempted, without much success. Ghazan now resorted to a form of that tried and tested device, so important in Saljūq times, the *iqṭā'*. He assigned to the detachments of the army the areas of agricultural land nearest to their summer and winter pastures. The soldiers were to reside on these holdings, and were to receive the produce of the land in lieu of salary. Rashīd al-Dīn alleges that this measure was popular among the Mongols, since most of them were now anxious to engage in the practice of agriculture. How seriously we are to take this claim is by no means easy to say. Nor can we be certain to what extent the distribution of *iqṭā's* was actually implemented, for this particular edict was issued only very shortly before Ghazan's early death in 703/1304.

We can be confident, then, that the abuses and illegalities that existed were known to Ghazan and his government; and we can see in some detail what Ghazan proposed to do to set matters right. What we cannot say with any degree of assurance is that the reforms intended and laid down by Ghazan were actually implemented. It would be extremely rash, bearing in mind the likely effectiveness of government in the thirteenth century, to assume that merely because a law was promulgated, anyone necessarily took any notice. In many cases Ghazan's was not the first attempt in Mongol times to rectify these abuses. The fact that such legislation had to be constantly repeated is perhaps some evidence of the limits to its success.

If the testimony of Rashīd al-Dīn were to be accepted at face value, we would indeed assume that all the state's troubles were totally put to rights by Ghazan's reforming *yarlīghs*. But we cannot afford to forget that Rashīd al-Dīn was the Īlkhān's leading minister. He was therefore closely involved in planning and implementing the reform programme, and while this means that his evidence about it is quite exceptionally well informed, it also implies that he is by no means an impartial witness.

Other historians of the period, such as Waṣṣāf and Ḥamd Allāh Mustawfī Qazwīnī, discuss the reforms, though not in such great detail as Rashīd al-Dīn; and no one else gives us the texts of the *yarlīghs*. All are agreed that they were of major importance, but they tend not to be quite so enthusiastic as the great minister. They are not so sure that the programme was an unqualified success. Ḥamd Allāh, who as a *mustawfī*, an audit official in the financial administration of the Ilkhanate, is likely to have had access to good sources, maintains that as the result of the reforms the revenues of the state rose from 17 million currency *dīnārs* at the time of Ghazan's accession to 21 million at his death. An increase of the order of 20–25 per cent seems a modest enough claim, and is indeed by no means implausible.

The likelihood is that Ghazan's work, together with his strong hand on the government, ensured at least a temporary measure of improvement in conditions, and that this was to some extent prolonged during the reigns of his brother and nephew. Rashīd al-Dīn remained in office to continue his and his royal master's work. He retained the position of *wazīr* throughout Öljeitü's reign, though his influence was not as unchallenged as it had been under Ghazan. He was obliged to share power with other officials: ultimately with Tāj al-Dīn ʿAlī Shāh, who in the end brought about his rival's downfall and death before himself achieving the unparalleled feat of dying of natural causes (though one later chronicler suggests that he was in fact poisoned).

We may hazard, then, that the Ilkhanate was a more efficient, and possibly a more humane, kingdom as a result of Ghazan's efforts. But there is not sufficient evidence to justify us in believing that the reforms brought about a total transformation in the character of Mongol rule. Probably more would have been achieved had Ghazan's reign lasted longer than a mere nine years. Nevertheless, he should be given credit for inaugurating the most sustained attempt made to rectify some of the disorders that the Mongol conquest and occupation had brought down upon Persia.

THE LAST ĪLKHĀNS

Ghazan left no sons, and was succeeded by his brother Öljeitü (reigned 703–16/1304–16). The last thirty years of the Ilkhanate's history are more difficult to document than the preceding fifty, for there are few major surviving sources for the period. For Öljeitü's reign we have a fairly detailed chronicle by Qāshānī, but for his son Abū Saʿīd we are obliged to resort very largely to histories written many years later, in the Timurid period. This is a serious disadvantage when we have to attempt an explanation of the presumed decline and the undoubted fall of the Mongol kingdom in Persia.

Öljeitü had at least two major achievements to his credit. He was responsible first of all for the last new addition to Mongol-ruled territory: his army conquered the province of Gīlān, on the Caspian coast. The Caspian provinces, because of the difficulties of their heavily wooded terrain and their inaccessibility behind the Alborz mountains, have often been able to resist the control of the Persian central government. This was almost as true in the early twentieth century as it had been in early Islamic times, and it is certainly significant that even the Mongols, the most formidable of conquerors, took so long to subdue Gīlān.

Secondly, Öljeitü bequeathed to Persia the most impressive piece of evidence which could be said to show that the Mongols were capable of construction as well as demolition. This was his own mausoleum at Sulṭāniyya. Öljeitü's religious pilgrimage was complex even by the standards of the time, and he had passed through Christian and Buddhist phases, not to mention his probable residual Shamanism, before spending some years oscillating between the Sunnī and the Shīʿī forms of Islam. It is said that during his Shīʿī period he planned to bring the remains of the early Shīʿī martyrs ʿAlī and Ḥusayn from their shrines in Iraq, and intended Sulṭāniyya to become a new centre of pilgrimage. This scheme, for whatever reasons, did not come to fruition. The mausoleum became his own. It was the central feature of his new capital and remains now as its only important surviving building. With its vast double-skinned dome, which some experts believe may have influenced the design of Brunelleschi's dome for Florence cathedral a hundred years later, it is a magnificent memorial, one of the finest buildings in Persia.

At the time of Öljeitü's death his successor Abū Saʿīd was only eleven years old. Initially, both his father's *wazīrs*, Rashīd al-Dīn and Tāj al-Dīn ʿAlī Shāh, were retained in office; but the former's fall and execution, at the age of seventy, soon followed. The dominant figure during the first decade of the reign was a leading Mongol *amīr*, Chopan. The period, in the absence of a strong and effective Īlkhān, saw the beginnings of the factional struggles which were to destroy the Ilkhanate utterly after the death of Abū Saʿīd. The two principal Mongol factions were Chopan's own, known as the Chopanids, and the followers of Ḥasan Jalayir, the Jalayirids. The Īlkhān endured his tutelage until 727/1327, when he acted to overthrow and kill Chopan and take over the reins of power himself.

For the remainder of his reign, until 736/1335, Abū Saʿīd seems to have ruled the Ilkhanate with considerable competence. He was ably assisted by Rashīd al-Dīn's son Ghiyāth al-Dīn, whom he appointed as *wazīr*. Writers later in the fourteenth century liked to portray Abū Saʿīd's time as something of a Golden Age, though admittedly this may reflect their experience of the troubles of the anarchic post-Ilkhanid period as much as it is a sober comment on the last Īlkhān's qualities, however real they may have been.

Even before the establishment of Abū Saʿīd's personal rule his government had achieved a notable change in the pattern of the Ilkhanate's foreign affairs: in 722/1322 peace was made with the Mamlūks. This proved enduring, and the apparently endless cycle of campaigns in Syria was terminated.

But all Abū Saʿīd's ability could not save his kingdom once he was dead. The factional struggles of his first years were certainly an ominous indication of what might happen if central control were relaxed, though there is virtually no sign during the reign that the Ilkhanate was in a state of decline. Nevertheless, the Ilkhanate can hardly be said to have survived Abū Saʿīd, and it may reasonably be suggested, therefore, that it fell without in any real sense having previously declined. Why was this?

The crucial reason is a simple one: Abū Saʿīd left no heir. This did not mean that the Mongol royal house was extinct; but the direct line of Hülegü had failed. Ghiyāth al-Dīn attempted to fill the vacuum by raising to the throne Arpa Ke'ün, a descendant of Chingiz Khān though not of Hülegü. This move gained insufficient support, and Īlkhān and minister fell together after a reign of only a few months. Thereafter a variety of Chingizid pretenders, many of them members of the house of Hülegü, put themselves forward or were promoted as figureheads by the various contending factions. None was able to gain control of the whole Ilkhanid legacy. Of the factions the most notable, ultimately, were the Jalayirids, who built up a strong position in Iraq and Āẕarbāy-jān which survived into the fifteenth century.

There seems little reason to suppose that, had Abū Saʿīd left a male heir who was generally acceptable to the Mongol *amīrs*, the Ilkhanate would necessarily have disintegrated in the 1330s. In the absence of an acknowledged Īlkhān, power in Persia was there for whoever had the strength to seize it. The situation was an open invitation to the factions that had already formed. The Ilkhanate was doomed by dynastic failure: an interesting demonstration of the historical importance, in some circumstances, of the highly placed individual.

THE MONGOL IMPACT ON PERSIA

It takes a very determined historical revisionist to make out much of a case in favour of the Mongols as rulers of Persia – though this has in fact been attempted. Contemporaries were in no doubt of what the verdict should be. Juwaynī, a historian who was also a lifelong servant of the Mongols, has often been accused of flattering them. Yet he wrote that "every town and every village has been several times subjected to pillage and massacre and has suffered this confusion for years, so that even though there be generation and increase until the Resurrection the population will not attain to a tenth part of what it was before."[1] This was at the beginning of the Ilkhanate. At its end, Ḥamd Allāh Mustawfī Qazwīnī, another Mongol government official, concluded that "there is no doubt that the destruction which happened on the emergence of the Mongol state and the general massacre that occurred at that time will not be repaired in a thousand years, even if no other calamity happens; and the world will not return to the condition in which it was before that event."[2]

The initial destruction was undoubtedly immense. We do not need to believe, with the chroniclers, that millions were massacred by the Mongols at each of the great cities of Khurāsān. Indeed, anyone who has looked at the size of some of the sites concerned, such as the walled area of Harāt, will be unable to believe them. Nevertheless these figures should be taken seriously, not as statistics but as evidence of the chroniclers' state of mind: clearly these massacres were on a scale quite outside their previous experience. There is no dissenting voice among our authorities, whether they were compiling their histories within the Mongol Empire or in the hostile neighbouring states; whether they were contemporary with the events or writing later.

It is no light matter to discount such unanimity. All that can be said in mitigation is that the destruction was patchy in its incidence. The areas attacked by Chingiz Khān himself and Tolui, especially Khurāsān, suffered most; but other areas, such as much of the south of Persia, never had to suffer a full-scale Mongol assault. Similarly, as we have seen, Hülegü's invasion was, for sound practical reasons, by no means as destructive as his grandfather's punitive expedition against the Khwārazm-shāh had been.

The impact of the invasions was not limited to massacre and destruction in the cities. Perhaps of more lasting significance for Persia, agriculture also suffered. There was some deliberate destruction, but probably more important was the flight of the peasants from their land. The result was that large tracts went completely out of cultivation, as Ghazan's attempt to encourage recultivation showed. The problem in Persia is that land that has been neglected may well not be easy to bring back into cultivation. Agriculture was, in the absence of large rivers or adequate rainfall, very dependent on the *qanāt* system of underground water channels. Since – as we saw in Chapter 1 – *qanāts* require constant skilled maintenance if they are to continue to operate, many will have been ruined, not necessarily by deliberate destruction but simply through long-term neglect because the peasants had fled. The character of Mongol rule was not such as to encourage them to return. Land left uncultivated for a long period could well revert to desert.

Similarly in the case of Iraq, it has traditionally been held that the Mongols were responsible for the destruction of the ancient system of irrigation. This was not *qanāt*-based but drew its water from the great rivers, the Tigris and Euphrates. It is unlikely that Hülegü deliberately destroyed the agricultural potential of Iraq though here, too, much damage could inadvertently have been done simply through lack of proper maintenance of the irrigation canals. It should be said, however, that the fertility and prosperity of Iraq at the time of the Mongol conquest were in any case in decay, and far from what they had been in the great days of the early ʿAbbasids. Whatever the immediate results of Hülegü's invasion, Iraq certainly did not flourish under Ilkhanid rule. It became a neglected frontier province.

Persia's ordeal was not at an end once the invasions proper were over. Ilkhanid government before the accession of Ghazan aimed at immediate exploitation of the wealth of Persia for the exclusive benefit of the conquerors. Mongol rule also involved a large increase in the nomadic sector of the population. Much formerly agricultural land was turned over to pasture: it could not be said of the Mongols, as it could of the Saljūqs, that the land they occupied as nomads was for the most part marginal from the agricultural point of view. It can be claimed that the nomadic influx into Persia in the Saljūq period was, on balance, of benefit to the economy. No such suggestion can be made in respect of the much greater nomadic immigrations that occurred in Mongol times.

A measure of reconstruction was eventually undertaken, and it is rightly associated with the reign of Ghazan Khān. Whatever our estimate of the effectiveness of Ghazan's reforms, he at least attempted to undo some of the damage his ancestors had inflicted on Persia. Perhaps as important was the change in attitude which seems, to some extent, to be evident. There does appear in the late Ilkhanid period to be a much greater degree of identification between the Mongols and their Persian subjects than in former times. It may be that Rashīd al-Dīn's assertion, when writing about Ghazan's allocation of *iqṭāʿs* to his army, that the Mongols were becoming favourably inclined towards agriculture, is a significant pointer towards changing attitudes. So is the occasional piece of evidence that – as for example in Fārs – some of the Mongols were intermarrying with the Persians. The conversion of the Mongols to Islam removed the most conspicuous point of difference between them and most of their subjects, and it must certainly have facilitated enormously the assimilation of the Mongols into Persian society. It is interesting to note that although the Ilkhanate did collapse, the Mongols were never driven out of Persia, as they were from China. Eventually they simply disappeared from view. Admittedly there were probably not very many of them in any case: the majority of the rank and file of the "Mongol" armies were no doubt Turks. But they do seem, ultimately, to have been successfully and fairly painlessly absorbed into the Turkish Muslim population of Persia.

Not everything in Ghazan's reform programme improved the Persian subjects' lot. One of its effects was to tie the peasants to the land, though this may have been no more than a formal regularization of what had previously been the customary practice. Even after the

Mongols had become Muslims, it has been noted that an increasing amount of property was constituted as *waqf*, supposedly inalienable religious endowment. Certainly an avowedly Muslim government would be less likely to expropriate *waqf* property than its infidel predecessor; but it has been suggested that this development may indicate that security of tenure was regarded as uncertain, and that there was still a lack of confidence in the justness of the Ilkhanid government, even after it had gone over to Islam.

Other positive points may be made in the Mongols' favour. The fact that Persia became, for a time, part of a vast Asian empire did mean that intellectual horizons were broadened. The scope of some of the historians of the Ilkhanate – such as Juwaynī, Waṣṣāf and above all Rashīd al-Dīn – was far wider than that of their predecessors, or indeed of their post-Mongol successors. Political, religious and cultural barriers were partially and temporarily lowered. Persia became a link in the chain that led from Europe to China, and the influence of motifs from Chinese landscape painting in Persian art of the fourteenth century, the first great age of Persian miniature painting, was highly beneficial.

In the last analysis, however, we may justly have our doubts over how impressed the Persian peasants, as they did their best to avoid the Mongol tax-collectors, would have been by developments in miniature painting. For Persia, the Mongol period was a disaster on a grand and unparalleled scale; though for the historian, at the safe distance of seven centuries, it is a disaster of great fascination.

NOTES

1. Juwaynī, *Ta'rīkh-i Jahān Gushā*, ed. M. M. Qazwīnī, vol. 1, Leiden and London 1912, 75: trans. J. A. Boyle, *The History of the World Conqueror*, vol. 1, Manchester 1958, 96–7.
2. Ḥamd Allāh Mustawfī Qazwīnī, *Nuzhat al-qulūb*, ed. G. Le Strange, Leiden and London 1915, 27.

CHAPTER NINE
The Empire of Tamerlane

THE POST-MONGOL VACUUM

The collapse of the Ilkhanate after the death of Abū Saʿīd in 736/1335 resulted in a series of factional struggles for control of the central government of Persia, struggles which had no decisive victor. Concepts of political legitimacy tended to require that the throne should remain the perquisite of the house of Chingiz Khān, if not of the Huleguid branch of it, and a series of Chingizids were briefly elevated in various parts of the land, most of them – with the exception of Togha Temür, who ruled in western Khurāsān until 754/1353 – as puppets or semi-puppets of the contending factions.

In these circumstances it was possible for local dynasties in different areas of the country to assert their independence. The Jalayirid faction succeeded in eliminating its principal rivals, the Chopanids, but it was not even then sufficiently powerful to prevent families which already held a position of influence in the more outlying provinces from going their own way.

Of these local successor states to the Ilkhanate the most significant was probably that of the Muzaffarids. The head of the family, Mubāriz al-Dīn, had gained control of the city of Yazd, in central Persia, during Abū Saʿīd's reign, and in the 1350s he was able to displace the Injuids, another local family, who had ruled in the southern province of Fārs since the early years of the century. Mubāriz al-Dīn established his capital at Shīrāz, in Fārs; he had already extended his power further east still to Kirmān. Iṣfahān, too, came under Muzaffarid rule, and when on two occasions their armies briefly managed to take Tabrīz, the old Ilkhanid capital, it might have seemed that a real central government was about to be re-established in Persia under Muzaffarid auspices. But they were unable to hold the north-west permanently against the

Jalayirids, who were based in Baghdad, and they remained no more than a formidable local power, only to fall victim to Tamerlane (Temür) after the death of their great ruler Shāh Shujāʿ in 786/1384.

In the north-east, in Khurāsān, another local family, the Karts of Harāt, had survived the end of Ilkhanid rule with their influence intact. They had governed Harāt as at least semi-autonomous representatives of the Mongols since the mid-thirteenth century, sometimes playing a significant if slightly ambiguous role in Ilkhanid politics. They too did not succeed in surviving the onslaught of Temür, and their power was finally suppressed by him in 785/1383.

More fortunate was a dynasty – if such it may be termed – to the west of them, at Sabzawār. This was the Sarbadārs (a name which means "heads on gallows"), who were an independent power from 736/1336 to 783/1381 and thereafter tributaries, with their power much reduced, of Temür. The Sarbadār state was a revolutionary Shīʿī polity without effective dynastic succession. It has been interpreted in various ways. A Marxist historian like I. P. Petrushevsky sees it as the result of a popular movement of social protest, essentially a peasant uprising against "feudal" oppression. J. M. Smith, by contrast, prefers to explain the establishment of the Sarbadār state as deriving from a revolt by the upper classes of the region against taxes they found objectionable. Whatever the truth of the matter, there is no denying the lower-class and, in some sense, the revolutionary element in what was going on.

Still, the Sarbadār leaders are perhaps hardly likely to have been proto-Lenins, though even so the Sarbadār phenomenon was an extraordinary one, an interesting example of what might happen in Persia when central political control was relaxed. In this connection it is perhaps worth pointing out that the decades immediately following the collapse of the Ilkhanate saw the arrival of the Black Death, in the Middle East as well as in Europe. Not a great deal of evidence has survived about its impact on Persia; but what there is gives good ground for supposing that mortality from the disease made its own contribution to the prevailing political instability of the period.

THE RISE OF TEMÜR

None of the local successor states to the Ilkhanate was destined to give Persia unified government. Unity of a sort did come, but it came from outside the old boundaries of the kingdom of Hülegü, from the territories of the Ilkhanate's eastern neighbour and traditional enemy. This was the Chaghatai Khanate of Central Asia, the part of the Mongol Empire allotted by Chingiz Khān to his second son Chaghatai and his descendants.

By the middle of the fourteenth century, the Chaghatai Khanate had fallen into two parts which were to a considerable extent separate entities. Different branches of the royal house ruled, or reigned, in the two halves. The eastern half, Mughulistān, retained quite consciously a good deal of the original Mongol ethos. Its society was still predominantly nomadic, and its people for the most part remained pagan, though Islam had made some progress. The western half, Transoxania, was very different: this, after all, was – unlike Mughulistān – an old-established centre of Islamic civilization. Though the ruling classes were the Chaghatais, the Turko-Mongol nomadic tribesmen, the bulk of the population consisted of sedentary peasants and city-dwellers. In Samarqand and Bukhārā Transoxania could boast the possession of two of the great cities of Islam and its people, settled and nomad alike, were Muslims.

In Mughulistān the Chaghatai khāns were still the rulers, but in Transoxania they had lost all effective control over affairs. Real power now rested in the hands of a variety of *amīrs*, men who were influential Chaghatai tribal magnates. At times a single *amīr* could become dominant, as in the case of Qazaghan, who was the major political influence in Transoxania for more than a decade before his death in 759/1358. But even such an *amīr* was hardly the ruler of Transoxania; he was rather a first among equals. As in the Ilkhanate after 736/1335, political legitimacy, if not actual power, continued to reside in the Chingizids; *amīrs* like Qazaghan therefore normally retained a member of the house of Chaghatai as nominal *khān*.

Temür – Tamerlane or Tamburlaine (Temür the Lame) in Western literature – was born near Shahr-i Sabz in Transoxania, traditionally if perhaps suspiciously in the same year in which the last "real" Īlkhān, Abū Saʿīd, died. He was a member of the Barlas, a tribe of Mongol origin which had become Turkish in speech and had adopted Islam. Despite the allegations of the inscription on his tomb in Samarqand he was not, and did not in his lifetime claim to be, a descendant of Chingiz Khān. Later in his career he married two Chingizid princesses, and thus acquired the title of *güregen* ("son-in-law"). Throughout his career this absence of royal prestige obliged him, like so many others, to acknowledge a Chaghatai prince as the nominal ruler, though he seems not to have bothered to appoint a successor when his tame Chaghataid, Sulṭān Maḥmūd, died, probably in 805/1402, three years before his own death. In due course, descent from Temür itself came to confer legitimacy, and his successors were ultimately able to dispense with the Chaghataid fiction.

The road to power in mid-fourteenth-century Transoxania was in some respects similar to what it had been in Mongolia at the time of Chingiz Khān; and the accounts we have of Temür's early career bear a striking – again possibly a suspicious – resemblance to the life of the young Chingiz. The class that mattered politically were the Chaghatai nomads. Unlike the twelfth-century Mongols, they were not ignorant of city life or unconscious of its potential financial benefits to them: they installed governors in cities, they used fortified strongpoints in warfare, and they collected taxes from the sedentary population. But the settled peoples were politically insignificant.

An ambitious Transoxanian nomad had first to acquire the chieftainship of his own tribe. To achieve this he had to build up a strong personal following of men who would accept his leadership because of his personal qualities, as Chingiz Khān had based his power on the support of his *nökers*. With his followers and his own tribe behind him, he could establish alliances with other tribes. As he became a power in the land, smaller tribes and military groupings deriving from the period of Mongol conquest and government (many of which had in the course of time become artificial tribes) would be attracted to his banner. Among the steppe peoples, nothing succeeded like success.

Part of Temür's achievement as conqueror and ruler is perhaps to be explained in terms of the support he always enjoyed from the people of Transoxania, in that they saw him as their most potent defender against the nomads, especially those of Mughulistān but also those of the Golden Horde to the north. The Chaghatai Khāns of Mughulistān had by no means accepted the division of the old khanate as definitive, and frequently interfered in the affairs of Transoxania. Indeed, Temür was not at all above exploiting this when it suited him: he owed his seizure of the Barlas leadership in 762/1361 largely to temporary Mughul support. But he had also built up his own personal following, starting as perhaps little more than a successful robber-chief, and he made appropriate alliances with other chiefs, such alliances often being cemented by marriage.

His principal ally and later rival was Ḥusayn, grandson of the *amīr* Qazaghan: Ḥusayn plays a part in Temür's career which is parallel to that of Jamuqa, Chingiz Khān's *anda* and later enemy, as portrayed in the *Secret History of the Mongols*. Like Chingiz's rise to power in Mongolia, Temür's had marked vicissitudes, but by 771–2/1370 he had become in effect the unchallenged ruler of Transoxania.

TEMÜR'S CONQUESTS

Like many another tribal unifier, Temür now had to face the question of what to do with his militarily effective but potentially unruly followers. His solution was the customary one: he would keep them agreeably and profitably occupied – and thus avoid any danger to his own supremacy – by embarking on a series of campaigns of conquest beyond his own boundaries. It is a remarkable fact that after 771–2/1370 Temür spent almost the whole of the remainder of his life, some thirty-five years, outside Transoxania.

Chingiz Khān, in organizing his superlative army, had to a considerable extent recast the old tribal structure of Mongolia by breaking up many of the tribes among his new military formations. Temür, in forming his army of conquest, acted in a similar though less thoroughgoing fashion. The old tribes and groupings did survive, but their original leaders were gradually eliminated. Instead, military leadership was entrusted to Temür's own followers and to members of his family – two groups which could be relied on, at least to some extent, to produce generals whose loyalty Temür could trust. It was no doubt possible that even members of this new elite might prove to have political ambitions of their own. This danger was reduced by keeping them constantly on campaign, out of Transoxania and away, therefore, from their traditional sphere of political activity.

Armies of Chaghatai nomads from Transoxania were in due course settled permanently in the newly conquered provinces. Temür's sons and grandsons were appointed as provincial governors, but even they (with good cause) were not trusted: *amīrs* were in place to supervise them, and their governorships were frequently changed, so that they should be unable to build up a strong local power base. With the Chaghatai armies no longer resident in Transoxania, other measures had to be taken for the protection of the home province. Temür's solution to this difficulty was to install there a new nomadic population made up of tribal levies transferred from the lands he had conquered, especially from Anatolia, Āẕarbāyjān and Iraq. Thus he both protected his homeland and reduced the numbers of effective and potentially hostile troops available to defeated rulers in other areas.

Temür's army seems to have followed the traditional steppe pattern in most respects. It was a largely cavalry army, though it included some infantry, and considerable emphasis was placed on its siege engineers. As we have seen, it incorporated contingents conscripted from the conquered regions. Like the Mongol army, it relied on its great mobility and on the skills of the steppe cavalry archer, who was trained by means of such activities as the great encircling hunts. It was organized decimally, with units such as the *hazāra* and the *tümen*, theoretically consisting of 1,000 and 10,000 men respectively. Again like Chingiz Khān's, Temür's armies relied on the terror of his name to induce speedy surrender. They adopted the same principle that the people of any city that surrendered on demand would be spared, while any that resisted could expect a bloody massacre. The principal difference between the two great conquerors in this respect was that Temür indulged in extreme refinements of cruelty which would have been alien to Chingiz's sense of efficiency, if nothing else.

It is, as usual in such cases, almost impossible to arrive at any accurate assessment of the size of Temür's army. We can safely if vaguely say that it was evidently very large: he could and did draw on the whole adult male nomadic population of Transoxania, as well as on the contingents of troops that were exacted from the conquered territories. Temür himself offered one estimate of the size of his army, which may perhaps deserve to be taken seriously: when he was campaigning against Tokhtamish, Khān of the Golden Horde, in 793/1391, his army is alleged to have been 200,000 strong. Something of the sort, even considering the logistical problems of moving about in such large numbers, is perhaps not implausible.

A chronological narrative of Temür's campaigns would be extremely confusing, and it will not be attempted here. This confusion is partly the result of the fact that Temür, as we have seen, spent so much of his time on campaign – and, unlike Chingiz Khān, he was unwilling to allow other generals to command major campaigns and thus possibly build up their own positions of power: he was almost always on the spot himself. But the other factor is that there is no clear sequence of conquest to be discerned. Temür was, in a sense, an inefficient conqueror in that he tended to have to subjugate the same territories over and over again. He began fighting in Persia in 783/1381, and was still doing so until not long before his last, abortive, campaign, against China. This is certainly no way in which to establish a coherent, flourishing and wide-ranging empire, but it may be that we have to see Temür's priorities as being different from this.

If, as has been argued, his chief preoccupation was the control of his own military elite, then his major concern will have been for an adequate series of military campaigns, with appropriate plunder, for them to fight. Thus they would be kept occupied and reasonably contented, and out of Transoxania. The devastation that was inflicted on the conquered provinces, and the consequent loss of tax revenue, would be very much a secondary consideration. The welfare of the conquered subjects would not, of course, be a consideration at all.

Temür seems to have shown little interest in more than temporary occupation even of some of the areas he continually devastated. The lands of the old Ilkhanate were his principal sphere of activity, and despite the damage that he constantly and deliberately inflicted there, he does appear to have intended that Persia and Iraq should form a permanent part of his empire. Garrisons were installed, governors appointed, local rulers deposed or confirmed in office.

It is one of the more perplexing features of Temür's career that he seems, although he was himself a nomad of Mongol descent, to have been aiming at the establishment of an empire consisting largely of the sedentary lands (though many of these certainly included areas where nomadism was prevalent). While it is true that he also did not attempt the permanent annexation of sedentary territories which he attacked but which had been outside the boundaries of the Mongol Empire, such as India, theories that seek to explain his activities as an attempt to refound the Mongol Empire under his own aegis fail to explain his apparent lack of interest in the occupation of the steppes of Mughulistān and the Golden Horde. He campaigned in those khanates, and soundly defeated his enemies there. But then he went away, content to have chastised the nomads.

This was certainly not the Chingizid method of building an empire. Indeed, there is a sense in which it was the exact opposite, for while Chingiz attacked the sedentary lands from a secure base in the steppe, Temür was quite dependent on the reliability of his base in largely sedentary Transoxania for his attacks on the tribes of the northern and eastern grasslands. Temür may have despised the agricultural population and the city-dwellers, and he may have treated them with a barbarity rarely seen before or since; but he was not an alien, assaulting the Islamic world from outside, as Chingiz Khān had been. This, be it said, is offered not in mitigation, still less justification, of Temür's appalling ferocity, but as perhaps a partial explanation of the form that ferocity took.

Temür's campaigns in the former Ilkhanate had various results, apart from massacre and destruction on a scale equivalent to, and perhaps exceeding, that inflicted during Chingiz Khān's subjugation of Khurāsān in 616–20/1219–23. He suppressed some of the most powerful of the local dynasties, such as the Muzaffarids and the Karts, perhaps thus ending any possibility that the ultimate successors to the Īlkhāns as rulers of Persia would be of sedentary origin. So far as the nomadic powers of the region were concerned, his activities were less decisive.

He greatly weakened the Jalayirids, but they survived and were to remain a power to be reckoned with for some few years after his death. The two nomad Türkmen confederations which had arisen in eastern Anatolia in the middle of the fourteenth century, the Qara-Qoyunlu and the Aq-Qoyunlu, also lived to fight another day (see Chapter 11). Temür's successors were to find that his victories over the Türkmens had been of a very temporary nature.

It is of course obvious enough that a sedentary enemy, however formidable he might be on the field of battle, was susceptible of a total defeat in a way that was not true of a confederation of nomadic tribes. Such confederations were characteristically fluid, and could dissolve or reform as circumstances dictated. A nomad chief could always flee with his followers, whose wealth was in portable livestock rather than in immovable agricultural land, and return later with the essence of his military power basically intact: the ruler of a city and its agricultural hinterland had to fight and die where he stood. If he fled, he simply became an impotent fugitive. If Temür had sought a definitive end to the nomad menace to Timurid power in western Persia, he would have needed to incorporate the nomads' manpower fully and on attractive terms into his own military machine, as Chingiz Khān had done after his conquest of the steppe tribes. But Temür and his followers were not, it would seem, interested in acquiring equal partners in conquest.

Beyond his numerous forays into former Ilkhanid territory and eastward for the restraint of Mughul depredations on Transoxania, his expeditions were led in almost every conceivable direction. Temür's neutralization of the danger to Transoxania from the Golden Horde was much bound up with the career of the Chingizid prince Tokhtamish, whom Temür adopted as his protégé, essentially as a means of keeping the Horde in internal turmoil lest a united army should turn its predatory attentions to the south. Tokhtamish's loyalty to his patron proved a wasting asset once he had succeeded in establishing his position as Khān of the Golden Horde, but Temür's campaigns against him were certainly effective in averting serious danger from that quarter.

Northern India was subjected, on the flimsiest of pretexts, to attack in 801/1398. Temür's assault on the Delhi sultanate was nothing more than a plundering expedition on a vast scale, an approach to India not uncharacteristic of Central Asian Muslim attitudes. Delhi was sacked and its legendary wealth carted off to Samarqand, and the sultanate, though not destroyed, was greatly weakened: much of the responsibility for the political chaos of its territories in the fifteenth century must be laid at Temür's door.

Syria, still part of the lands of the Mamlūk sultanate, was invaded and briefly conquered. No attempt was made to incorporate the province into Temür's empire, nor did he go on to attack the Mamlūk heartland in Egypt. The expedition did, however, leave one perhaps surprising memorial. In Damascus Temür met the north African historian, philosopher and proto-sociologist Ibn Khaldūn. Fortunately for posterity, Ibn Khaldūn wrote an account of their meeting and of the conversations they had, which is one of our most fascinating sources for Temür's career. It is especially important in that Ibn Khaldūn, aside from being one of the most intelligent and learned of medieval Muslims, was able to stand apart from the court-centred and panegyrical approach to Temür which characterizes so many of the Persian sources. He was impressed by Temür, but he stopped a long way short of idolatry.

An ephemeral campaign with more far-reaching consequences was that against the Ottoman Empire. This culminated in the battle of Ankara in 804/1402, at which Temür both defeated and captured Sulṭān Bayezid. In his usual fashion he did not absorb Anatolia into his empire: instead, power was returned to some of the local rulers who had been displaced by the expanding Ottoman state. Ottoman rule survived in the Balkans, well away from Temür, and over the next decades Bayezid's successors were able gradually to recover their position in Anatolia. But this took time, and there can be little doubt that Temür's intervention had one effect quite unintended by him. The last vestiges of Byzantine territory, and the city of Constantinople itself, would almost certainly have fallen to Bayezid had he not had to face Temür's invasion. Temür, in effect, granted Constantinople a half-century reprieve: the city remained in Christian hands until its capture by Sulṭān Meḥmed II in 857/1453.

By the latter part of Temür's reign there was still one of the great Asian powers with which he had not come into conflict: the greatest of them all, China, now under the rule of the native Chinese Ming Dynasty, which had evicted the Yüan Mongols in 1368. He resolved that China, too, should bow the knee. To attempt the conquest of China from a base in Transoxania looks very like megalomania, though if Temür was in reality trying to emulate the career of Chingiz Khān, he may have felt that he had to make an assault on the land which had always been the primary target of the east Asian steppe nomads. Whether Temür had conquest and occupation, or simply raid and plunder, in mind we shall never know. The great expedition set off from Transoxania, but when in 807/1405 it had reached Utrār, on the Jaxartes River, Temür died, the invasion was abandoned, and his empire was plunged into confusion as the members of his family hastened to make good their claims to the imperial inheritance.

So ended a career of military conquest perhaps unequalled in the consistency of its success. Temür had taken on all comers and vanquished them all without exception. There can be little doubt that he ranks with the greatest generals in the history of the world. Nor can there be much doubt that he had campaigned with a degree of brutality unmatched until the twentieth century. He was the last of the great nomad conquerors, those leaders whose armies of highly trained steppe cavalry archers made them virtually invincible in the field. Within the next two centuries the military balance was to shift decisively in favour of the great sedentary states, as the development of gunpowder and firearms ultimately reduced the mounted archer to obsolescence.

THE CHARACTER OF TEMÜR'S EMPIRE

Chingiz Khān, like Temür, had been a great military conqueror, directly responsible for massacre and destruction on a vast scale. But he had also been a state builder. He had laid institutional foundations for his empire and made adequate arrangements for the succession after his death. His empire continued to expand for fifty years after its founder had passed from the scene. By contrast, Temür's empire was a purely personal creation which, as a whole, failed to survive him.

Temür's chief concern seems to have been his own supremacy. His state depended entirely on his presence at the top. He allowed none of his sons and grandsons sufficient power or prestige to enable them to succeed him without a lengthy period of civil war. He refused to permit even the possibility of the creation of an alternative centre of power. His achievement was militarily effective, but institutionally it was far from constructive. His system of government was designed to assure his own personal power, not to function apart from him.

Like earlier eastern conquerors of Persia, he made extensive use of the old-established Persian bureaucracy in the administration of his empire. But the bureaucracy by no means exercised the influence it had had in the Ilkhanid period: there was no Timurid equivalent to Rashīd al-Dīn. The Persian bureaucrats did indeed manage much of the basic work of government and finance, but they were not given their head. Chaghatai *amīrs* fulfilled many of the functions that Persians might have expected to have under their control: there was no clear distinction between the civil and the military sphere, as was perhaps inevitable in a state which essentially existed as a permanent military campaign.

Nor do offices seem to have had clearly defined functions: as in other periods, *darughas*, for example – city governors – might be found acting as army commanders. The possession of an official title did not necessarily indicate the use to which Temür might put its holder. The system, if it was a system, appears to have been designed as much as anything to ensure that only limited amounts of power were in the hands of any one man. Those who had extensive military responsibilities were not also given substantial power in the government of the provinces, and office-holders were constantly moved around to prevent the establishment of local bases of support.

Temür himself, though illiterate, seems to have been a cultured man according to his lights. He encouraged the writing of history in Persian, especially in order to celebrate his own exploits. He was fond of chess and devoted to the construction of architectural masterpieces in his capital, Samarqand, even though he himself was rarely to be seen there. Indeed, the world was plundered for the greater glory of Samarqand, around which suburbs were erected named after the great cities of the Islamic world, many of which Temür had had the pleasure of sacking. The architecture was on a grandiose scale: his great mosque, the Bībī Khānum, had a colossal dome which was shattered by earthquake even during his lifetime. There were, then, signs even during Temür's reign of the cultural efflorescence which was to be the most striking feature of the reigns of his descendants.

We may feel that the fact that Temür was a Muslim, and the product of Islamic civilization, makes his career the more culpable as compared with that of the pagan Chingiz Khān: he had, perhaps, less excuse. He entertained a great, even a superstitious, reverence for *ṣūfī shaykhs*: such men were sometimes the only individuals who could expect to survive defying him. One of them, Sayyid Baraka, was so close to Temür that they were buried next to each other in the conqueror's great mausoleum, the Gūr-i Mīr, in Samarqand. Temür's own religious persuasion is difficult to discern: he professed a reverence for ʿAlī and the Shīʿī *imāms*, and on occasion attacked Sunnīs on what were represented as religious grounds. But at other times he attacked Shīʿīs on Sunnī grounds. All in all he remains one of the most complex, puzzling and unattractive figures in the history of Persia and Central Asia.

CHAPTER TEN

Persia in the Fifteenth Century: the Timurids

If Temür had been a constructive empire-builder as well as a destructive conqueror, it might have been possible to write the history of fifteenth-century Persia in a coherent and unified way. But he was not, and it is not. Temür's successors, the Timurids (Tīmūr is the Persian form of the Turkish name Temür) retained control of part of his dominions, including the eastern provinces of Persia. But however hard they tried, they were unable to hold on to his western conquests. For the western half of Persia the fifteenth century is the era of the Türkmen dynasties, the Qara-Qoyunlu and the Aq-Qoyunlu. Persia therefore – if we are prepared to indulge in oversimplification – fell into two parts, a Timurid and a Türkmen. If some of the resulting confusion is to be evaded by the historian, as it could not be by the men of the time, those two parts have to be considered to some extent separately.

SHĀH RUKH: STABILITY IN THE EAST

Temür, as we have seen, appears to have given little effective thought to what might happen after his own death, and he allowed none of his descendants the prestige and resources necessary for a reasonably uncontested bid for the throne. He was survived by only one of his sons, the youngest, Shāh Rukh, so named, according to a famous story, because at the time of his birth Temür was playing chess – the English word is derived from *shāh* – and had just castled – *rukh*, rook is Persian for the castle in chess. However picturesque the circumstances of his birth may have been, Shāh Rukh was not a favourite son and was not his father's choice as his successor. Temür had in fact varied his designation for the succession. At the time of his death it rested on one of his numerous grandsons, Pīr Muḥammad. The other Timurid princes saw no reason why they should accept this, and civil war ensued.

Pīr Muḥammad was speedily set aside by his cousin Khalīl Sulṭān, and the main struggle was between him and Shāh Rukh, who in 807/1405 was powerfully ensconced as governor of Khurāsān. Shāh Rukh eliminated Khalīl Sulṭān within a few years, but it took him well over a decade to establish an unchallengeable supremacy. From his base at Harāt he took Māzandarān on the Caspian in 809/1406–7, Transoxania with Temür's capital of Samarqand in 811/1409, Fārs in south Persia in 817/1414, Kirmān further east in 819/1416; and for a time from 823/1420 he was able to hold Āẕarbāyjān in the north-west. He had proved himself a skilful politician and a competent soldier, though neither he nor any of the Timurids came near to equalling the generalship of the founder of the dynasty.

Shāh Rukh moved the capital of the Timurid empire from Samarqand to Harāt, now in western Afghanistan, his own favoured stronghold. There he and his principal wife Gawhar Shād acted as lavish and enthusiastic patrons of the arts, especially architecture. In Harāt itself they erected a number of magnificent buildings, several of which still survived, in varying states of rather agreeable disrepair, at least until the end of the 1970s. Better preserved is Gawhar Shād's mosque at the shrine of the Shīʿī Imām Riḍā at Mashhad, in eastern Persia. The Timurid period excelled especially in the production of mosaic tilework, and some of the best of this is to be seen at Mashhad by anyone who is able to gain entrance to the mosque. Shāh Rukh's son Bāysunqur, who predeceased him in 837/1433, was also a notable artistic patron and himself an acknowledged master of the art of Persian calligraphy.

So if Shāh Rukh did not seek to emulate his father's military exploits, he does seem to have wanted to outdo his cultural achievements and to repair some of the damage caused by Temür's life of incessant campaigning. He saw himself as an Islamic monarch rather than as a Central Asian *khān* in the tradition of Chingiz: he is reputed to have refused to have any truck with the *Yāsā*, the pagan Mongol laws or customs ascribed to Chingiz Khān, declaring instead his allegiance to the *sharīʿa*, the law of Islam.

As far as the political circumstances of the time permitted, Shāh Rukh was a peaceful ruler, and after he had finally succeeded in establishing his possession of the Timurid inheritance he gave his dominions three decades of welcome stability. He had some limited success in western Persia, where he mounted three campaigns between 823/1420 and 838/1434. He could not eliminate the Qara-Qoyunlu, but he was at least able to contain them. After 838/1434 the Qara-Qoyunlu ruler of

Tabrīz had the status of a rather independent Timurid governor; and the Türkmen were further held in check by the establishment of a long-standing alliance between Shāh Rukh and the Qara-Qoyunlu's principal rivals, the Aq-Qoyunlu. Shāh Rukh had not kept Temür's empire intact, but he had in some fashion retained much more of it than any of his successors were able to do.

With the imperial capital transferred to Harāt, Samarqand was left in the hands of the heir to the throne, Shāh Rukh's son Ulugh Beg. Transoxania in this period was virtually an independent Timurid principality, in which Shāh Rukh interfered very little. He and his son had widely different attitudes, for Ulugh Beg, unlike his father, favoured the old Mongol traditions. A Chingizid puppet-*khān* was enthroned in Ulugh Beg's Samarqand: no such antiquarian approaches to sovereignty were tolerated in Harāt. Under his rule Samarqand, too, became a centre of cultural activity. Ulugh Beg himself had strong scientific interests, and in collaboration with four scholars he produced a volume of astronomical tables which long remained in use: a Latin edition was published in England as late as the seventeenth century. He built an observatory at Samarqand, the impressive remains of which are still to be seen. Like his father he was a patron of architecture, and *madrasas*, religious colleges, commissioned by him exist both at Samarqand and at Bukhārā.

SHĀH RUKH'S SUCCESSORS

On Shāh Rukh's death in 850/1447, as when Temür himself died, the Timurid world was plunged into political chaos. Ulugh Beg, being Shāh Rukh's only surviving son, regarded himself as his father's successor, but he had to fight for the inheritance throughout his short reign and managed to lay hands on only part of Shāh Rukh's empire. He had no control over central or southern Persia, and his grip even on Khurāsān was very uncertain. In any case his reign was to be brought to a speedy and ignominious conclusion at the hands of his estranged son, ʿAbd al-Laṭīf, who revolted against him. Ulugh Beg was obliged to surrender, and was executed at his son's instigation, on a trumped-up legal pretext. ʿAbd al-Laṭīf's brother ʿAbd al-ʿAzīz, Ulugh Beg's favourite son, was also done to death. Even in the Timurid world of the fifteenth century, patricide and fratricide were thought to be altogether too much, and few were surprised or displeased when ʿAbd al-Laṭīf was himself killed in the following year.

The throne now passed briefly through the hands of another of Shāh Rukh's grandsons, and then away from that branch of the Timurid family. In 855/1451 it was seized by Abū Saʿīd, a grandson of Temür's son Mīrānshāh. This success he had achieved with the help of the Özbegs from the north, under their leader Abū'l-Khayr. It was those same Özbegs who at the end of the century would evict the Timurids from Transoxania (see Chapter 12), a conquest to the permanence of which the existence of the Soviet republic of Uzbekistan bears witness.

It took Abū Saʿīd several years to capture Shāh Rukh's old capital of Harāt; he was not securely in possession of the city until 863/1459, though two years previously he had caused Shāh Rukh's aged and distinguished widow, Gawhar Shād, to be murdered there. In 862/1458, at a singularly low point in Timurid fortunes, the capital was briefly occupied by the greatest of the Qara-Qoyunlu rulers, Jahān Shāh. Even at its greatest extent, the empire under Abū Saʿīd had shrunk again. He controlled only Transoxania and Khurāsān, together with – at the end of his reign – Māzandarān in the north and Sīstān in the south, and even this was far from remaining unchallenged. In Transoxania the most powerful political influence was a *ṣūfī shaykh* of Samarqand, Khwāja Aḥrār of the Naqshbandī order.

When in 872/1467 Jahān Shāh was killed in battle with the Aq-Qoyunlu ruler Uzun Ḥasan, Abū Saʿīd yielded fatally to the temptation to attempt the restoration of Timurid power in Āẕarbāyjān before Aq-Qoyunlu power could be fully established. The invasion, which had been urged on Abū Saʿīd by Khwāja Aḥrār, was a disastrous failure. In 873/1469 Abū Saʿīd was defeated and captured by Uzun Ḥasan, who handed him over to a grandson of Gawhar Shād for avenging execution. Abū Saʿīd had managed to maintain some kind of a position, necessarily through constant warfare, for eighteen years. As a result he had given a limited stability to the lands he controlled, and like Shāh Rukh he had favoured and patronized cultural activity. He was hardly, perhaps, a really notable ruler, but given the difficulties of his time he was not a negligible figure.

On his death the throne again shifted to a different branch of the Timurid family: any Timurid prince, if he gave signs of ambition and political and military competence, could hope to acquire a following. We should probably see here a vestige of the old Central Asian Turkish notion that political sovereignty was to be regarded as the possession of the ruling family as a whole rather than of any individual member of it.

This time the ruler was Ḥusayn Bāyqarā, a grandson of Temür's son ʿUmar Shaykh. At least in the cultural field, he was perhaps the most notable of the later Timurids. He ruled in Harāt from 875/1470 until his death in 911/1506. He exercised no power in western Persia, where the Aq-Qoyunlu were enjoying their heyday: he was careful to remain on excellent terms with Uzun Ḥasan. Nor did he control the original heartland of Transoxania, where a variety of Timurid princelings contended with each other: the throne in Samarqand was occupied by the family of Abū Saʿīd, though the real power there was held by Khwāja Aḥrār until his death in 895/1490. Towards the end of the century the Özbeg conquest of Transoxania began.

In his early years Ḥusayn Bāyqarā was an able soldier – this was still a prerequisite for possession of the throne – though he was partially paralysed for the last twenty years of his life. As a patron of the arts he spread his net far and wide. The celebrated Mīr ʿAlī Shīr Nawāʾī was employed in high office; he was a figure of more than political importance who is credited with the virtual creation of Chaghatai Turkish as a literary language. Jāmī, the last of the great classical poets of Persia, flourished under Ḥusayn's rule, and is buried just outside Harāt. Ḥusayn encouraged historians and miniature painters. One of the greatest of the latter, Bihzād, worked at Harāt before moving to the new Ṣafawid capital of Tabrīz on the fall of the Timurid kingdom: in this way the artistic traditions of Timurid Khurāsān were carried over into the Ṣafawid period and continued to flourish, especially under the first two Ṣafawid shāhs.

The death of Ḥusayn Bāyqarā in 911/1506 marked the effective end of Timurid rule in the eastern Islamic world. For a few years it was not clear who was to succeed them, but in 916/1510 the first shāh of the Ṣafawid dynasty, Ismāʿīl I, drove the Özbegs out of Khurāsān and established the River Oxus as Persia's eastern frontier. Most of the Persian and Afghan lands of the Timurid family fell into Ṣafawid hands.

THE TIMURID ACHIEVEMENT

The Timurids had, on the whole, deserved better of Persia than anyone might reasonably have expected. Their dynasty had got off to the worst possible start with the appalling career of Temür, but for all their internecine struggles, many of them had done much to atone for the destruction inflicted by their ancestor. Western writers have sometimes thought it justifiable to speak in terms of a "Timurid Renaissance", and it is perhaps relevant to point out that political fragmentation seems to have been no obstacle to cultural achievement, any more than it was in Italy during the same period.

Painting, calligraphy, architecture, poetry and the writing of history all flourished. The Timurid courts resembled those of the Īlkhāns in their patronage of history, even if they produced nothing of quite the same quality as the *Jāmiʿ al-tawārīkh* of Rashīd al-Dīn. Temür had set the fashion by commissioning the writing of a history of his own military career called *Ẓafar-nāma*, the Book of Victory, by Niẓām al-Dīn Shāmī. Other notable historians wrote at the courts of his successors. The most accomplished of them was Ḥāfiẓ Abrū, who worked at the court of Shāh Rukh and consciously carried on where Rashīd al-Dīn had left off a century before. Further historians of importance included Sharaf al-Dīn ʿAlī Yazdī, ʿAbd al-Razzāq Samarqandī and, at the court of Ḥusayn Bāyqarā, Mīrkhwānd and his grandson Khwāndamīr, who like Bihzād continued his work under the new Ṣafawid rulers, before ultimately departing to India.

The Turkish political tradition which gave every member of the ruling house a stake in the state meant that, whoever had managed to establish himself, for the time being, as paramount Timurid, many other princes would still be acting as governors of cities or of whole provinces. Hence there were a variety of courts at which cultural patronage might be practised. The main institutional device whereby this distribution of power was organized was the *suyūrghāl*, a development of the older *iqṭāʿ*.

The word, as we have seen, is Mongolian in origin, and in the time of Chingiz Khān meant "favour" or "reward". In Timurid times, however, it meant the assignment of a city, an area of land, even a province, to some prince or other powerful *amīr* or influential person. It carried the obligation, at least in theory, that its holder would provide on demand a specified number of troops. The authority conferred on the holder of a *suyūrghāl* was very extensive, perhaps more so than in the days of the Saljūq *iqṭāʿ*. Such grants came to be regarded as hereditary. Thus it was that so many princes were able, during an interregnum, to make a bid for the throne: they had a firm local power base. Equally, however, it was difficult in a period of such fragmentation of political authority to maintain a strong central government.

In such circumstances it is perhaps surprising that the Timurids contrived to hold on to as much of Temür's legacy as they did, and for as long as a century. This is probably to be ascribed in part to the fact that – whatever their deficiencies as rulers – many of the Timurids were very competent military leaders. But this might have availed them little had they been obliged to face a really formidable enemy. In this respect Temür's work survived him. No enemy arose in the east until the Özbegs began their penetration of Transoxania. In the west, both the

Jalayirids and the Türkmen confederations, though not destroyed by Temür, had had their strength greatly weakened by him. The Jalayirids were soon swept from the scene, but the Türkmen groups remained dangerous, and would probably have been more so had the Qara-Qoyunlu and the Aq-Qoyunlu not had to contend with each other as well as, in the later fifteenth century, the power of the Ottoman Empire to the west of them. How dangerous the Türkmen armies could be was graphically demonstrated by Jahān Shāh's occupation of Harāt in 862/1458; and Shāh Ismāʿīl's campaigns in the first years of the sixteenth century showed that Khurāsān was not permanently beyond the reach of a ruler based in Āẕarbāyjān.

There was one remarkable postscript to the Timurid story. One of the princes who had been driven out of Transoxania by the Özbegs was Bābur, a descendant not only of Temür but also, on his mother's side, of Chingiz Khān. Despite this unpromising ancestry he was a man of attractive character, if his celebrated Chaghatai Turkish autobiography, the *Bābur-nāma*, is to be believed.

Bābur reluctantly withdrew from Transoxania, though neither he nor his successors easily gave up their dream of recovering Samarqand, which he had occupied three times during his early career (see Chapter 12). He moved to Kābul (where he was eventually buried) and from there went on to invade northern India, winning a great victory over the sulṭān of Delhi at Pānīpat in 932/1526. Thus he became the founder of the Mughal Empire, and descendants of Temür and Chingiz ruled or reigned in India until the last Timurid king of Delhi was deposed after the suppression of the Indian Mutiny of 1857.

CHAPTER ELEVEN

Persia in the Fifteenth Century: the Türkmen Dynasties and the Rise of the Ṣafawids

In the western part of the old Ilkhanid territories, Mongol rule was replaced neither by that of local city-based dynasties nor, except very temporarily, by Temür. The effective successors to the Īlkhāns were three tribal groups: the Jalayirids, initially the most important, of Mongol origin; and the two Türkmen groups, the Qara-Qoyunlu ("Black Sheep") and the Aq-Qoyunlu ("White Sheep"). It was these latter – two nomadic, or at least semi-nomadic, Türkmen confederations – that, starting from very insignificant beginnings, were to dominate the political history of western Persia, Iraq and eastern Anatolia between the death of Temür in 807/1405 and the accession of the first Ṣafawid shāh in 907/1501. They evolved in parallel and in rivalry with one another, reaching the height of their power in succession and very largely at the other's expense. The Qara-Qoyunlu were a more short-lived power than the Aq-Qoyunlu, and they achieved hegemony earlier. Their history, as is often the case with losers, is less well documented than that of their more successful rivals. It will be discussed first.

THE QARA-QOYUNLU CONFEDERATION

The origins of the Qara-Qoyunlu confederation are hidden in what seems likely to remain impenetrable obscurity. Its ruling family is given the name Baharlu or Barani in the sources, but there seems no certainty over whether this family, or clan, predates the Mongol invasion or was part of the human wave swept westward by Chingiz Khān and Hülegü. Be that as it may, the Qara-Qoyunlu are first seen as an identifiable grouping of importance in the period of the collapse of the Ilkhanate after the death in 736/1335 of Abū Saʿīd.

They made their way initially as clients of the Jalayirids, who had become the leading power in Iraq and Āẕarbāyjān: their particular patron was the Jalayirid ruler Shaykh Uways (reigned 757–76/1356–74). Their own territorial centre was in the vicinity of Lake Van in eastern Anatolia, part of what is now Turkey. Their leader at this time was one Bayrām Khwāja (died 782/1380). His successor, Qara Muḥammad, remained close to the Jalayirids, though more as an ally than as a subordinate power. He consolidated the Qara-Qoyunlu position, but was killed in 791/1389.

It was his son Qara Yūsuf who had to cope with the menace to Qara-Qoyunlu power presented by Temür. Unlike his Aq-Qoyunlu rivals, he chose to oppose Temür, was predictably and repeatedly defeated, and was twice obliged to save himself by flight. On the first occasion he took refuge with the Ottomans, on the second in Mamlūk Syria. In this way he lived to fight another day: an option, as we have seen, always available to a nomadic chief (provided he could recover control of his nomadic followers if, as in Qara Yūsuf's case, he did not take them with him into exile), whereas it was much more difficult for a sedentary ruler to do other than fight for his kingdom where it was. Temür, then, did not eliminate the Qara-Qoyunlu by defeating them in battle. He could have done this only by one of the two expedients employed in his day by Chingiz Khān: near-total extermination or equally total incorporation of the manpower of the defeated enemy into his own forces. Temür did not attempt either.

The Mamlūks adopted a rather unwelcoming attitude towards their uninvited guest, whose earlier activities had included attacks on their territory. They therefore imprisoned him, together with the Jalayirid ruler Aḥmad, who had also saved himself from Temür by flight. In prison the two reached an agreement about their respective spheres of influence when they should return to power: the Jalayirids should have Iraq, the Qara-Qoyunlu Āẕarbāyjān. In 806/1404 they were released and returned to their homeland, which had been entrusted by Temür to his grandson Abā Bakr, whose power, once the strong hand of Temür himself had disappeared, Qara Yūsuf was able to eliminate by 810/1408. The agreement with Aḥmad Jalayir did not last: Qara Yūsuf defeated and executed him in 813/1410. This marked the end of the Jalayirids.

Qara Yūsuf was now able to occupy large areas in Anatolia, Āẕarbāyjān, Mesopotamia and Iraq. In 822/1419 he even invaded western Persia, provoking Shāh Rukh to march against him; but in the following year he died. A degree of fragmentation now ensued, but Qara Yūsuf had laid good foundations and from the 1440s the Qara-

Qoyunlu, now under Jahān Shāh, were able to reach the summit of their power.

Paradoxically, although there was normally an alliance between the Timurids and the Aq-Qoyunlu against the Qara-Qoyunlu, Jahān Shāh owed his rise to power to Shāh Rukh, who had appointed him governor of Āẕarbāyjān in an attempt to settle the turbulent affairs of western Persia. Building on this, and taking over the position established by Qara Yūsuf, he was able to throw off his Timurid allegiance and to build up, in the two decades following the death of Shāh Rukh in 850/1447, something that might almost be termed an empire. It included much of eastern Anatolia, north-western, western and central Persia, and Iraq. Its capital was at Tabrīz.

Jahān Shāh, despite his Persian name (it means "king of the world") seems to have seen his kingdom as being in the direct line of succession to the Ilkhanate, by way of the Jalayirids, the forms of whose official documents were closely followed by the Qara-Qoyunlu chancery. He called himself not only *sulṭān*, a specifically Islamic title, but also *khaqan*, an unmistakably Turko-Mongol one. It would seem that even now, a century and more after the disintegration of the Ilkhanate, political legitimacy was still, in the eyes of some, inextricably bound up with Mongol rule.

Qara-Qoyunlu leaders before Jahān Shāh were not noted for their cultural achievements, but he did go some way towards emulating the activities of the Timurids in this respect. He gave patronage to scholars and poets, even writing poetry himself, and he engaged in building work. Substantial fragments remain in Tabrīz of his Blue Mosque, the tilework of which is perhaps equal in quality to the best products of the Timurid workshops.

There has been much controversy over Jahān Shāh's religious allegiance. He has often been described as a Shīʿī, being opposed in this respect as in others to the allegedly Sunnī Aq-Qoyunlu. This now seems to be a misunderstanding of the situation. It is true that some favour was shown to Shīʿism within his dominions, and that he on occasion had Shīʿī inscriptions put on his coins. But during this period, which was one of considerable religious flux, the expression of a reverence for ʿAlī and even for the later Shīʿī *imāms* does not seem to have been thought incompatible with a more or less orthodox Sunnism. Jahān Shāh's "Shīʿī" coins often had Sunnī inscriptions on the other side. We have to refrain, when considering the fifteenth century, from reading into it the rigidity of religious allegiance that was more characteristic of the sixteenth and later centuries.

During the latter part of Jahān Shāh's reign the head of the other

Türkmen confederation, Uzun Ḥasan Aq-Qoyunlu, had been steadily consolidating his position, as we shall see. Jahān Shāh eventually decided that Uzun Ḥasan would have to be checked, and marched against him in 872/1467. He does not, however, seem to have taken his enemy sufficiently seriously. Jahān Shāh was surprised when encamped with only a small force, defeated and killed. Within a short space of time it became evident that the strength of the Qara-Qoyunlu empire, if not illusory, was entirely dependent on the remarkable individual at its head. Qara-Qoyunlu power died with Jahān Shāh. The future lay, for the time being at least, with the Aq-Qoyunlu.

THE AQ-QOYUNLU CONFEDERATION

The ruling clan of the Aq-Qoyunlu had the name Bayandur. Their origins, like those of the Qara-Qoyunlu leaders, are veiled in obscurity. Like them, they may well have found their way to eastern Anatolia in the wake of the Mongol invasions. In the fourteenth century they are found in Armenia and Diyārbakr, with their centre at the town of Āmid, to the west of the Qara-Qoyunlu homeland. One of their early chiefs, Ṭūr ʿAlī, held the rank of *amīr* under the Īlkhān Ghazan Khān. Such were the Aq-Qoyunlu beginnings. They did not develop as speedily as the Qara-Qoyunlu, perhaps because they lacked an influential patron such as the Jalayirids had been to the Qara-Qoyunlu.

Before long, too, an inherent weakness in the Aq-Qoyunlu confederation manifested itself. It could not easily evolve an adequate mechanism for ensuring peaceful succession: over and again the death of the head of the confederation was followed by years of civil war. Conceivably these wars were examples of the steppe principle that the chief most fitted to lead was he who had convincingly demonstrated his fitness by eliminating the other candidates. Such a war broke out in 791/1389, and was not resolved until the victory of Qara ʿUthmān in 805/1403. In these circumstances it is hardly surprising that the rise of the Aq-Qoyunlu was very far from uninterrupted.

Qara ʿUthmān's long reign (805–39/1403–35) saw a considerable expansion. The Aq-Qoyunlu had decided, unlike their Qara-Qoyunlu rivals, to submit to Temür. They received the reward of Timurid favour, and for much of Qara ʿUthmān's reign they were in alliance with Shāh Rukh against the Qara-Qoyunlu and the Mamlūks of Egypt. Their capital was at Āmid, where it remained until the reign of Uzun Ḥasan, but they were also able to acquire other important towns, notably Mārdīn and Erzerum. The possession of these gave the Aq-Qoyunlu control of important trade routes. So Qara ʿUthmān's reign had seen a substantial if unspectacular advance in the fortunes of his confederation.

But there was no doubt that the Qara-Qoyunlu were still the stronger of the two groupings, a fact that was emphasized when they defeated and killed Qara ʿUthmān in battle in 839/1435 and his death was followed by twenty-two years of civil war, in which no fewer than eleven claimants contended for the Aq-Qoyunlu throne. This was a period of weakness which coincided with the apogee of Qara-Qoyunlu power under Jahān Shāh.

From 856/1452, however, the situation began gradually to change. In that year Uzun Ḥasan seized Āmid and thereafter his rise, though slow, was steady. At a great battle on the Tigris in 861/1457 he defeated his principal rival, Jahāngīr, who had Qara-Qoyunlu support; he was clearly now the leading figure among the Aq-Qoyunlu.

His first task was to re-establish the shattered principality of Qara ʿUthmān. This took him ten years, and culminated in his decisive victory over Jahān Shāh in 872/1467. The succeeding two years saw him extend his power in such a way as to alarm the Timurid ruler Abū Saʿīd, who marched against him but was defeated and killed in 873/1469. Uzun Ḥasan, now unstoppable, was able to occupy Iraq and the whole of Persia as far east as Fārs and Kirmān. Khurāsān and Transoxania remained in Timurid control and Uzun Ḥasan made no attempt to over-extend himself in that direction, as Jahān Shāh had in 862/1458.

One potential enemy remained: the Ottoman Empire. Here Uzun Ḥasan finally met his match. The Ottomans defeated him in battle at Bashkent in 878/1473, a victory whose decisiveness has often, rightly or wrongly, been attributed to the effectiveness of the Ottoman artillery. The battle put a term to Aq-Qoyunlu expansion but did not result in Uzun Ḥasan's overthrow, nor in any significant territorial losses. The Ottomans showed little inclination to follow up their victory. The incident did, however, cost Uzun Ḥasan some of his prestige, and in the last years of his reign he had to deal with a number of internal revolts. He died in 882/1478.

Tabrīz, the traditional Mongol-Turkish centre, became Uzun Ḥasan's capital. In 876/1472 it saw the arrival of an embassy from Venice. There were intensive negotiations to try to organize a European-Aq-Qoyunlu pincer movement against the Ottomans: it was a little reminiscent of attempts to arrange a Christian-Mongol alliance against the Mamlūks during the Ilkhanid period. As at that time, the negotiations were apparently entered into quite seriously on both sides, though with not much greater practical effect. The Venetians seem to have been perhaps overimpressed by the splendour of Uzun Ḥasan's court, and do not seem later to have appreciated how serious his defeat at Bashkent had been.

Decline now set in: the Aq-Qoyunlu empire, like that of Jahān Shāh, proved too dependent on the man at the top. Uzun Ḥasan's death was followed by the almost obligatory civil war, in which by 886/1481 Yaʿqūb had emerged victorious. He reigned until 896/1490. Factions continued to struggle for power during his reign, and the Aq-Qoyunlu realm withdrew into a kind of isolationism. There was no further territorial expansion, but much internal prosperity, reflected in the opulence of court life in Tabrīz and in patronage of the arts.

Trouble arose towards the end of the reign. Yaʿqūb's minister Qāḍī ʿĪsā brought in a series of administrative reforms, which were interpreted as an attack on the influential nomadic sector of the population. Their aim was to eradicate any traces of the old Mongol *Yāsā* and to restore the full operation of the Muslim *sharīʿa*. There was much resentment and vigorous opposition to the reforms. Yaʿqūb himself died in mysterious circumstances in the following year.

Civil war inevitably ensued. Rustam had established himself as ruler by 899/1494, but he had little control over the outlying provinces of the empire. He fell and was killed in 902/1497. For the next ten years there were simultaneous claimants in various parts of the empire. A triple partition was attempted in 906/1500, but it was too late to save Aq-Qoyunlu rule. The young head of the Ṣafawī *ṣūfī* order, Ismāʿīl, had come out of hiding in 905/1499, and the Aq-Qoyunlu succumbed to the attack of an organization which had once been their client. Ismāʿīl defeated Alwand Aq-Qoyunlu at Sharūr in 907/1501 and in the same year took Tabrīz – the incident from which his accession, and the beginning of the Ṣafawid dynasty, is usually dated – and Baghdad in 914/1508. The last nominal Aq-Qoyunlu ruler, Murād, was killed in 920/1514.

The Aq-Qoyunlu army was perhaps the last in Persia to be constructed on the traditional Mongol, nomadic lines. It was a predominantly cavalry force organized in units arranged decimally. Its size has been variously estimated. Different observers in 878/1473 put the same army at 40,000 and 300,000 respectively. A more reliable estimate is perhaps offered by the evidence of a review held in Fārs in 881/1476. This seems to suggest an army of 25,000 cavalry and 10,000 infantry. It has been argued that if the contingents from the provinces are added in, Uzun Ḥasan may have had at his disposal an army of something like 100,000 men.

If the army was of the traditional steppe type – unlike the Ottoman army which defeated it – the bureaucracy, equally traditionally, was of the usual Persian sedentary sort. It is possible that the difficulties involved in satisfactorily integrating the steppe and sedentary elements in the state proved insuperable – witness the resistance to Qāḍī ʿĪsā's reforms – and that this is part of the explanation of why the Aq-Qoyunlu failed to construct a durable polity. Certainly they did fail; but in many ways the Ṣafawid empire, which succeeded most conspicuously, should be seen as a successor state to the Aq-Qoyunlu confederation.

THE RISE OF THE ṢAFAWIDS

The rise of the Ṣafawid *ṣūfī* order to become the ruling dynasty of Persia presents historians with problems which they are still very far from solving. How was it that an order of Sunnī religious mystics became, two centuries later, a militantly Shīʿī "secular" dynasty? The stages in the process are not by any means clear as yet.

Shaykh Ṣafī al-Dīn (650–735/1252–1334), after whom the order was named, was probably of Kurdish ancestry. His ancestors seem to have lived in Āẕarbāyjān since the eleventh century. He attached himself to Shaykh Zāhid Gīlānī, the head of a Sunnī *ṣūfī* organization in Tālish, at the south-western corner of the Caspian Sea. After Shaykh Zāhid's death in 700/1301, Shaykh Ṣafī assumed the headship of the organization and moved to Ardabīl, between Tabrīz and the Caspian, where he lived for the rest of his life and where his shrine is still the town's architectural centrepiece.

Shaykh Ṣafī was a late Ilkhanid figure, one of some importance as a religious leader in the Īlkhāns' home province during the period immediately after the Mongols had gone over to Islam. He seems to have been held in great respect by some of the Mongols, who like many converts from steppe Shamanism tended to have a marked preference for the popular varieties of Ṣufism as against the more "orthodox" Islam of the *ʿulamāʾ*.

The influence he was able to exercise is amply demonstrated in the biography of him written by a member of the order, Ibn Bazzāz, after his death. This, the *Ṣafwat al-ṣafāʾ*, contains a wealth of anecdotes about Shaykh Ṣafī's activities and wonder-working deeds. Whatever the literal truth of these stories, they provide not only a picture of how the founder of the order was seen by his followers but also an insight into the social history of the period such as is rarely to be found in the dynastic chronicles.

There is no reason to suppose that Shaykh Ṣafī, however suspiciously he may have been regarded, as a *ṣūfī*, by the *ʿulamāʾ*, was a Shīʿī, or had any claim to ʿAlid descent. The fact that he was actually of the Sunnī persuasion is indeed made very clear in the authoritative *Ṣafwat al-ṣafāʾ*. This proved most inconvenient to his Shīʿī descendants after they had seized the throne of Persia. In the sixteenth century revised versions of the book were therefore produced in which Shaykh Ṣafī is represented as having professed more suitable views. Fortunately, not all the manuscripts of the authentic version were destroyed.

The early heads of the Ṣafawid order were long-lived, and between Ṣafī's death in 735/1334 and 851/1447 possibly only three of them ruled. They consolidated the order's position in Āẕarbāyjān, and its land holdings became very extensive. The until recently unsuspected survival of a large cache of documents in the shrine of Shaykh Ṣafī at Ardabīl, which his son Ṣadr al-Dīn had built, provides some very rare archival evidence of this process. This is supplemented by a sixteenth-century register of the order's properties, the *Ṣarīḥ al-milk*. From these sources it is evident that by the mid-fifteenth century the Ṣafawid *shaykhs* had become extremely wealthy.

Until the death of the fourth head of the order, Ibrāhīm, in 851/1447, it had been a highly successful if more or less conventional Sunnī *ṣūfī* organization, gradually acquiring disciples and property in a not especially unworldly fashion. Its leaders had shown little sign of specifically political involvement in the tangled affairs of the Türkmen era. This now began to change.

According to the official Ṣafawid version of history, Ibrāhīm's successor was his son Junayd; but in fact the actual head of the order at Ardabīl throughout Junayd's life was his uncle Jaʿfar, with whom he was at daggers drawn. Jaʿfar had been installed with Qara-Qoyunlu support; Junayd was expelled from Ardabīl, and obliged to go on his travels. It was this itinerant period, which recent research suggests lasted from 851/1447 to 863/1459, that was crucial in the transformation of the Ṣafawid order from a peaceful and essentially "apolitical" *ṣūfī* organization to a militant, though not yet necessarily a Shīʿī, political movement.

Junayd spent his long years of exile initially in eastern Anatolia, but mainly in northern Syria. There he recruited considerable numbers of devoted followers from the Türkmen tribesmen of those regions. What these Türkmen appear to have been devoted to is Junayd himself. We now begin to see the emergence of extremist religious beliefs in the

Ṣafawid context, in which not only ʿAlī, the first Shīʿī *imām*, but also Junayd himself, are regarded as partaking of the divine nature.

It is tempting to call this Shīʿism, but several caveats need to be borne in mind. First of all, as we saw in the case of Jahān Shāh Qara-Qoyunlu, reverence for ʿAlī and the Shīʿī *imāms* was not seen, in the fifteenth century, as being incompatible with something approximating to orthodox Sunnī belief. Secondly, the attributes granted to Junayd by his followers would have been anathema to a respectable Twelver Shīʿī no less than to a Sunnī. Thirdly, tracking down evidence of Shīʿī belief is always a hazardous business because of the doctrine of *taqiyya*, tactical dissimulation, whereby a Shīʿī who was in any danger was permitted, even obliged, to conceal his true beliefs. In so far as Shīʿīs practised *taqiyya* successfully, their existence is concealed from us. What we should say, therefore, is that Junayd's followers professed an extremist and militant form of popular Islam which may have contained some elements of Shīʿī origin. Of the extremism and the militancy, at least, there could be no doubt in the light of Junayd's activities in the very short time left to him after his return to Āẕarbāyjān.

It was perhaps natural, in the light of the hostility shown him by the Qara-Qoyunlu, now at the height of their power, that Junayd should have sought to ally himself with Uzun Ḥasan Aq-Qoyunlu. What is less obvious is why Uzun Ḥasan should have viewed such a proposal with favour: indeed, according to the Ottoman historian ʿĀshiqpashazāde, his first reaction was to imprison Junayd. Nevertheless, Uzun Ḥasan gave him his sister in marriage, thus inaugurating a long-term relationship between the Aq-Qoyunlu and the Ṣafawids. One can only conclude – since there is no indication that Uzun Ḥasan was either a Shīʿī or impressed by his new brother-in-law's weirder religious pretensions – that the Türkmen following he had built up during the previous decade made Junayd an ally worth having; or conceivably that Uzun Ḥasan's own Türkmen followers were impressed by Junayd.

A militant Muslim force needed an enemy, and preferably an infidel enemy, to test its steel on. Junayd's men certainly regarded themselves as *ghāzīs*, fighters for the faith. The nearest available potential adversaries that fitted the bill were the Christians of the Caucasus, against whom Junayd proceeded to mount a raid. Unfortunately he had to cross the territory of the Muslim Shīrwān-shāh in order to reach the infidel. In doing so he fell foul of the Shīrwān-shāh, and was killed in battle with him in 864/1460.

His infant son Ḥaydar was brought up at Uzun Ḥasan's court and in due course married to his daughter, thus strengthening the family relationship between the two houses. After going to Ardabīl, Ḥaydar is said to have invented the *tāj*, a red twelve-gored hat for his followers to wear (hence the tribesmen who supported the Ṣafawids were called *Qizilbash*, "red-heads" in Turkish). At least in retrospect, this was seen as being in honour of the twelve Shīʿī *imāms* and thus as an indication of the Shīʿī convictions of Ḥaydar and the Ṣafawid movement. This may be so, but it has to be remembered both that Ḥaydar had been brought up away from Shīʿī influences and that, as we have seen, respect for the *imāms* did not necessarily imply Shīʿī allegiance. In any case, Uzun Ḥasan is alleged – although admittedly only by later sources which on such a point should be regarded as dubious – to have worn the *tāj*, an odd thing for a Sunnī monarch to have done if it was regarded at the time as an unequivocally Shīʿī symbol.

The friendship between the Aq-Qoyunlu and the Ṣafawids did not survive far into the reign of Yaʿqūb Aq-Qoyunlu. It may be that Yaʿqūb regarded Ḥaydar as a potential danger to his own power. At any rate, when Ḥaydar marched to emulate his father in mounting a *ghazā* raid into the Caucasus in 893/1488, Yaʿqūb provided the Shīrwān-shāh, the successor to Junayd's enemy, with aid. Like his father, Ḥaydar was killed in battle by the Shīrwān-shāh.

Ḥaydar's son Sulṭān ʿAlī succeeded him as head of the Ṣafawid order; but between 894/1489 and 898/1493 he was imprisoned, with his brothers, in the Aq-Qoyunlu fortress of Iṣṭakhr in distant Fārs. Sulṭān ʿAlī was killed by the Aq-Qoyunlu in 899/1494. His younger brother Ismāʿīl, aged only seven but now the head of the order, fled for refuge to Gīlān, on the Caspian coast, where he was given asylum by a local Shīʿī ruler. There he remained until 905/1499, being educated by a tutor who was also presumably a Shīʿī of some sort. Thus we can say of Ismāʿīl, as we cannot of any of his predecessors, that during his formative years he was thoroughly exposed to specifically Shīʿī influences. This is not to say that Ismāʿīl's own beliefs were of an orthodox Shīʿī kind. To judge from the poetry he wrote in Turkish, under the pseudonym Khaṭāʾī, he was a true grandson of Junayd in regarding himself as in some sense divine: a view evidently shared by the Türkmen followers who put him on the throne of Persia.

There can be little doubt that when the twelve-year-old Ismāʿīl rode out of Gīlān in 905/1499, both to pay the family debt of vengeance on the Shīrwān-shāh and ultimately to seize Tabrīz from his Aq-Qoyunlu relatives, the religious appeal of a young God-King counted for much among the Türkmens. It is also possible to argue that the appeal of the Ṣafawid movement to some of the nomadic Türkmen tribesmen of eastern Anatolia was strong in a period in which the alternative was the acceptance of an increasingly rigid and bureaucratic Ottoman system of government and taxation. Even so, it is perhaps unlikely that Ismāʿīl, for all his charisma, could have achieved so much had it not been for the collapse and factionalism of the Aq-Qoyunlu.

A new era in Persian history was inaugurated by the accession of Shāh Ismāʿīl I. He seized the throne as the divine leader of a Türkmen religious movement which held to a very strange form of Islamic belief. It was not this creed which Ismāʿīl imposed on his newly acquired kingdom: but that is another story.

CHAPTER TWELVE

Shāh Ismāʿīl I and the Establishment of Shīʿism

THE FORMATION OF THE ṢAFAWID EMPIRE

Ṣafawid rule over Persia is conventionally dated from Shāh Ismāʿīl's capture of Tabrīz in the aftermath of his victory over the Aq-Qoyunlu ruler Alwand at Sharūr in 907/1501. But there was still a very long way to go before Ismāʿīl could be regarded as anything more than a potential successor to the Aq-Qoyunlu in Āẕarbāyjān. Nor, for some years, was the geographical shape of the new state by any means clear. It may be that Ismāʿīl's expectation was that he would be able to set up an essentially Türkmen empire after the Aq-Qoyunlu pattern, consisting of eastern Anatolia, Āẕarbāyjān, western Persia and Iraq. After all, the military following on which he depended was Türkmen in composition, he had fixed his capital at Tabrīz, the now traditional Türkmen centre on the periphery of Persia proper, and he may have seen himself as in some sense the legitimate successor to his Aq-Qoyunlu grandfather, Uzun Ḥasan.

The direction of Ismāʿīl's early campaigns certainly suggested that it was the Türkmen heritage he was primarily interested in. The defeat of Alwand had not finally ended the danger from the Aq-Qoyunlu. With Āẕarbāyjān secure for the time being, the Ṣafawid forces marched south, where they met and defeated Murād Aq-Qoyunlu at Hamadān in 908/1503. This led to the establishment of Ṣafawid rule in western Persia. In 913/1507 Ismāʿīl turned his attention back towards the west, to the old Aq-Qoyunlu heartland in Diyārbakr and their former centres in the cities of Āmid and Mārdīn. This advance into eastern Anatolia meant that Ṣafawid power now reached as far as the frontiers of the Ottoman Empire, but for the time being a clash with the Ottomans was avoided.

Next it was the turn of Iraq. Baghdad was taken in 914/1508, and thereafter the Mushaʿshaʿ, a Shīʿite power in Khūzistān in the south-west of Persia, whose religious notions were dangerously similar to those of the Ṣafawid order, were brought to submission. By 914/1508, then, Shāh Ismāʿīl was effectively the ruler of most of the territories that had constituted his grandfather's Türkmen empire. But the year 916/1510 saw what was to prove a decisive shift towards the east. In Khurāsān the Timurids were no more: since 911/1506 the real enemy was Muḥammad Shaybānī Khān, ruler of the Özbegs, who were to remain dangerous eastern adversaries of the Ṣafawids at least until the end of the sixteenth century.

THE RISE OF THE ÖZBEGS

By the late fourteenth century the tribes of the steppes west and north of the Caspian, in what is now Kazakhstan, had become known to Muslim writers as Özbegs. This name may have had some connection with the great fourteenth-century Khān Özbeg of the Golden Horde, though other explanations have been offered such as that they believed themselves to have had a hundred (*öz*) chiefs (*beg*). In the aftermath of Temür's defeat of Tokhtamish in 797/1395, factional strife fractured the Golden Horde. Among the Özbeg groupings that arose at this time was one headed by the descendants of Shiban (the name was later Arabicized as Shaybān), a brother of Batu, founder of the Golden Horde. Another Özbeg group was known as the Kazakhs (the word "Cossack" is derived from this term).

By 831/1428 a certain Abū'l-Khayr, who was the chief Shaybanid prince, had succeeded in unifying a number of Özbeg tribes. Following the usual practice, he at once embarked on a career of territorial expansion. He attacked the Timurids to the south, invading Khwārazm and sacking the city of Urganj in the 1430s and occupying the Jaxartes River area, in the east of Transoxania, in 849–50/1446. He moved his capital to the city of Sighnāq, in this region, and attempted to consolidate his power by centralizing the government of his new empire and reducing the independence of the tribal chieftains who had joined his confederation. After the death of the Timurid Shāh Rukh in 850/1447 he took advantage of the political confusion to invade Transoxania, though he was unable to establish himself there. Nevertheless he continued to intervene in the affairs of the Timurid empire, and in 855/1451 Abū Saʿīd was able to seize the throne only with his help.

Some Kazakh clans – under the leadership of two Mongol princes,

Janibeg and Qarai – had refused to accept the new order, possibly discerning an unacceptable trend towards sedentarization. They fled to the eastern Chaghatai khanate in Mughulistān. Abū'l-Khayr was much weakened by these defections from his ranks and was consequently to suffer defeat in 861/1456–7 at the hands of the Oirat Mongols, who were advancing from western Mongolia. He never really recovered from this setback. In 872–3/1468 he died while on campaign against the Kazakhs and their allies from Mughulistān. His death was followed by internecine warfare among the tribes which had formed his confederation, and its power collapsed. For the time being Özbeg expansion was at an end, and of Abū'l-Khayr's family only his grandson Muḥammad Shaybānī, born about 855/1451, survived.

After the disaster of 872–3/1468 Muḥammad Shaybānī lived for a time as little more than a bandit. But he was able gradually to build up a substantial following, and from 891/1486 he began raiding Timurid territory in force. In the 1490s he was able to occupy the Jaxartes territory and to prepare for a full-scale invasion of Transoxania. After marching unsuccessfully against Samarqand in 904/1499, in 905/1500 he abandoned the ancestral steppes for ever. The vacuum on the steppes was filled by the Kazakhs, who remained there and after whom the modern Soviet republic of Kazakhstan is named.

The conquest of Transoxania took several years: Samarqand itself had to be occupied twice, in 905/1500 and 906/1501. A considerable effort to resist the Özbegs was made by the Timurid Bābur, whose lifelong ambition it was to be the ruler of Samarqand. But in 910/1504 he admitted defeat, for the time being, and withdrew to Kābul. In 910/1504–5 Muḥammad Shaybānī took Khwārazm, and was poised to invade Khurāsān. There the last great Timurid, Ḥusayn Bāyqarā, died in 911/1506. In 912/1507 the Özbeg forces entered his capital, Harāt. By 913–14/1508 they controlled the whole of Khurāsān, and had laid Persia waste as far west and south as Dāmghān and Kirmān. They were even able to inflict severe damage on the Kazakhs in the steppes to the north. By 914–15/1509 it must have seemed that the Shaybanid Özbegs had succeeded to the whole Timurid inheritance in the east: they looked invincible. In fact it fell to the equally triumphant Shāh Ismāʿīl to bring Muḥammad Shaybānī's career to an inglorious end.

SHĀH ISMĀʿĪL VERSUS ÖZBEGS AND OTTOMANS

Perhaps Ismāʿīl might have been prepared to tolerate a Timurid neighbour that offered no real threat to his own power: Uzun Ḥasan and

Ḥusayn Bāyqarā had contrived to co-exist without undue strain on either side. But Muḥammad Shaybānī's expanding Özbeg empire was another matter. Ismāʿīl evidently concluded that to ignore the new, confident and – dangerously for the Ṣafawids – Sunnī state to the east was an unacceptable risk. In 916/1510 he marched into Khurāsān and met Muḥammad Shaybānī in battle near Marv. The Özbegs were defeated and their ruler killed. Ismāʿīl had his skull set in gold and fashioned into a drinking cup – a way of treating a dead enemy that had a very long steppe pedigree behind it. He despatched this gruesome trophy to his other great enemy, the Ottoman sulṭān.

Harāt surrendered to the Ṣafawid forces, but Ismāʿīl seems to have decided that to attempt to carry the war into Transoxania would tax his resources too far. He accepted the River Oxus as the boundary between the Ṣafawid and Özbeg empires. Khurāsān became a Ṣafawid province. Although Shāh Ismāʿīl did not intervene directly in Transoxania, he did encourage Bābur to take advantage of the confusion which had followed the defeat and death of Muḥammad Shaybānī. In 917/1511 Bābur invaded, and was able, for the last time, to enter Samarqand. But whether because, as a protégé of Ismāʿīl, he had been obliged to declare himself a Shīʿī, or because of the harsh economic measures he found it necessary to take, Bābur received a hostile reception from the populace and was driven out before long by Muḥammad Shaybānī's nephew ʿUbayd Allāh. This time there was to be no return: the future, for Bābur and his Timurid descendants, lay in India (see Chapter 11).

In 918/1512 Özbeg troops under ʿUbayd Allāh invaded Khurāsān once more. This time they had more success: at Ghujduwān they defeated the Ṣafawid army, though on this occasion Ismāʿīl was not in command. A few months later, in 919/1513, he marched east again in person. The Özbegs withdrew without fighting, and the Ṣafawid-Özbeg frontier was stabilized, at least for a time.

Despite the defeat of 918/1512 and the failure of Bābur, Ismāʿīl's policy in Khurāsān could on the whole be counted a considerable success. He had contained, if he had not destroyed, a formidable enemy, and had acquired a vast province for his empire, one that had not for many years been held by the rulers of western Persia. But it could not be pretended that the Özbegs were Ṣafawid Persia's most dangerous adversary. A state whose centre was still in Āẕarbāyjān and eastern Anatolia clearly had much more to fear from the Ottoman Empire.

The root cause of the conflict between the two empires lay in the fact that so large a proportion of the supporters of the Ṣafawid cause came from among the Türkmen tribesmen of eastern and central Anatolia, near to, or actually inside, Ottoman territory. This meant not only that the Ottoman state was losing valuable manpower to its neighbour, but also that the loyalty to the Ottomans of many of those who remained could not be relied on. As early as 907–8/1502 there had been mass deportations of Qizilbash to southern Greece, where they would be out of harm's way.

In 917/1511 and 918/1512 major Qizilbash revolts broke out in Ottoman Anatolia, in the latter stages with active Ṣafawid support. The devastation caused was immense. The reasons for these events seem to have been as much social and economic as specifically political or religious. Severe economic distress, plague and famine, had alienated the Türkmen of Anatolia; and they had a further grievance in that the policy of the Ottoman government towards its nomadic subjects was to restrict their freedom of movement and bring them firmly under the bureaucratic control of the central administration. In these circumstances the appeal of the Ṣafawids was not simply a religious one. Türkmen tribesmen may have followed Shāh Ismāʿīl because they regarded him as divine, but they also found the tribally oriented Ṣafawid political enterprise altogether more attractive than submission to the government in Constantinople. Their prospects in Ṣafawid Persia were good: they had none as subjects of the Ottoman sulṭān.

The Qizilbash revolts exhausted the patience of the Ottomans. They helped to precipitate the abdication in 918/1512 of Sulṭān Bayezid in favour of his formidable son Selim ("the Grim"), who was destined not only to deal with the menace from Persia but also to add Syria and Egypt to the Ottoman dominions.

Selim first of all inaugurated a savage repression of the Qizilbash, executing many and deporting others. He then prepared to confront Shāh Ismāʿīl directly, marching across Anatolia towards Āẕarbāyjān in 920/1514. It was a long march, and the logistical problems, in the face of a Ṣafawid scorched earth policy, were great. Nevertheless Ismāʿīl chose to accept battle at Chāldirān, an encounter which was to have permanent consequences both for the future of the Ṣafawid empire and for the political geography of the Middle East down to the present day.

Whatever we may make of the figures quoted in contemporary sources, it seems clear that the Ottoman army at Chāldirān was much larger than its Ṣafawid opponent. Perhaps as important as relative size was the nature of the two armies' composition. The Ṣafawids still mobilized a force essentially of the traditional Turko-Mongol type: its strength lay in its cavalry archers. The Ottomans, on the other hand, had, as well as cavalry, the Janissaries, infantry armed with hand guns, and field artillery. The Ṣafawids, on this occasion, had no guns, though they had in the past used them, at least in siege warfare.

The Ottoman victory was total. Shāh Ismāʿīl escaped from the field, but his army was crushed and many of his high-ranking officers killed. The conventional explanation of the scale of the defeat is in terms partly of the numerical superiority of the Ottomans and partly of their guns: Chāldirān is seen above all else as the victory of modern military technology over the outdated steppe ways of warfare. There may be something in this, and it should be remembered that the Ottoman artillery had also made a contribution to the defeat of Uzun Ḥasan Aq-Qoyunlu at Bashkent in 878/1473. But the superiority of the guns ought not, at this date, to be pressed too far. It may well be that what was really dangerous to the Ṣafawids about the Ottoman field artillery was not so much what came out of the guns' barrels as the fact that, chained together, they formed an effective barrier to cavalry charges and a safe refuge behind which the Janissary musketeers could shelter while loading and firing.

In the aftermath of Chāldirān Selim marched into Āẕarbāyjān and occupied Tabrīz. But his troops, never very enthusiastic about the campaign, proved unwilling to winter there, and he withdrew westwards. Ismāʿīl was able to reoccupy his capital unopposed. What, then, were the consequences of the battle of Chāldirān?

The first was a major and definitive readjustment of the Perso-Turkish frontier. The eastern Anatolian provinces, homeland of the Qara-Qoyunlu and the Aq-Qoyunlu, the principal Qizilbash recruiting ground, became and remained Ottoman territory. The present border between Iran and Turkey is a result of Chāldirān: there was no such frontier before 920/1514. This meant a decisive change in the shape of the Ṣafawid empire. It was no longer the old Türkmen state with Khurāsān added on: instead it was something more like Iran as we think of it today, although Shāh Ismāʿīl still controlled Iraq, as well as lands in the Caucasus and in the east which Persia later lost. Tabrīz, the capital, was now almost a border city, hazardously close to the enemy – a consideration which no doubt influenced the transfer of the capital, under Ismāʿīl's successors, first to Qazwīn and then to Iṣfahān. Inevitably, although the Türkmen element in the Ṣafawid polity was still of immense importance, this shift of the centre of gravity eastwards also resulted, in time, in the state becoming more "Persian" and less "Turkish" in character.

The second consequence, the one most frequently remarked on, is the effect the defeat had on Shāh Ismāʿīl himself and on his status in the eyes of his Qizilbash followers. We read that Ismāʿīl sank into a deep depression, that he never smiled again, and so forth, though this is hardly borne out by the testimony of European ambassadors who saw him in the years after Chāldirān. It is indeed true that he did not, in the ten remaining years of his life, take the field again in person, and this may be significant.

So far as his status is concerned, belief among the Qizilbash in the shāh's divinity must certainly have been damaged by the defeat: gods are not usually expected to lose battles, and Chāldirān cost Ismāʿīl his previously well-deserved reputation for invincibility. But this should not be exaggerated. Both his father and his grandfather had been defeated and killed in battle, without this having any discernible detrimental effect on the religious appeal of the Ṣafawid cause. As late as the 1540s, well into the reign of Ismāʿīl's son and successor Ṭahmāsp I, the Italian traveller Michel Membrè observed practices at the Ṣafawid court which clearly indicated that the old beliefs of the Qizilbash had not as yet been destroyed either by Chāldirān or by the establishment of the much more staid and sober Twelver variety of Shīʿism.

If the shāh's loss of personal status was as serious as is sometimes maintained, one might have expected the Ṣafawid state to have collapsed in the aftermath of the Ottoman victory, but in fact nothing of the sort occurred. It would seem that even by 920/1514 the regime was resting on foundations more varied and durable than the mere loyalty of the Qizilbash tribesmen. This was just as well, since the state had to endure, and did endure, two long periods of weak central government and Qizilbash factional struggles before the century was out.

FOUNDATIONS OF ṢAFAWID POWER

The Ṣafawid state established by Shāh Ismāʿīl relied on three elements for the maintenance of its power. The first, without which the Ṣafawid family could never have seized control of Persia, was the loyalty of the Qizilbash tribesmen to the shāh in his capacity as head of the Ṣafawid order, descendant of ʿAlī, even divine being. The acquisition of political power required above all, in the first instance, the necessary military capability, and this the Qizilbash provided. There were a host of clan and tribal affiliations, but the Qizilbash were organized, up to a point, into a number of broad tribal groupings – Rūmlū, Shāmlū, Afshār, Qājār, and so forth.

After the conquest of Persia many of the Qizilbash groups were granted grazing lands, especially in the north-west of the country, which not only contained the grasslands traditionally most favoured by nomads but was also the area nearest to the point of greatest danger to the state, the Ottoman frontier. Whole provinces were granted to tribal chiefs as governors, in return for the obligation to provide the shāh with troops. The most powerful tribal leaders took office in the central government, near to the person of the shāh, the source of all authority and patronage. At court, and increasingly without much direct relevance to original tribal loyalties and bases of power, factions developed and alliances were forged. The Qizilbash leaders long remained a potent force within the state, and not always one that the shāh found possible to control as he might have wished. But they, and the military forces they held at their disposal, could not easily be dispensed with.

"The empire", a Chinese bureaucrat is supposed to have said to the Mongol khān Ögedei, "has been conquered on horseback, but it cannot be governed on horseback." As all nomadic and semi-nomadic dynasties had found, this was no less true of Persia than of China. The local bureaucracy, recruited especially from members of the urban population of the cities of central Persia, was an essential part of the machinery of government once the initial period of conquest was over.

In the Ṣafawid case the truth of this was accepted right from the start. Before the battle of Sharūr, Shams al-Dīn Zakariyā Kujujī, a Persian who was *wazīr* to the Aq-Qoyunlu, had arrived at Ismāʿīl's camp to reveal the parlous state of confusion that prevailed at the Türkmen court and to encourage Ismāʿīl to attack. He received his reward by being appointed to the same post in the new Ṣafawid government, and men of his origin and training proceeded to staff the main administrative – as distinct from military – offices (though the distinction was in practice by no means absolute). In this way Ismāʿīl ensured that there should be a strong thread of administrative continuity between his government and that of his Türkmen predecessors.

This did not mean that no significant changes were made. Some modifications to the system of government had to be implemented to take account of the fact that Persia was now, in a sense, being governed as a theocracy, in which the shāh was also the head of a *ṣūfī* order and his military followers his disciples.

One of the principal results of this perhaps anomalous situation was the creation of the office of *wakīl*, deputy to the shāh. He was deputy as head of the government – that is, he was a kind of *wazīr*. But he was not only the chief executive of the government: he also in some instances acted as commander-in-chief of the armed forces. It was in this role that the *wakīl* Yār Aḥmad Khūzānī led the Ṣafawid army to a defeat which resulted in his own death at the battle of Ghujduwān in 918/1512.

What is interesting is that Yār Aḥmad Khūzānī, like almost all the early Ṣafawid *wakīls*, was a Persian: it is clear enough that to say that all military responsibility fell to the Türkmen chiefs and all civil posts to the Persian bureaucrats is far too simple. Indeed, such appointments to the wakilate are an indication that Shāh Ismāʿīl was consciously attempting to shift power away from the Qizilbash towards the more reliable and less militarily dangerous Persians. He could not do without the Qizilbash, but the bureaucracy was in some ways a more secure foundation for his regime. The Qizilbash themselves certainly saw the advancement of Persians to the highest office as an affront to themselves: two Persian *wakīls* were murdered by them.

THE IMPOSITION OF TWELVER SHĪʿISM

The Ṣafawid state's third and most distinctive foundation was its new official faith, the Twelver variety of Shīʿism, whose adherents accept a line of twelve infallible *imāms*, beginning with ʿAlī and ending with Muḥammad al-Mahdī, who disappeared (but did not die) in about 264/878 and whose return the faithful expect. Everybody is now well aware that late-twentieth-century Iran is a Shīʿī country, and for this the religious policy of Shāh Ismāʿīl is directly responsible.

There seems no reason to doubt that a large majority of the Persian people in 907/1501 adhered to the Sunnī branch of the Islamic faith. The advent of the Ṣafawid dynasty brought with it compulsory conversion to Shīʿism. Why this should have been so is not immediately obvious: the form of Shīʿism chosen by Shāh Ismāʿīl was not the faith of his Qizilbash followers. Possibly Ismāʿīl had been influenced by the Shīʿī environment in which he had lived in Gīlān before marching against the Aq-Qoyunlu; or he may have felt that Twelver Shīʿism was at least nearer to Qizilbash belief than Sunnism was.

It has sometimes been suggested that Ismāʿīl's motives were in reality, in the modern Western sense, "political": that he saw in Shīʿism a convenient source of identity, a means of differentiating his kingdom from its Sunnī neighbours, Ottoman and Özbeg. Bernard Lewis has some wise words about such reasoning: "When modern man ceased to accord first place to religion in his own concerns, he also ceased to believe that other men, in other times, could ever truly have done so, and so he began to re-examine the great religious movements of the past in search of interests and motives acceptable to modern minds."[1] There is no evidence whatever to lead us to suppose that Ismāʿīl was motivated by cynical notions of political manipulation, or indeed that to draw such a distinction between "politics" and "religion" would have occurred to him. This, however, is not to say that the adoption of Shīʿism did not, in time, play its part in helping to define the political and cultural identity of "Persia", as against other Muslim countries.

It may be said, with some justice, that the ground had been prepared for the acceptance of Shīʿism during the previous two centuries, a period in which veneration of ʿAlī and the other eleven Shīʿī *imāms* had become popular and widespread, and was not thought incompatible with adherence to Sunnism. But there was no Shīʿī religious establishment in Persia on which Shāh Ismāʿīl could call for assistance when, on taking possession of Tabrīz in 907/1501, he declared Twelver Shīʿism not only the official but the compulsory religion of his new empire. This did not prevent the speedy enforcement of Ismāʿīl's policy.

The shāh is said to have threatened that death would be the penalty for any opposition to his wishes with respect to religion. If anyone had thought this an empty threat, they were soon to be disabused. As the Ṣafawid forces marched across Persia, Shīʿism was imposed at the point of the sword. Sunnīs who were reluctant to see the error of their ways were treated with great brutality. Many were executed.

In these circumstances the speed at which Persia apparently became a Shīʿī country is hardly a matter for surprise. If Shāh Ismāʿīl's motives are unlikely to have been "secular", the same may well not have been true of all those Persians who hastened to declare their allegiance to the official faith. They had that most powerful of motives, the wish to save their own lives and property. But a good many leading Persians seem to have taken a more positive view than this. Before long we see the emergence of a class of what have been called Persian "clerical notables" – wealthy *ʿulamāʾ*, originally Sunnī, who adhered to Shīʿism and rose to high rank in the new religious establishment, holding positions as *qāḍīs* and even the supreme religious dignity, that of *ṣadr*. The *ṣadr* was appointed by the government to oversee the religious institution, in particular the administration of *waqf* property and of the *sharīʿa*. Some scholars believe that for a time he had also to supervise the imposition of Shīʿism and root out heresy and Sunnism. On occasion both the *ṣadr* and *qāḍīs* would hold military commands, which indicates that it was not only the distinction between civil and military office that was not always clearly maintained.

But such opportunistic defectors from Sunnism, useful and indeed essential as they were, could not provide the theological and legal backbone for the new Shīʿī establishment. No one in Persia could do this. Shāh Ismāʿīl had to look elsewhere. He imported Shīʿī *ʿulamāʾ*

from the Arab lands, from Baḥrayn, from Ḥilla in Iraq, and above all from Jabal ʿĀmil in Lebanon. Many of the leading theologians and lawyers of the Ṣafawid period were of ʿĀmilī origin, including the most influential religious figure of Ismāʿīl's own time, al-Karakī. The religious brain drain to Persia long continued: it was not a merely temporary phenomenon.

The position of the Ṣafawid shāh, a ruler who claimed descent from the *imāms* and regarded himself – and was officially regarded – as their representative on earth, was not one that could easily be reconciled with Twelver Shīʿī theology and law. But the creation of a new Shīʿī state, in which impoverished if learned theologians and lawyers could expect employment and a sympathetic hearing, was not to be lightly despised. For the most part the immigrant *ʿulamāʾ* kept to themselves any reservations they may have felt, except on occasion in works (in Arabic) on law, intended for their fellow-scholars rather than for a wider Persian readership.

At what stage the majority of the Persian people became actually, as well as nominally, attached to the Shīʿī version of their faith is impossible to say without the ability to make windows into the souls of men long dead. The process was probably a slow one, and was never total. Sunnī communities, especially among some of the tribal peoples, remain in Persia to the present day. It was still possible for Shāh Ismāʿīl II to mount an admittedly abortive attempt to return to Sunnism during his brief reign (984–5/1576–7). But Nādir Shāh in the eighteenth century failed to move Persia in a Sunnī direction, and it would probably be fair to suggest that Persia was irrevocably Shīʿī well before the end of the Ṣafawid period. Certainly the Persian people's allegiance to that faith has remained firm ever since.

Shāh Ismāʿīl died suddenly in 930/1524, still only in his thirties. His achievement, despite the failure at Chāldirān, had been very great. He had founded a dynasty which ruled for over two centuries – far longer than any other Persian dynasty in the Islamic period. He had secured its territory within borders which may not have been what he was aiming at, but which his successors did not extend, and which approximate to those of modern Persia before the contractions of the nineteenth century. He had begun the process of organizing his kingdom so as to ensure that it would survive times of adversity. He had promoted the adoption of a new official faith for his country, admittedly by methods that were unsavoury; but the effects were enduring. All in all, he had left more of a mark on Persia than most of its rulers have managed to do. What he had not done, as his successors were to discover, was to solve the problem of how a dynasty which had come to power at the head of an army of Türkmen tribesmen might prevent those same tribesmen from becoming a menace to the stability of the state they had helped establish.

NOTE

1. B. Lewis, *The Assassins: a Radical Sect in Islam*, London 1967, 136.

CHAPTER THIRTEEN

Crisis, Recovery and Crisis (930–995/1524–1587)

On Shāh Ismāʿīl's death in 930/1524, his ten-year-old son ascended the throne as Ṭahmāsp I. The young boy could not of course exercise effective personal rule, and ten years of crisis, both internal and external, ensued. Control of the central government became a prize to be grasped by contending factions of Qizilbash *amīrs*, and Persia's foreign enemies, Ottoman and Özbeg, did not fail to take advantage of the situation. It might have seemed that the dynasty was on the verge of collapse, but in fact Ṭahmāsp's victory over the factions at the end of this period ushered in forty years of comparative stability. Ṭahmāsp, however, did not succeed in finding a permanent solution to the problems of his minority, and his death was the prelude to a further time of internal chaos and external assault which looked even more likely to bring the regime to an inglorious end. Recovery this time, however, was yet more strikingly dramatic: the reign of Shāh ʿAbbās I (995–1038/1587–1629) proved to be the high point of Ṣafawid power and prestige. ʿAbbās's achievement made it possible for Ṣafawid rule to survive a succession of largely ineffective shāhs for a further century.

A DECADE OF QIZILBASH FACTION, 930–940/1524–1533

At the beginning of Ṭahmāsp's reign his *atabeg*, a member of the Rūmlū Qizilbash tribe, seized power, taking office as chief *amīr* (*amīr al-umarāʾ*). For a time he made an alliance with two other tribal leaders, representing the Ustajlū and the Takkalū. But this did not last, and in 933/1527 Chūha Sulṭān Takkalū managed to establish the dominance of his faction, which lasted until 937/1530–1.

In the meantime the old enemy to the east had not been inactive. After Muḥammad Shaybānī had been killed in 916/1510, no one figure was able to dominate the politics of Özbeg Transoxania as he had done. The leading contender for power was Muḥammad Shaybānī's nephew ʿUbayd Allāh, but he was never able to establish an absolute supremacy over the other Özbeg *khāns*. An agreement was arrived at among them that, irrespective of where real power actually lay, the supreme khanate should be vested in the senior living Shaybanid. Although ʿUbayd Allāh was certainly the single most influential Özbeg, he occupied the highest titular dignity only for the last seven years of his life (940–7/1533–40).

ʿUbayd Allāh mounted no fewer than five invasions of Khurāsān between 930/1524 and 944/1537: division in Tabrīz provided him with an excellent opportunity for wreaking havoc in, and even attempting to annex permanently, what was for the Ṣafawid government a distant province. The first incursion, at the beginning of the reign, was not pressed to a conclusion, but in 934/1528 ʿUbayd Allāh marched in again, this time apparently aiming at a full-scale occupation of Khurāsān. He took Mashhad, and subjected Harāt to a siege. A Persian relief force went to the city's aid, the young shāh accompanying it in person; and he is said to have distinguished himself at the ensuing battle of Jām, where the Ṣafawid army was victorious, possibly owing in part to its use of artillery (which Shāh Ismāʿīl had obtained from the Portuguese). It would seem that the Persians had learned a lesson from the battle of Chāldirān. The Özbegs, too, knew that guns were becoming important, but they were handicapped by their inability to manufacture them domestically; and no other state was prepared to guarantee them a supply of such armaments.

The Ṣafawid troops were unable to benefit as much from this victory as they might have, for they were obliged to hasten back to the west to deal with a Qizilbash revolt in Baghdad. This was especially dangerous since the rebel leader had acknowledged the authority of the Ottoman sulṭān and Ṣafawid governments were always aware that the Ottomans, at least potentially, were a much more serious menace to their survival than the Özbegs could ever be. As it happened the revolt was quickly put down, without there being overt Ottoman intervention; but ʿUbayd Allāh had taken the opportunity to invade again. He withdrew in the following year (936/1530), on the return of the Persian army.

Not long after this, Chūha Sulṭān Takkalū was overthrown and killed. This was followed by a general massacre of Takkalū tribesmen. The dominant Qizilbash faction was now led by Ḥusayn Khān Shāmlū.

A refugee Takkalū *amīr* fled to the Ottoman court, and urged the sulṭān to intervene in Persia. The danger from the west was increasing. Then in 938/1532 the Özbegs invaded yet again, occupying most of Khurāsān apart from the city of Harāt, which they besieged. They did not withdraw for over a year, during which they were not challenged: evidently the Ottoman menace was thought too great for it to be safe to concentrate Ṣafawid military resources on the affairs of Khurāsān.

In 940/1533 a further bout of internal strife occurred, in the course of which Ḥusayn Khān Shāmlū was overthrown and executed on the shāh's orders. This time the end result was not the usual one: the ultimate beneficiary was not another Qizilbash faction, but the shāh himself. By now he was old and experienced enough to assert his own authority over the state. Although the danger to the empire's stability which the feuding Qizilbash posed had not by any means been eliminated, as events after Ṭahmāsp's death were to show, there now followed four decades in which the position of the shāh as the real head of the government was successfully maintained. It was as well: Ṭahmāsp seized power from his *amīrs* just in time to face the worst Ṣafawid nightmare: a full-scale Ottoman invasion.

THE EFFECTIVE RULE OF ṬAHMĀSP I, 940–984/1533–1576

Until 940/1533 the principal concern of the Ottoman sulṭān, Süleyman the Magnificent, had been military operations in south-east Europe, which had involved the siege of Vienna in 936/1529. Peace with the Holy Roman Emperor enabled him to turn his attention to the Persians. In 941/1534 the Ottoman Grand Vizier invaded Āẕarbāyjān and occupied Tabrīz. The sulṭān himself arrived soon after, but was faced with snowstorms in Āẕarbāyjān and marched south to take Baghdad. Ṭahmāsp was in Khurāsān, leading operations against the Özbegs. He had also to cope with the last manifestations of Qizilbash revolt; this time the rebels were in touch with the Ottomans.

Ṭahmāsp took care not to face Süleyman in a pitched battle: his prospects in such a situation were not good. The Ottoman problem was one of holding their conquests once they had withdrawn their troops back to Ottoman territory. At the end of 1535 the sulṭān marched home. He managed to retain some of his conquests: Baghdad and Mesopotamia, apart from a short period in the next century, were now to be part of the Ottoman Empire. But Āẕarbāyjān and the Ṣafawid capital returned to Persian rule. From Ṭahmāsp's point of view it was not a wholly unsatisfactory outcome.

So much for the west. But there remained the recurring problem of war on two widely separated fronts: the end of 1535 saw ʿUbayd Allāh and the Özbegs in Khurāsān again. The ground had been well prepared for them. As part of the last convulsion of Qizilbash faction, Ṭahmāsp's brother Sām Mīrzā, who was governor of Khurāsān, had revolted with his *amīrs*. They had oppressed the population in and around Harāt with such severity that the people had themselves revolted against their rulers, so successfully that they were able to besiege Harāt and join forces with ʿUbayd Allāh when he marched into Persian territory. This is a remarkable event: it provides one of the few glimpses that our largely court-centred Persian sources allow us of the nature and extent of popular discontent in Ṣafawid times.

Harāt was surrendered to the rebels and the Özbegs. But even though ʿUbayd Allāh was now supreme *khān* in name as well as in fact, his power remained limited, and when news came that Shāh Ṭahmāsp was on the march he was unable to prevent his *amīrs* from insisting on abandoning Khurāsān and returning to Transoxania. Part of his forces, the temporarily allied troops of another Shaybanid khanate in Khwārazm, even changed sides, joining the Qizilbash in attacking ʿUbayd Allāh.

This all served to demonstrate that the Özbeg menace, though serious, did not in itself pose a real threat to the existence of the Ṣafawid state. ʿUbayd Allāh may perhaps have hoped to conquer and occupy Khurāsān, but he was always hamstrung by the fact that many other Özbegs saw that province as no more than a rich source of plunder. Ṭahmāsp was able in 943–4/1537 not only to retake Khurāsān but even, for a time, to seize Qandahār (now in southern Afghanistan) from the Mughals. ʿUbayd Allāh died in 947/1540: the Özbeg challenge to the integrity of Persia receded for many years.

The same was not, however, true of the Ottomans. Süleyman mounted two further invasions of Persia. In 955/1548 he had the assistance of the shāh's brother Alqāṣ Mīrzā, who was in revolt. Again Tabrīz was captured, but again the Turks retreated. Once more Ṭahmāsp's tactics of avoiding set-piece battles but making life impossible for the Ottomans by scorched earth tactics had proved effective. A final Ottoman campaign in 961/1554 was even less successful. Süleyman gave up: in 962/1555 he made the Treaty of Amāsya with Ṭahmāsp.

Mesopotamia, Baghdad, and the great Shīʿī shrines in Iraq were lost by Persia, but Āẕarbāyjān was saved. The shāh had fought off his two great foreign enemies and enjoyed, for the remaining two decades of his life, external peace. In the meantime he had transferred the capital from the all too vulnerable Tabrīz to the more centrally placed city of Qazwīn, where it remained for half a century. The move was no doubt dictated mainly by strategic considerations, but it perhaps serves also, as we have seen, to emphasize the increasingly "Persian" as against the originally "Türkmen" character of the regime.

The middle years of Ṭahmāsp's reign saw the beginnings of the introduction into the Ṣafawid power structure of a new "ethnic" element to add to the Türkmen Qizilbash and the Persian bureaucrats. Older scholarship tended to represent the internal strife of the first Ṣafawid century in something approaching racial terms: in Vladimir Minorsky's oft-quoted phrase: "like oil and water, the Turcomans and Persians did not mix freely."[1] More recent research has suggested that this contrast is too stark. There were indeed latent tensions between the largely military Türkmen and the largely bureaucratic Persians in the ruling elite, and these did from time to time erupt into active hostility. But as the century progressed it was less and less true that the factions that formed were based simply on racial or tribal loyalties. Persian bureaucrats married into leading Qizilbash families; local, provincial loyalties developed in the decentralized governmental system that characterized the early Ṣafawid period; alliances were formed between powerful individuals. Ṣafawid politics cannot be convincingly explained in crude racial terms.

None of this is very surprising. There was nothing new about a situation in which Persia was ruled by a Turkish military class and a Persian bureaucracy: in Shāh Ṭahmāsp's time this had been the case in much of Persia for five hundred years. It was in fact the norm. Persian society and culture had had constant practice at coping with such a state of affairs, and was quite sufficiently resilient to be able to do so without breaking under the strain. The principal difference from the past was perhaps that this time the ruling house itself – because of its beginnings in a religious order rather than a tribe, and possibly also because of its non-Turkish origin (though this was very remote) – was less closely identified than were its predecessors with the Turkish element.

Yet this, too, began to change in Ṭahmāsp's reign. Although the loyalty of the Qizilbash to the shāh in his capacity as head of the Ṣafawid order may well have remained stronger than is sometimes supposed, we see the first signs among them of an appeal to the *Shāh-savanī*, "those who love the shāh" – a name adopted much later by a nomadic tribal group in Āẕarbāyjān. This, then, implied the growth of loyalty to the shāh as monarch rather than as *ṣūfī* master. Much – indeed, too much – has been made of this in the past by historians who wished to emphasize the decisive role in Persian history of its monarchical tradition, though this view is no longer as fashionable as it once was. But it is certainly fair to say that the "secular" status of the Ṣafawid shāhs as monarchs increased as their "religious" role gradually diminished.

If a dual elite of Turks and Persians was a common enough phenomenon, the introduction of a third element was an innovation. But it was an innovation based on time-hallowed Ṣafawid tradition, that of holy war against the Christian infidel in the Caucasus. In the 1540s and 1550s Shāh Ṭahmāsp mounted four major expeditions against this area, bringing back tens of thousands of Georgian, Circassian and Armenian prisoners as slaves. Here were the makings of the new element.

Many of the female prisoners entered harems, some of them the royal harem, where they became the mothers of princes and a force to be reckoned with in court politics, especially at times of crisis in the succession. Some of the male prisoners were converted, in name or otherwise, to Islam, and were trained at court. After Ṭahmāsp's time they were allowed to rise to high office in the state, even to the rank of provincial governor. Some scholars believe that they could enter the shāh's bodyguard, the *qūrchīs*. This was a small standing army, independent of the Qizilbash levies and with its membership selected from the various Qizilbash tribes. At this period the importance of their commander, the *qūrchī-bāshī*, was increasing. It was in this matter of the military recruitment of non-Türkmen to provide a possibly reliable counterweight to the unruly Qizilbash that Ṭahmāsp, whether consciously or not, laid foundations that were to be built on with decisive effect by his grandson ʿAbbās I.

Ṭahmāsp died in 984/1576 after a reign of fifty-two years. He does not seem to have been, personally, an especially attractive figure, though he is given credit for generous artistic patronage, at least in the first part of his reign: a celebrated example is what is known as the Houghton *Shāh-nāma*, an illustrated manuscript produced for him which contains some of the very finest of all Persian miniatures. He is often accused of parsimony and religious bigotry, and he has been described as weak or diffident. Yet he had fought and mastered the Qizilbash factions, at least for his own lifetime, and had retained intact almost all the territory bequeathed to him by his father in the face of determined assaults by powerful neighbours.

He had survived, and the empire had survived with him. The events of the next decade showed that the problems of his minority had not yet been solved permanently; but his achievement was by no means an insignificant one. The Ṣafawid empire might well have collapsed either at the beginning of his reign or in the years after his death. The fact that it did not was at least in part the result of Shāh Ṭahmāsp's long and patient efforts.

RENEWED CRISIS, 984–995/1576–1587

Ṭahmāsp does not seem to have left any very clear arrangements for the succession. Inevitably, therefore, factions gathered around the two contenders, his sons Ḥaydar and Ismāʿīl. Each faction had Qizilbash support, in addition to which the Georgians at court supported Ḥaydar, and some Circassians backed Ismāʿīl. A third brother, Muḥammad Khudābanda, being nearly blind, was not regarded as a serious candidate. Ṭahmāsp had evidently had considerable reservations about Ismāʿīl, since he had had him imprisoned for the last twenty years of his reign. But Ḥaydar was murdered and Ismāʿīl duly became shāh.

Ṭahmāsp's presumed doubts about his son were speedily shown to be only too well founded. He acted, during his mercifully short reign, with such brutality that it is often supposed that he was in fact mad. Apart from his attempt to return to Sunnism – not in itself necessarily a sign of insanity – he mounted a reign of terror, not only against the supporters of the defeated faction but also against his own family. Possibly following the Ottoman precedent of the elimination, for reasons of political stability, of superfluous princes, he proceeded to execute his brothers and cousins. But after a little over a year on the throne, he died under what are usually called mysterious circumstances: it may well be that he was murdered.

His death came only just in time to save the life of his one surviving brother, Muḥammad Khudābanda, and of three of Muḥammad's own sons (one had already been murdered). Muḥammad now became shāh and reigned, though he can hardly be said to have ruled, for the next ten years.

The shāh stayed in the background. The foreground was occupied by contending factions in which various Qizilbash groups, the late shāh's sister Parī Khān Khānum, Muḥammad's wife Mahd-i ʿUlyā, the Persian chief minister Mīrzā Salmān and the crown prince Ḥamza Mīrzā (who was murdered in 994/1586), all played their part.

The Ottomans and the Özbegs did not neglect their opportunity. The Ottoman armies invaded Persian territory in 986/1578, and the war was not brought to an end until 998/1590. Large areas of northern and western Persia were lost to them, and Tabrīz was taken yet again.

The Özbegs, under their formidable ruler ʿAbd Allāh II, invaded Khurāsān and besieged Harāt. It was very like the bad old days of the 1530s, but the disasters had no effect on the virulence of factional strugglings in the territory remaining to the Persians. The most important revolt occurred in Khurāsān, where Muḥammad Khudābanda's son ʿAbbās Mīrzā had been sent as governor, supervised by a Qizilbash *amīr* of the Shāmlū tribe, ʿAlī Qulī Khān. In 989/1581 ʿAlī Qulī declared ʿAbbās shāh; Khurāsān had effectively seceded from the central government. ʿAlī Qulī eventually submitted, being allowed to retain his office; but the situation in Khurāsān continued to simmer.

In 995/1587 another Qizilbash *amīr*, Murshid Qulī Khān Ustājlū, who was governor of Mashhad and had gained custody of prince ʿAbbās, reactivated the revolt. This time it was successful. He and ʿAbbās marched on Qazwīn. Muḥammad was deposed and his son enthroned as Shāh ʿAbbās. Muḥammad, who seems never to have taken much interest in the business of being ruler of Persia, meekly acquiesced. His son appears to have treated him fairly generously, though accounts differ. Murshid Qulī Khān must have thought that he had acquired for himself a malleable sixteen-year-old royal puppet. He could not have been more mistaken.

NOTE

1. V. Minorsky (ed. and trans.), *Tadhkirat al-Mulūk*, London 1943, 188.

CHAPTER FOURTEEN

The Apogee of the Ṣafawid Empire: the Reign of Shāh ʿAbbās I (995–1038/1587–1629)

It might have been doubted whether there was actually a Ṣafawid empire in existence in 995/1587 for Shāh ʿAbbās to rule. External enemies were in occupation of nearly half of what had been Ṣafawid territory in the time of Shāh Ṭahmāsp. So far as the unoccupied areas of the country were concerned, factional fighting among the Türkmen *amīrs* had reached the proportions of civil war, and the rump of Persia could very well at this point have dissolved into a conglomeration of small Türkmen principalities. Only a quite remarkably strong and determined personality could have put all this to rights. Shāh ʿAbbās was such a man, but even with him at the head of affairs the process of recovery and reconstruction took many years.

THE RECONQUEST OF PERSIA

ʿAbbās was not strong enough, at the outset of his reign, to make any significant inroads against the Ottomans, and in any case he could not hope to fight simultaneously a two-front war against both Ottomans and Özbegs. Indeed, he could hardly expect to achieve much militarily until he had begun the internal reorganization of his empire: but this was a lengthy process which will be considered as a whole later. The Özbegs were, as ever, the less formidable of Persia's two by now traditional enemies: ʿAbbās therefore resolved to tackle them first. To free his hands for this, he was obliged to make a humiliating peace with the Ottomans in 998/1590. Vast areas of western and northern Persia, including Tabrīz, the original Ṣafawid capital, were ceded to the Ottoman Empire. Although most of Āẕarbāyjān was lost, ʿAbbās did manage to retain the town of Ardabīl, headquarters of the Ṣafawid order and site of the shrine of Shaykh Ṣafī al-Dīn. But there were not many sops to Persian sensibilities in the peace treaty. It was simply an acknowledgement of the political realities: a step that was, for the time being, necessary if Shāh ʿAbbās and the dynasty were to survive at all.

Success against the Özbegs was by no means immediate. They remained for a decade in occupation of most of Khurāsān, as well as of Sīstān further south. In addition, Qandahār was again lost to the Mughals. It was not until the death of the able Özbeg *khān* ʿAbd Allāh in 1007/1598 that it was possible to recover substantial parts of these lands for Persia. Harāt was retaken in 1007/1598 and by 1011/1602–3, although things had not all gone the Ṣafawid way, the eastern frontier had been stabilized. ʿAbbās was materially helped in this by the prevailing disunity among the various Özbeg *khāns*: he was able to make alliances with a number of those who controlled areas near the frontier, at Marv, Balkh, and Astarābād. This real if limited success was finally followed, though not until 1031/1622, by the recovery of Qandahār from the Mughals.

With the eastern border reasonably secure, it remained to mount a counter-attack on the Ottomans. The war began in 1012/1603 and was a long one, but on the whole the Persians were successful. The Ottoman forces sustained a crushing defeat at Ṣūfiyān, near Tabrīz, in 1014/1605, and north-west Persia was reoccupied. By 1015/1607 the Ottoman troops had been driven from most of the territory that had been defined as Persian by the Treaty of Amāsya. But the war dragged on, and the Ottomans did not recognize ʿAbbās's right to the reconquered lands until 1027/1618.

Hostilities even then were not at an end: in the 1620s ʿAbbās was strong enough to take Diyārbakr and, in 1033/1623, Baghdad, which had long been lost. In the previous year the island of Hurmūz in the Persian Gulf, an important centre of international trade, was taken from the Portuguese, though not without the help of an English fleet. By the end of the reign in 1038/1629 Persia once more had the borders established over a century earlier during the time of Shāh Ismāʿīl I. It had recovered all that had been lost since the death of Shāh Ṭahmāsp in 984/1576, and had even expanded its borders significantly.

INTERNAL REORGANIZATION

This was a considerable achievement as far as it went, but such victories did not in themselves solve the long-standing internal problems of the

Ṣafawid regime: military success and internal restructuring unavoidably went together. If Shāh ʿAbbās had restricted his efforts to the military sphere – to attempting to drive out the Özbegs and the Ottomans – he might have enjoyed an ephemeral success (though he might equally have enjoyed no success at all). But the potential of another descent into Qizilbash factional fighting, opening the way to more loss of territory to the neighbouring powers, would still have been there. As it was, the reforms that ʿAbbās inaugurated formed an important part of a major social transformation, one which enabled the Ṣafawid dynasty to survive for a century after his death, despite the on the whole unimpressive quality of his successors on the throne.

The immediate spur to action was the need to bring the turbulent Qizilbash *amīrs* under effective royal control. Right from the start of his reign ʿAbbās showed that he intended to achieve this, but the measures he took went far beyond the mere containment of fractious tribal chieftains. Action against rebel and ex-rebel Qizilbash began immediately. ʿAbbās's patron, Murshid Qulī Khān, was appointed *wakīl*, and with his assistance the shāh took reprisals especially against those Qizilbash he held responsible for the murder of his brother Ḥamza, during the previous reign. But not long after this ʿAbbās evidently decided that Murshid Qulī Khān himself was becoming an over-mighty subject, and the *wakīl* was killed on royal orders.

The fundamental problem of the regime was a direct legacy of the way in which it had come to power in Persia: its military dependence on the Qizilbash tribesmen whose support had been the mainstay first of the Ṣafawid order and then of the dynasty. The religious basis of loyalty to the shāh in his capacity as head of the Ṣafawid order had not disappeared, but by the time of Shāh ʿAbbās it was clearly much weaker than it had been a century earlier. We now hear more of the *Shāh-savanī* appeal – let those who love the shāh rally to his assistance.

But still such support could not necessarily be counted on. The Qizilbash had repeatedly proved fickle, and their undoubted allegiance to the Ṣafawid family did not appear in practice to preclude supporting a Ṣafawid prince against the reigning shāh. The circumstances of ʿAbbās's own accession would have made that fact sufficiently clear to him. What the dynasty needed if it were to achieve political stability was a counterweight to the Qizilbash, a strong military force recruited from other sections of the population, on whose loyalty to himself the shāh could rely even if he were to face a Qizilbash revolt.

ʿAbbās found his source of recruitment chiefly in the Caucasians. Here he was following the precedent laid down, at least in embryo, in the reign of Ṭahmāsp. The Georgians, Armenians and Circassians who now became so important were in part the descendants of those who had been taken prisoner at that time. But their numbers were considerably augmented by further batches of prisoners taken by ʿAbbās himself during campaigns in Armenia in 1012/1603–4 and Georgia in 1023/1614 and 1025/1616.

The forces ʿAbbās inherited did not, with the exception of the comparatively small force of *qūrchīs* (who were Türkmen chosen from among the Qizilbash tribes), constitute a standing army. According to the established system, the shāh called on the various Qizilbash chiefs for levies as and when required. But the new units that were founded from Caucasian *ghulām* (military slave) manpower were to be a permanent army, answerable to and paid by the shāh himself.

The process began right at the beginning of the reign. Figures for the size of the new units have been worked out, and are certainly worthy of quotation, though they should not be regarded as wholly reliable. The first formation was a *ghulām* unit, eventually 10,000 strong, whose members were called *qullar*. This was a cavalry force. Other innovations followed later. The shāh himself acquired a personal bodyguard of 3,000 *qullar*; a corps of artillerymen (*tūpchīs*) was formed, 12,000 strong, with some 500 guns; and a corps of 12,000 infantry, armed with muskets, was recruited from a variety of sources including the Persian peasantry. This made up, at least in theory, a standing army of some 37,000 men. Pietro della Valle, a highly acute Italian traveller who visited Persia during ʿAbbās's reign, reckoned that in his time the army – presumably including provincial troops, mainly Qizilbash – consisted of 70–80,000 combatants, of whom 40–50,000 could be mobilized for use on any one campaign.

The payment of the new and permanent forces required a radical change in the way in which the Ṣafawid empire was administered. The shāh did not pay the Qizilbash troops directly: they were maintained from the revenues of provinces which were granted to the tribal chiefs as assignments (now known as *tiyūl* rather than *suyūrghāl*). Such provinces were termed *mamālik*. This was something like a version of the administrative *iqṭāʿ* of Saljūq times: the Qizilbash chiefs supplied, or were expected to supply, a fixed number of troops when summoned to do so, but in return they ruled their *tiyūl* provinces as governors. During periods of weak central government, which were all too frequent during Ṣafawid times, this could involve a major diminution of the shāh's real control over his empire.

When, therefore, it was decided to pay the *ghulām* troops directly from the royal treasury, there was nothing approaching sufficient revenue available to the shāh for the purpose. The central government received very little from the *mamālik* provinces, what there was being paid into the state treasury for the general expenses of the empire, rather than into the shāh's personal treasury. Such provincial tax revenue was administered by the *Dīwān-i mamālik*. The expenses of the royal household were met from the crown lands (*khāṣṣa*), which were administered directly by the shāh. Such lands existed before Shāh ʿAbbās's reign, and had at times been increased. But during the chaotic period before 995/1587 they had been considerably eroded. The remedy for the problem of military salaries was evidently to increase the amount of *khāṣṣa* land available. The principal means of achieving this was inevitably a substantial transfer of *mamālik* land to the category of *khāṣṣa*.

This could not be done overnight, but eventually very large areas of Persia became *khāṣṣa* land. Between 996/1588 and 1014/1606 such provinces as Qazwīn, Kāshān, part of Kirmān, Yazd, and Qum ceased to be *mamālik*. The whole of their revenue now went neither to the state treasury nor to the Qizilbash *amīrs* as the yield of their *tiyūls*: it was paid directly to the shāh. ʿAbbās had the resources necessary for the maintenance of his new military forces.

The implications of the great *mamālik–khāṣṣa* transfer were not, of course, solely fiscal. Provinces that came under the direct rule of the shāh also ceased to be at the disposal of the Qizilbash *amīrs*. The balance of power between the shāh and the Qizilbash shifted radically. In this context it is also worth noting a further measure that Shāh ʿAbbās took. Until his reign, under the previous decentralized approach to the administration of the empire, local Persian families had retained a considerable degree of autonomy in certain parts of the country. This, too, was drastically curtailed. Areas in the Caspian provinces, Luristān, Lār and Sīstān were taken into direct rule. Real autonomy was left only to the hereditary governors (*wālīs*) in Georgia, Kurdistān, Khūzistān and the remaining part of Luristān.

The administration of the Ṣafawid empire had, in fact, been centralized in the hands of the shāh to an extent previously unparalleled. As long as the shāh himself was a strong ruler, he would now have the power and resources to meet and crush any internal challenge. Even if the shāh himself was ineffective, as many of ʿAbbās's successors indeed were, it would no longer be as easy as it had been during the sixteenth century for the Qizilbash or anyone else to usurp the crown's prerogatives. Shāh ʿAbbās had laid foundations which would help ensure the survival of the dynasty for a century after his death.

As the new *ghulām* contingents were recruited and organized, and arrangements made for their payment, so the position of their leaders in the state was gradually enhanced. The most notable of the early *ghulāms* was a Georgian, Allāhvirdī Khān, who was the *qullar-āqāsī*, the commander of the first major new military force to be established. He not only became commander-in-chief but was appointed provincial governor of Fārs, his governorship eventually extending as far as the Persian Gulf. His son, Imām Qulī Khān, inherited many of his honours.

By the end of the reign, the proportion of provincial governorships held by *ghulāms* was something like half the total, and it has been calculated that they constituted some 20 per cent of all the important *amīrs*. According to information which has been extracted from the most important historian of the reign, Iskandar Beg Munshī, of the 89 principal *amīrs*, 74 were Qizilbash and 15 *ghulām*. It is important to note here both how great had been the inroads on power and influence made by the new military class and the fact that the Qizilbash, however, had by no means been totally superseded. Their stranglehold over the state had been broken by Shāh ʿAbbās's vigorous and effective measures, and he had further weakened them by, in some cases, breaking up the tribes and settling them in widely separated parts of the country. The Qājār tribe, for example, was divided into three, and the branches settled in Ganja, Astarābād and Marv. Even so, the Qizilbash tribes remained an important, if less central, element in the state, and continued to supply necessary contingents to the armed forces.

THE NEW CAPITAL

During the years up to 1006/1598 Shāh ʿAbbās transferred the capital from Qazwīn to Iṣfahān. Qazwīn had been the capital for half a century, but it does not seem to have become in any way a great metropolis, as Tabrīz had been before it. As we saw earlier, Shāh Ṭahmāsp's motives for moving from Tabrīz are reasonably clear. But ʿAbbās's reasons for making a further move are less obvious. He is said to have had a strong personal liking for Iṣfahān, and he may have felt that to shift to his favourite city would give him his best opportunity for building his ideal capital. Iṣfahān was more centrally placed than Qazwīn, which may have been a relevant factor; and it is situated in a fertile and well-watered area, with (unusually for a town on the Persian plateau) a river, the Zāyanda-rūd, flowing through it.

Iṣfahān was, of course, already a great and famous city with a long and distinguished history behind it, including a period as capital under the Saljūqs. For all the efforts of Shāh ʿAbbās and his successors, the most impressive and interesting building in the city remains one that was already there when ʿAbbās arrived: the Friday Mosque, the Masjid-i Jāmiʿ, which was built over a very long period but whose most striking features, perhaps, are the two magnificent brick dome chambers of the Saljūq period and the highly elaborate stucco *miḥrāb* commissioned by the Īlkhān Öljeitü.

Nevertheless, Iṣfahān is to this day, to a considerable extent, Shāh ʿAbbās's city. It is an impressive example of imperial town planning. A wide, straight thoroughfare, the Chahār Bāgh ("Four Gardens", indicating its leafy character in the Ṣafawid period) leads north from the Zāyanda-rūd across a bridge, named after Allāhvirdī Khān. Off the Chahār Bāgh and to its right is the centre of the Ṣafawid city: the great square, the Maydān. This, which is some distance to the south of the Friday Mosque and the old city centre, is ʿAbbās's most spectacular creation. The square was used as a polo ground (the marble goalposts are still *in situ*), and the shāh watched the sport from the balcony of the ʿĀlī Qāpū, the entrance to a royal palace, on the west side of the square. On the east side is a beautiful little mosque, the Shaykh Luṭf Allāh, named after and built in honour of ʿAbbās's father-in-law from Jabal ʿĀmil. To the north is the imposing entrance to the bazaar (and the sides of the square, too, were lined with shops).

On the south side is the Royal Mosque, the Masjid-i Shāh, which for all the solid architectural merit of the Friday Mosque is perhaps the most striking of the sights of Iṣfahān. Not everyone approves of the mosque: Robert Byron, author of a famous classic of Persian travel literature published in the 1930s, wrote of its "huge acreage of coarse floral tilework".[1] It is certainly true that Ṣafawid painted tiles, to the fastidious eye of the art historian, must yield place to the mosaic work of the Timurid era. The Royal Mosque was erected, comparatively speaking, in a hurry: no doubt ʿAbbās was anxious to see his great building substantially complete in his own lifetime. And it would certainly be true to say of the Royal Mosque, as of a good many Ṣafawid buildings, that it is in a sense "film-set" architecture: it does not seem so impressive if one looks round the back. But for many visitors to Iṣfahān their first sight of the Masjid-i Shāh remains overwhelming and incomparably memorable.

But Iṣfahān was not merely a centre for the court and for culture. It was also a thriving economic hub. This aspect of its life was vigorously encouraged by Shāh ʿAbbās, especially through his policy of population transfers. Of particular importance was the removal of 3,000 industrious Armenian families from the city of Julfā in the north-west to "New Julfā", their own suburb south of the Zāyanda-rūd in Iṣfahān. It remains an Armenian enclave today, its churches exhibiting the unusual sight of Ṣafawid-style domes topped by a cross.

The most detailed and perceptive accounts of Iṣfahān in Shāh ʿAbbās's time and after are those of some of the Europeans who came to Ṣafawid Persia in increasing numbers during this period. There were three distinct, though often interrelated, points of contact: trade, diplomacy, and simply travel for its own sake. To put these into context it is necessary to look back to the earlier Ṣafawid period.

The background to the international commercial history of the sixteenth century was created by the great Portuguese voyages, the most famous landmark being Vasco da Gama's establishment of a feasible sea-route to India in 1498. The sixteenth century was one of Portuguese commercial dominance in the Indian Ocean. In 913–14/1507 Albuquerque took the strategically placed island of Hurmūz in the Persian Gulf, and from 921/1515 it became a Portuguese base. Later the Portuguese also acquired Baḥrayn. Shāh Ismāʿīl reluctantly accepted the presence of a European power on the southern coast of his empire: as he had no navy, he had little alternative. In time the creation of the sea-routes damaged the overland trade routes across Asia which passed through Ṣafawid territory, though according to one distinguished economic historian they continued to flourish until the establishment of the great European India Companies in the early seventeenth century.[2] The English attempted to turn the Ottoman flank by trading overland with Persia through Russia: a Russia Company was founded, and its representative, Anthony Jenkinson, was in Russia and Central Asia in 1557 and in Persia in 1561 and 1562.

The English East India Company was founded in 1600, and the Dutch equivalent in 1602. The Portuguese trading monopoly was soon broken: in 1024/1615 the English East India Company secured a foothold in the Persian market, and in the following year an agreement was made with Shāh ʿAbbās for the exchange of English cloth for Persian silk through the Gulf port of Jāsk. In 1031/1622, as we have seen, the Company assisted the Persians in evicting the Portuguese from Hurmūz. But after the death of Shāh ʿAbbās the Dutch were able to seize the initiative, establishing a spice factory at the late shāh's port of Bandar ʿAbbās.

Such trading links, and the wish for others, brought European envoys to Iṣfahān, as did proposals for alliances with Persia against the Ottomans; though for such purposes the distances and the difficulties of communication proved too great, and little tangible was achieved on the purely political front. But ambassadors and others who left written accounts of their journeys, especially after 1600, provide the historian with a most important body of source material on Ṣafawid life and politics: on the court, the character and appearance of the shāhs, and on the architecture of the period (much of which no longer survives).

It is worth mentioning some of the most significant of these. In 1598 two English brothers, Anthony and Robert Sherley, arrived. Anthony was sent back to England as Shāh ʿAbbās's ambassador the following year, and his supposed influence on the organization and equipment of the Ṣafawid armed forces has been shown to be a myth. But his brother remained for much longer, and may well have exercised some influence in the development of the new corps and their firearms. Ultimately he returned to England, from where he was sent back by Charles I with an embassy under Sir Dodmore Cotton, of which another member, Sir Thomas Herbert, left a valuable account.

The period also saw a number of Europeans in Persia who were travelling simply for the pleasure of the experience. The most interesting of these to leave a description of Shāh ʿAbbās and Persia in his time was Pietro della Valle, mentioned earlier. In the later seventeenth century there came the traveller who left the fullest of all accounts of Ṣafawid Persia – it fills ten volumes in the standard edition – John (Jean) Chardin. Chardin was a Huguenot, who came to Persia as a jewel merchant and lived in Iṣfahān in 1666–7 and again between 1672 and 1677. He knew the Persian language, and left a remarkably complete description of the Iṣfahān of his day, even employing two *mullās* to provide him with information about the mosques of the city (which, as a non-Muslim, he was unable to enter himself). He finally died in England, driven from France because of his Protestantism; but he died as Sir John and is buried in Westminster Abbey.

Lastly, missionaries should be mentioned. Although Shāh ʿAbbās was by no means a tolerant ruler when it came to dealing with Sunnīs or with deviant Shīʿīs, he is often, perhaps justly, contrasted with his grandfather Shāh Ṭahmāsp in respect of his attitude towards non-Muslims – though he was not always tolerant of Armenian Christians. A Carmelite mission long survived in Iṣfahān; it left records which cover a considerable period; and in the middle and later seventeenth century a Capuchin, Raphael du Mans, lived in Persia for over fifty years (1644–96). He wrote, for Louis XIV of France's minister Colbert, a description of the *Estat de la Perse en 1660.*

This is very far from exhausting the important European travellers of the time: a complete catalogue would make a long list. The historian particularly of the second century of Ṣafawid rule would be in a poor way without such sources, for surviving chronicles are few and most of the state archives were destroyed when Iṣfahān fell to the Afghans in

1135/1722. It is no doubt true to say that the European observers "did not necessarily ask the kind of questions that interest historians today and rarely reached levels of Persian cultural and intellectual life beyond the Court and provincial officialdom",[3] but something of the sort is, regrettably, true of most sources for the pre-modern history of the Middle East, whatever their origin; and we have much reason to be grateful to these venturesome sixteenth- and seventeenth-century envoys, merchants, missionaries and tourists.

THE LEGACY OF SHĀH ʿABBĀS

Most of what has so far been said in this chapter has been very favourable towards Shāh ʿAbbās; and indeed the overall verdict on the achievement of this most remarkable monarch must be a positive one. Starting in what must have seemed at the beginning of his reign an almost hopeless situation, he had built up his kingdom to a position in the world which it had rarely reached before and was never to approach again. He had driven out formidable foreign enemies and secured Persia's frontiers. He had dealt decisively with the menace of factionalism which had plagued the Ṣafawid state since its foundation. In so doing he had initiated something of a social transformation in at least some levels of Persian society, and had built up royal absolutism until it was virtually unchallengeable. He had provided the necessary environment and encouragement for a flourishing economy and, perhaps, for at least a tolerable life for most of his subjects. He had made his new capital one of the world's great cities, and in that setting he had made it possible for the arts to flourish. In an age and a place where so much depended on the ability and strength of the ruler, much of this must in justice be ascribed to Shāh ʿAbbās as an individual: there is no reason for supposing that similar stability and prosperity would necessarily have come about had some other prince succeeded Muḥammad Khudābanda. All the signs in 995/1587 pointed to a gloomy future for Persia.

But part of his legacy was undeniably malign in its effects. He is remembered, like the great Sasanian Khusraw Anushirvan, as a monarch who dealt out firm but impartial justice to his people. But this benevolence, which always tended towards unpredictability, did not extend to his leading followers, who sometimes faced arbitrary execution, or even to his own family. It would appear that the experiences of ʿAbbās's youth, and in particular the circumstances of his own accession to the throne, had left him with an incurably distrustful temperament.

In 1024/1615 he had his eldest son, the heir-apparent Ṣafī Mīrzā, murdered on suspicion of plotting rebellion. The prince was almost certainly innocent, as his father realized when it was too late; and remorse for this act clouded the latter years of his reign. Two other sons were blinded for similar reasons, and since blinding was felt to disqualify a prince from the succession and the remaining two sons predeceased their father, there was no prince of the next generation available to succeed ʿAbbās in 1038/1629.

Even more destructive to the future of the regime was the general policy towards princes of the royal house which ʿAbbās inaugurated. In the early part of his reign, as was normal, they were employed to govern provinces; but signs of revolt, coupled no doubt with a recollection of how he had himself been able to displace his father, persuaded ʿAbbās to end this practice. Instead the princes were immured in the harem, and the leading men of the kingdom were kept away from them. So future shāhs (with the exception of ʿAbbās II, who came to the throne as a child) grew up ill-educated, with no experience of government, administration, or the world in general, and excessively under the influence of women and eunuchs. Their low quality as rulers, in such circumstances, is hardly a matter for surprise; and the fact that the Ṣafawid state nevertheless survived its greatest shāh for a century is no small tribute to the solidity of the work he had done.

NOTES

1. R. Byron, *The Road to Oxiana*, London 1937, 197.
2. See N. Steensgaard, *The Asian Trade Revolution of the Seventeenth Century*, Chicago and London 1974.
3. J. D. Gurney, "Pietro della Valle: the limits of perception", *BSOAS* XLIX/1, 1986, 103.

CHAPTER FIFTEEN

The Second Century of Ṣafawid Rule

THE CHARACTER OF THE PERIOD

The death of Shāh ʿAbbās I in 1038/1629 has too often been seen as the beginning of the end of the Ṣafawid dynasty, the start of an inexorable decline leading to a catastrophic fall in 1135/1722. But as H. R. Roemer says, "this view is emphatically not justified".[1] It may be that historians have been, subconsciously, unduly mesmerized by the potent formulation of Edward Gibbon. In fact, as we saw in Chapter 8, the Ilkhanid empire in Persia appears to have fallen without having previously declined; and while the Ṣafawid empire certainly did decline, a decline which lasted for almost half the entire length of the dynasty lacks a good deal in usefulness as an explanatory device. Ṣafawid rule survived Shāh ʿAbbās by ninety-three years: this is longer than the whole Ilkhanid period, and not much shorter than the duration of Saljūq rule in Persia. If we are to understand the second Ṣafawid century, we must do better than a simple "decline and fall".

It is undoubtedly true that, with the qualified exception of ʿAbbās II, none of the shāhs of the seventeenth century was of ʿAbbās I's calibre as a ruler, a fact for which the latter's policy of immuring the princes of the royal family in the harem was at least partly responsible. In a governmental system based on an autocratic monarchy, this was of no little moment; and as a result of Shāh ʿAbbās's administrative reforms, more power was centred on the court and the capital than in the sixteenth century. The personal qualities of the reigning monarch did matter. Yet despite a series of shāhs who, to say the least, did not possess ʿAbbās's outstanding ability, the governmental machine continued to function, and the regime faced no serious threats. The strength, effectiveness and durability of ʿAbbās's achievements must certainly be numbered among the reasons for this.

Perhaps of equal importance was the fact that after the reign of Ṣafī I (1038–52/1629–42), Ṣafawid Persia had to face no major external challenges to its security during the remainder of the seventeenth century. War broke out with the Ottomans, always Persia's most dangerous enemy, in 1038–9/1629, and fighting continued sporadically for the next decade. In 1048/1638 Baghdad fell, and finally ceased to be a Persian possession, remaining part of the Ottoman Empire until the First World War. In the following year the Treaty of Ẕuhāb was signed. The Persians had to reconcile themselves to the loss of the whole of what is now Iraq, but a Perso-Ottoman border which is approximately that now existing between Persia and Iraq was established; and there were no more Ottoman–Ṣafawid wars.

On the other side of the empire, the frontier with the Özbegs had also ceased to give much cause for concern. The Persians continued to be intermittently involved in the affairs of the Özbeg rulers of both Khīva and Bukhārā (which was now under the Janid family, who had succeeded the Shaybanids). Predatory raids by the Özbegs into Persian territory were a constant feature of the eastern frontier zone; but so they had been ever since the beginning of the Ṣafawid period, and in the seventeenth century no Özbeg conquest of Khurāsān seems to have been envisaged. Certainly no such conquest occurred, or seemed likely. Likewise relations with the Mughals, despite the continuing dispute between the two empires over the possession of Qandahār, were of only a peripheral nature. Overall, the Ṣafawid dynasty had little to fear, after 1049/1639, from foreign enemies; and indeed it was ultimately to be overthrown not by those enemies but by a group of its own subjects.

Historians of Persia have tended to neglect the seventeenth century: not, perhaps, so much because the period was a sorry one of degeneration and decline as because very little that is really striking actually happened. This means that there is not a great deal of political history to relate, though this does not, of course, necessarily apply to social, economic, religious or cultural history. But such a lack of event ought by no means to be regarded as a damning judgement on the Ṣafawid regime of the day. Indeed, the opposite may well be more just. The Chinese curse is well known: "May you live in interesting times". The seventeenth century was not an interesting time in Persian history – for which the Persians, in the light of the turbulence of the sixteenth and previous centuries, may well have been profoundly thankful. If one were required to choose a time in the Persian past during which it would have been tolerable to live, quite a convincing case could be made out for the mid-seventeenth century.

SHĀH ʿABBĀS'S SUCCESSORS

Since circumstances, natural and unnatural, dictated that not one of Shāh ʿAbbās's sons or brothers was available to succeed him on the throne, it passed to his grandson, a son of the murdered Ṣafī Mīrzā, who became Shāh Ṣafī I. It is interesting to note that according to contemporary accounts of Ṣafī's accession, members of the Ṣafawid order played a significant part, and that Ṣafawid *ṣūfī* observances were to be seen at the enthronement. We should be wary of assuming that the original *ṣūfī* inspiration of the dynasty was yet a totally spent force. Ṣafī was the first of the shāhs to have spent his upbringing in the harem and the effects of this showed themselves in his lack of interest in affairs of state, or apparently in much else apart from drink and drugs (indulgence in the former killed him when he was not much more than thirty years old).

Effective power was therefore exercised by the holders of high civil and military office. But such functionaries were far from enjoying real security of tenure or even of life and property: one use to which Ṣafī did put his theoretically autocratic powers was the arbitrary execution of any who had aroused his suspicion or dislike. Most of the royal princes, including those who had already been blinded and who were thus hardly a danger to the shāh, were murdered, as were many high officials. One of the most spectacular falls from grace was that of the immensely rich and powerful Imām Qulī Khān, son of Allāhvirdī Khān, who was executed with most of his sons in 1042–3/1632. This made it possible to incorporate the province of Fārs, which he had ruled and on the revenues of which he and his father had presumably maintained *ghulām* troops for the shāh's use, into the category of *khāṣṣa*. The process of creating more and more *khāṣṣa* land, begun by Shāh ʿAbbās, continued throughout the later Ṣafawid period, which would seem to imply that the central government was by no means reduced to impotence.

It was perhaps fortunate for Persia that in 1044–5/1634 Mīrzā Muḥammad Taqī, known as Ṣārū Taqī, became chief minister and managed to remain in office well into the next reign. He became the strongest influence on government. Ṣārū Taqī had his faults, and he made powerful enemies (though this does not at all imply that he was a bad minister: he may have been all too efficient for some tastes). He acquired a rare reputation not only for competence but also for personal integrity and incorruptibility; and since he also retained the confidence of the capricious Ṣafī, he was able to achieve a good deal, and is said to have raised the state revenue to unexampled heights.

When Ṣafī I died in 1052/1642, the Ṣafawid state was still in a healthy condition. It had weathered the last major war with the Ottoman Empire, albeit with considerable territorial losses, and it was enjoying, on the whole, efficient government despite the great failings of the shāh as a ruler. Ṣafī was succeeded by his son, ʿAbbās II, during whose reign later Ṣafawid Persia reached the height of its prosperity.

The new shāh had of course been incarcerated in the harem, as was now the normal practice; but since he emerged while still a small boy, his upbringing did not have the deleterious effects on his character that a longer stay there might have produced. Since he was so young, ʿAbbās was not for some years to exercise much influence on government; but for the first three years of the reign Ṣārū Taqī was still at the helm, and when ʿAbbās eventually took personal charge of affairs, he was to prove a ruler of remarkable ability, well able to bear comparison with any member of the dynasty apart from his great-grandfather and namesake.

Ṣārū Taqī was murdered by a faction led by the *qūrchī-bāshī* in 1055/1645. His successor was a more easy-going *wazīr*, Khalīfa Sulṭān, who had held the post before. He remained in office until his death nine years later, but in fact no one dominated affairs of state as Ṣārū Taqī had done. Eventually the shāh himself, with increasing years and experience, became the leading figure in his own government: he did not show his father's reluctance to involve himself in the day-to-day running of the empire.

The twenty-four years of ʿAbbās II's reign were predominantly peaceful. The shāh resisted the temptation to embroil Persia in the politics of Ottoman Iraq, though he was presented with opportunities for doing so had he wished. He preferred to preserve the lasting peace made with the Ottomans in 1049/1639. The only major foreign adventure occurred in the east. The Mughals of India, even after a century and a half, were still reluctant to renounce their Timurid heritage in Central Asia, and in the 1640s there was an attempt by the forces of the Emperor Shāh Jahān to intervene in Özbeg Transoxania. This was unsuccessful and seems to have provoked ʿAbbās into mounting, in 1058/1648, an expedition against the long-contested city of Qandahār. The city was taken, and remained in Persian hands for the remainder of the Ṣafawid period. It was never again to form part of the Mughal Empire. This apart, the only significant military involvements of the reign were caused by internal troubles, notably in the Georgian territories of the Caucasus which were in varying degrees subject to Persian control.

One criticism that can be levelled at ʿAbbās II is that – no doubt because he had to fight no major wars, but had usually only to mount fairly minor punitive expeditions – he allowed the quality of the Ṣafawid armed forces to begin to decline. It was no longer as necessary as it had been to keep a large, well-trained – and therefore expensive – army in a state of constant readiness. This decline was especially noticeable in the artillery corps. The process of degeneration was a slow one, but there is a celebrated story that at a military parade at the end of the reign, the same troops had to be marched past the shāh several times.

ʿAbbās continued to absorb more parts of the country into his *khāṣṣa*, and he took an unusually personal interest in the proper administration of his estates. He would on occasion intervene to protect the peasants against corrupt or unduly avaricious officials. The shāh's concern with the equitable dispensation of justice is a characteristic remarked on by both Persian and foreign observers at the time. He involved himself deeply in this, as in other aspects of administration. Although he did act with great cruelty on occasion, and observed the usual customs of blinding and murder in respect of superfluous members of the Ṣafawid house, he can be said, so far as the mass of his subjects were concerned, to have done what was in his power to provide them with even-handed and efficient government. Had he lived as long as his great namesake, he would have ruled Persia until nearly the end of the century. At the risk of exaggerating the importance of a single individual even in an absolute monarchy, it is possible to speculate that the history of Persia might then have been very different.

Unfortunately he was not immune from what had become the normal vices of the Ṣafawid court: drink, drugs, and excessive sexual indulgence. Such activities may have owed something to an old belief of the Ṣafawid order: that its head, the shāh, could do no wrong, and that therefore the prohibitions of Islamic law did not apply to him. Certainly the, at times, dissolute behaviour of the court aroused the disapproval of the Shīʿī *ʿulamāʾ*. Nor were they best pleased with the shāh's religious tolerance, from which the Christians, though not always the Jews, benefited. It is interesting that in ʿAbbās's reign we see the expression of a religious view of the place of the monarchy in Persia which, in a rather different form, was to come into its own over three centuries later. The traveller Chardin reports hearing the opinion that "Our kings are impious and unjust, their rule is a tyranny to which God has subjected us as a punishment after having withdrawn from the world the lawful successor of the Prophet. The supreme throne of the world belongs only to a *mujtahid*, a man possessed of sanctity and knowledge above the common rule of men. It is true that since the *mujtahid* is holy and by consequence peaceful, there must be a king to wield the sword, to exercise justice, but this he must do only as the minister and subordinate of the former."[2]

There does not seem to be evidence that such a view was dominant among the *ʿulamāʾ*, or that the position of the shāh was in reality threatened by its expression. But the fact that a foreigner like Chardin both heard it and thought it worth reporting is worthy of note. It is perhaps a pointer to the enhanced position of influence secured by the leading Shīʿī figures later in the century. It also foreshadows the developments within Shīʿism, particularly with reference to the status of *mujtahid* – one qualified to exercise independent judgement in matters of the faith, and worthy to be emulated – which were to occur after the fall of the dynasty and are discussed in Chapter 16.

Shāh ʿAbbās II died, aged only thirty-three, in 1077/1666, possibly of syphilis. He left behind him a deservedly impressive reputation as a ruler, and at least two notable architectural monuments in Iṣfahān which still exist. These are the Khājū bridge over the Zāyanda-rūd, an elaborate and pleasing combined bridge and weir, and the charming palace called the Chihil Sutūn ("Forty Pillars" – there are in fact twenty: the number is made up by their reflection in the pool in front of the building). There is no denying that with ʿAbbās's death the decline of the Ṣafawid dynasty did begin, though it was still to survive for more than half a century.

The new shāh was ʿAbbās's eldest son, Ṣafī Mīrzā, who initially took the title of Ṣafī II. He is usually known, however, as Sulaymān, since the first year and a half of his reign were so disastrous that he thought it advisable to start again in 1078/1668 with a different title. In a way he may well have considered that this measure proved something of a success, if what the shāh sought was a quiet life. It did not turn him into a vigorous and able ruler: Sulaymān had all his father's vices and more, and none of his good qualities or his abilities as a ruler. He was in his late teens at the time of his accession, and had of course spent his life in the company solely of the women and eunuchs of the harem.

The new shāh could perhaps hardly be held responsible for the immediate troubles of his reign: a sudden rise in food prices, outbreaks of famine and disease, an earthquake, raids by the Cossacks into the Caucasus. His inability to deal with such difficulties did not change as time went on. But as it happened, albeit a great deal more by luck than judgement, there were few more really serious disasters to face. The shāh withdrew increasingly back into the harem, and became virtually inaccessible to his ministers. In so far as policy was made, it was much influenced by those who did have access to the shāh – the women and eunuchs, who spent an enjoyable reign intriguing among themselves. Inevitably the efficiency and justice which had been so comparatively striking a feature of his father's reign began to disappear as effective control from the centre vanished. Corruption and oppression increased; the military capacity of the state continued to decline.

Yet despite this gloomy picture, no chickens came home to roost. Sulaymān reigned for twenty-eight years, for the most part in peace. Like ʿAbbās II he was wise enough to steer clear of foreign entanglements, declining to meddle in Ottoman affairs and so preserving the peace of 1049/1639. The usual Özbeg raids were of little consequence. Georgia was quiet. Whatever the deficiencies of the administration of the country, there were no internal troubles of any significance during the reign. One can only conclude that the work of Sulaymān's predecessors, especially the two Shāhs ʿAbbās, had been sufficiently solid to last through at least one reign of inefficiency and corruption. As in the reign of Shāh Ṣafī I, incompetent direction at the head of affairs was not in itself, apparently, enough to wreck the state or to make life intolerable for the mass of the shāh's subjects – at least in the short run. The Ṣafawid empire, when Sulaymān died in 1105/1694, could still be handed over intact to yet another inadequate ruler. He was to be the last.

SULṬĀN ḤUSAYN AND THE FALL OF THE ṢAFAWID DYNASTY

In many ways Shāh Sulṭān Ḥusayn was regrettably similar in character to his father. The story goes that he was installed as ruler by the court eunuchs, who preferred him to his potentially able and energetic younger brother, ʿAbbās Mīrzā, because of their wish for a quiet life and a shāh who would be likely to prove easily manageable. Where Sulṭān Ḥusayn did differ from Sulaymān was in the extent to which he was under the influence of the Shīʿī *ʿulamāʾ*: in this reign we see in them a further element added to the struggling factions at the Ṣafawid court.

The importance of the *ʿulamāʾ* in state affairs had been growing. We hear no more of the mutterings of religious discontent that had occasionally surfaced during the time of ʿAbbās II. A new post had been created for them, that of *mullā-bāshī*, the holder of which ranked high in the religious establishment. In the early years of Sulṭān Ḥusayn's reign one *mullā* above all, Muḥammad Bāqir Majlisī, was dominant. The shāh was very much under his sway, and allowed him his head when it came to determining religious policy. At Majlisī's instance the old comparative tolerance became a thing of the past. Christians and Jews were badly treated, but so were philosophers and other Muslims who were thought to be insufficiently orthodox by the standards of the *mujtahids*. These included *ṣūfīs*, though it is true that state disapproval of the *ṣūfī* orders went back at least as far as the reign of ʿAbbās I. More serious in its political consequences was the fact that the Sunnīs, too, came under pressure at the hands of the Shīʿī *ʿulamāʾ*.

The conversion of the Muslims of the Ṣafawid empire to Shīʿism had never been complete. In particular, most of the shāh's subjects in what is now Afghanistan remained Sunnī. The new anti-Sunnī policy of the government played its part in sparking off a series of revolts in that region of the empire. These were for a time held in check, especially after the appointment in 1116/1704 as governor of the area of the general Gurgīn Khān, who like many of the leading military figures in the last years of the Ṣafawids was of Georgian origin – indeed, he had formerly been King Giorgi XI of Kartlia, in Georgia. But the shāh failed to give Gurgīn Khān effective support, and revolt soon broke out again. For much of the reign the Ghilzai Afghans in Qandahār were effectively independent, and if they were only a limited danger to the state it was partly because they were at daggers drawn with another group of Afghan rebels, the Abdālīs of Harāt.

By 1132/1720 revolts and political unrest had broken out at a number of points on the periphery of the empire – in the Caucasus, in Kurdistān, in Khūzistān, in the south-east – and the Imām of ʿUmān was menacing the shores of the Persian Gulf. The government in Iṣfahān hardly knew where to turn or what, if anything, to do. The chief minister, Fatḥ ʿAlī Khān Dāghistānī, and his nephew Luṭf ʿAlī Khān, who was governor of Fārs, initially decided to beat off the threat from ʿUmān. But in the meantime the danger from the Afghans materialized again, though the *wazīr* and his nephew were overthrown by a court intrigue before they could do much to counter it.

A young Ghilzai prince, Maḥmūd, was now in command in Qandahār. He had marched as far as Kirmān in 1131/1719, but had had to return home to deal with local opposition. In 1133–4/1721 he set off again, whether or not with the actual intention of trying to overthrow his Ṣafawid overlord is difficult to say with certainty. He failed to take Kirmān and Yazd, but marched on towards Iṣfahān nevertheless. In Jumādā I 1134/March 1722 he met the Ṣafawid army at Gulnābād, some miles to the east of the capital.

Despite the decay of the Ṣafawid forces during the previous decades, the result of the battle ought not to have been in much doubt. The Persian army was far larger than Maḥmūd's, and was equipped with artillery. It contained at least a substantial number of experienced troops. It was indeed successful in the early stages of the battle, but before long it became apparent that the absence of a unified command on the Persian side was to prove fatal. The better co-ordinated Afghans eventually won the day, and the routed Persians fled in the direction of Iṣfahān. After a few days Maḥmūd followed and besieged the city. The shāh had lost a battle; but he lost the war, his throne, and ultimately his life only because he failed to take any further effective measures against the enemy.

The siege lasted for seven months, many of the inhabitants of Iṣfahān dying in the latter stages from disease and starvation. In October Sulṭān Ḥusayn surrendered and abdicated, declaring Maḥmūd his successor as shāh of Persia. There was a good deal of destruction in the city – including, it is said, the dumping of the state archives in the Zāyanda-rūd; though the sack was perhaps not much of one by the standards of Chingiz Khān or Tamerlane. Ṣafawid princes lingered on for many years as pawns on the political chessboard, but the rule of Persia's longest-lasting dynasty since the rise of Islam was at an end. It was more of a collapse than a defeat and conquest; and the Ghilzais were soon to find that seizing the capital and the person of the shāh did not make them the effective rulers of the empire. It was a singularly inglorious end to a reign which had had few redeeming features. Perhaps only those who have seen Sulṭān Ḥusayn's mother's Madrasa-i Chahār Bāgh, the last great Ṣafawid building – indeed, perhaps the last great Persian building to date – will find it possible to grant him some small degree of indulgence.

The reasons for the fall of the Ṣafawid dynasty will have been apparent from the above narrative – the decline in the personal qualities of the rulers, due in part to their upbringing in the harem; linked with this, the excessive influence on government of the women and eunuchs of the harem; the decay of governmental efficiency and the disastrous reduction in effectiveness of the military forces. It would probably be true to say that a determined assault from outside could have overthrown the Ṣafawids at almost any time since the death of Shāh ʿAbbās II. It just so happened, fortunately for the shāhs and for the Persian people, that before Maḥmūd Ghilzai set off for Iṣfahān with his less than formidable army, no one had tried.

NOTES

1. H. R. Roemer, "The Safavid period", in P. Jackson and L. Lockhart (eds), *The Cambridge History of Iran, 6: The Timurid and Safavid Periods*, Cambridge 1986, 278.
2. J. Chardin, *Voyages . . . en Perse, et autres lieux de l'Orient*, ed. L. Langlès, Paris, 1811, vol. 5, 215–16.

CHAPTER SIXTEEN

Persia in the Eighteenth Century

The eighteenth century was not a happy period for Persia. After the fall of the degenerate Ṣafawid regime, no man or group succeeded in restoring real stability over the whole country for many decades. Nādir Shāh did indeed restore political unity and even, for the last time to date, extended Persia's borders. But unity under Nādir was probably in some respects as undesirable as anarchy. Much of the country enjoyed a time of reasonably benevolent government at the hands of Karīm Khān Zand, but not until the accession of Āghā Muḥammad Khān Qājār, towards the end of the century, were both unity and stability, of a sort, recovered. This did not mean that the period was entirely sterile: in particular, there were important developments within Shīʿī Islam in Persia which were to have their effect down to the present day.

THE CAREER OF NĀDIR SHĀH

The Ghilzai Afghans who, as it were by chance, had overthrown the Ṣafawid empire in 1134–5/1722 did not retain control of Persia for very long. In fact, they did not control a good deal of the country at all. They did have possession of the person of the last fully fledged Ṣafawid shāh, Sulṭān Ḥusayn; and he had indeed acknowledged, albeit under duress, Maḥmūd Ghilzai as his successor. The Afghans had also seized a number of other Ṣafawid princes when they took Iṣfahān. These were imprisoned together with the former shāh, who was for the moment well treated. But later Maḥmūd killed many of the princes, some of them with his own hands; and in the following year (1139/1726) his successor had Sulṭān Ḥusayn executed.

The last, however, had not been heard of the Ṣafawids, though no representative of that house was ever again to recover real power. The dynasty had reigned over Persia for the quite unusually long period of two and a quarter centuries. It was difficult for Persians to accustom themselves to the idea that the rule of the descendants of Shāh Ismāʿīl and Shāh ʿAbbās was no more. Despite the decay and degeneracy of the last decades of Ṣafawid rule, the prestige of the dynasty which had not only proved so long-lasting but had been responsible for the introduction of the now firmly established state religion did not evaporate overnight. For some time to come, many of those who were struggling for power in Persia claimed to be acting on behalf of the "rightful" Ṣafawid claimant, and kept tame Ṣafawids at their courts for purposes of display and to lend legitimacy to their ambitions.

Soon after the fall of Iṣfahān a Ṣafawid prince declared himself shāh in the north of the country, which the Afghans had not succeeded in occupying. Other external enemies of Persia had not missed their chance: Russian forces had marched into the north-west of the country, and the Ottomans had seized much of the west, reaching as far as the region of Hamadān and Kirmānshāh.

Maḥmūd Ghilzai was murdered in 1137/1725 and was succeeded as shāh of the parts of Persia under Afghan rule, an area centred on Iṣfahān, by his nephew Ashraf. But Ashraf's power was precarious, for he failed to hold the Ghilzai home base of Qandahār, where a son of Maḥmūd was able to seize the throne. In 1142/1729 Ashraf was overthrown by Nādir Khān Afshār, and in 1142–3/1730 the second and last Afghan shāh, too, was murdered. The short-lived period of Ghilzai government, or misgovernment, in Persia was at an end.

Nādir Khān, who now moved into prominence, was a member of one of the great Qizilbash tribes, the Afshār. An able general, he assembled an army in the north of Persia and after rallying to the support of the Ṣafawid claimant in the north, Ṭahmāsp II, he overthrew his principal rival, Fatḥ ʿAlī Khān of the Qājār Qizilbash tribe. He adopted the name Ṭahmāsp-qulī, the slave of Ṭahmāsp. Nādir's was a singularly unservile form of slavery, but he did acknowledge Ṭahmāsp II as shāh, at least in name, until 1145/1732, and thereafter for the next four years he recognized Ṭahmāsp's infant son, who was called ʿAbbās III.

But by 1148/1736 Nādir evidently felt that his own position had been established so firmly that he no longer needed to hide behind a nominal Ṣafawid shāh. He therefore held an assembly, called by the Mongol term *quriltai*, at Mūghān in Āẕarbāyjān. The notables present at the *quriltai* – military commanders, officials, *ʿulamāʾ* – did what was expected of them and declared Nādir the first shāh of the Afshār dynasty. He had already embarked on what was to prove a spectacular career of military conquest.

He had turned his attention first to the Ottomans. In 1142–3/1730 he reconquered western and northern Persia from them, as far as Tabrīz. In 1145/1732–3 he besieged Baghdad – without success, but the threat was enough to persuade the Ottomans to agree to return to the Perso-Ottoman frontier as it had been in 1049/1639. This agreement was not immediately ratified by the government in Constantinople, but it was finally accepted after there had been further fighting in the north in 1148–9/1736. There was no clash with the Russians, who were still in occupation of parts of north Persia. They withdrew when it became clear that the areas they had held would not be taken by the Ottomans but would fall to Nādir, who seemed to them to be less of a threat.

Next Nādir marched against the Afghans. Initially his aim was the recovery of Qandahār for the Persian crown, but when this was achieved (1150/1738) he went on to take Ghazna, Kābul and Peshawar. These advances pointed him in the direction of the legendary riches of India. There the Mughal Empire was past its peak, and Nādir was able to take Lahore, then marching on to meet and defeat the Mughal forces at Karnāl (1151/1739). He seized and sacked Delhi, the Mughal capital, and marched home with a prodigious quantity of loot, including the famous Peacock Throne of the Mughal emperors. He made no attempt to remain and rule India: this was simply a plundering expedition on a massive scale, like Temür's in 801/1398.

In 1153/1740 Nādir attacked that traditional enemy of the shāhs of Persia, the Özbegs of Transoxania. He took the cities of Bukhārā and Khīva, leaving the Khān of Bukhārā as a subject ruler. But the lands up to the Oxus River he annexed to Persia. Lastly, Nādir's troops occupied ʿUmān between 1149/1736 and 1157/1744. The result of the conquests was to move the centre of gravity of the Persian empire substantially to the east, where Nādir resettled considerable numbers of tribespeople from western Persia. He decided, therefore, to transfer the capital to Mashhad, in Khurāsān. The new capital also had the advantage for Nādir that it was conveniently close to his favourite refuge, the formidable mountain fortress known as Kalāt-i Nādirī.

Despite the fact that the capital was now situated in a city whose greatest pride – indeed, whose reason for existence – was the presence of the tomb of the eighth Shīʿī *imām*, Riḍā, Nādir Shāh made a last attempt to move Persia away from state-sponsored Twelver Shīʿism. What he tried to have accepted was a little more subtle than a mere abandonment of Shīʿism in favour of Sunnism: the approach he favoured was that of integrating Shīʿism into Sunnism as a fifth *madhhab* (school of law) to add to the four Sunnī schools. It would be called Jaʿfarī, after the generally respected sixth Shīʿī *imām*, Jaʿfar al-Ṣādiq. This involved, at the very least, the abandonment on the part of the Shīʿīs of some of their practices which were most offensive to the Sunnīs, notably *sabb* and *rafḍ* (vilification of the first three caliphs and the denial of their legitimacy).

Nādir's scheme was exceedingly ill-received in Persia, and no one in the Sunnī world would have anything to do with it except, temporarily, the religious authorities in Iraq, who under duress during Nādir's invasion agreed to accept the Twelvers as a fifth *madhhab*. Ultimately the plan came to nothing, and it is not easy to say with certainty what Nādir's motives in trying to half-reverse the Ṣafawid religious settlement may have been. Nādir himself, as a member of a leading Qizilbash tribe, was from as Shīʿī a background as anyone. It has been suggested that he was attempting to reduce the religious prestige of the Ṣafawid dynasty which he had displaced; or that he felt the "legitimation" of Persian Shīʿism to be a necessary preliminary to a general conquest and unification of the Muslim world under his leadership. There is also the consideration that many of Nādir's soldiers, especially the Afghans, were Sunnīs; it may perhaps have been thought politic to conciliate them in this way.

Nādir Shāh had succeeded in welding together an impressive and highly successful army of Shīʿī Persians and Sunnī Afghans. There can be no dispute about the very high degree of competence he possessed as a military leader. But in no other respect is it possible to find much that is positive to say about him. He showed little if any concern for the general welfare of the country or his subjects. He made enormous demands for taxation on a land much of which was devastated, imposing the death penalty on those who failed to pay. He concentrated all power in his own hands, in this way accentuating a decline in the efficiency of the traditional Persian bureaucracy.

In Nādir's later years, revolts began to break out against his oppressive rule. He became gradually less sane and more cruel. Towards the end, even his own tribesmen felt that he was too dangerous a man to be near. A group of Qizilbash murdered him in 1160/1747. There was now nothing to keep his army together. One of the Afghan leaders, Aḥmad Khān, left Persia and returned home, where he founded the Durrānī empire: he has some claim to be regarded as the founder of modern Afghanistan. Nādir's family proved unable to maintain the Afshār dynasty as rulers of Persia; but one of them, the blind Shāh Rukh, did manage to keep hold of the capital, Mashhad, and of the province of Khurāsān, for nearly fifty years.

KARĪM KHĀN ZAND

The principal leader to emerge in Persia from the chaos that followed the murder of Nādir Shāh had served in Nādir's army, though he had not been one of his generals. This was Karīm Khān, a member of the Zand tribe, a minor pastoral people who lived near the town of Malāyir, in the foothills of the Zagros mountains of western Persia. The Zands were an Iranian people, and their decades of dominance were one of the few periods, between the arrival of the Saljūqs and the twentieth century, during which effective political power was exercised by a dynasty that can be regarded as in some sense ethnically "Persian".

Initially the Zands were allied with a more important group of western Persian pastoralists, the Bakhtiyārī. Karīm Khān and ʿAlī Mardān Khān Bakhtiyārī acted as regents for a nominal Ṣafawid ruler, Ismāʿīl III. But the alliance did not endure. ʿAlī Mardān was killed in 1167/1754, and in the years following Karīm Khān eliminated several other contenders for power in the region. The most important of these were Āzād Khān, an Afghan who had seized Āẕarbāyjān, and Muḥammad Ḥasan Khān Qājār. The latter was the father of Āghā Muḥammad Khān, the first shāh of the Qājār dynasty which at the end of the century was to displace both the Zands and the rule of the Afshārs in Khurāsān. It has been argued, with some plausibility, that it would have been better in the long run for Persia had Muḥammad Ḥasan been able to establish a Qājār dynasty in mid-century. The country might then have been spared much anarchy and suffering as well, perhaps, as the appalling cruelties of Āghā Muḥammad. But this is speculation, not history.

What is not speculation is the fact that Karīm Khān did provide much of Persia with, a no doubt, welcome interlude, lasting for a quarter of a century, of reasonably just government. Karīm Khān has always had the reputation of having been Persia's "good" ruler, and though the competition for that title is not, perhaps, impossibly strong, such a favourable view does on the whole seem to be justified. There was, though, a time in the early 1760s when, for whatever reason, Karīm was almost as dangerous to be near as Nādir Shāh in his last days. It has been suggested that this was the result of illness, and it may be so: in any case, this behaviour on Karīm's part was certainly an uncharacteristic aberration.

Karīm Khān made Shīrāz, in the south of the country, his capital, and there he built extensively. Surviving buildings of importance include his mosque (the Masjid-i Wakīl) and bazaar (the Bāzār-i Wakīl). The architecture of the dynasty has its admirers, and it is certainly pleasant enough in its way. As the names of the buildings indicate, Karīm did not take the title of shāh. He was content to be called *wakīl*, deputy or representative, theoretically of a Ṣafawid shāh: he maintained Ismāʿīl III as nominal ruler.

He did, however, change the form of his title from 1179/1765. Previously he had been *wakīl al-dawla*; thereafter he was *wakīl al-raʿāyā*. Since *dawla* means, among other things, "the dynasty", and *raʿāyā* "the subjects", it has been argued that Karīm came to regard himself as "a representative of the people rather than a delegate of the government".[1] This may have an anachronistically democratic ring about it, but it is possible that Karīm was indeed making some kind of bid for popular support.

The rule of Karīm Khān saw the re-establishment of Twelver Shīʿism after the failure of Nādir Shāh's curious experiment. This was appropriately symbolized by the naming of the twelve quarters of Shīrāz after the twelve Shīʿī *imāms*. Such patronage on the part of the secular power was no doubt welcome, though the Shīʿī establishment was not dependent on and associated with the ruling house as it had been in Ṣafawid times. Karīm Khān made no claim to descent from the *imāms*, nor had his family been responsible for the imposition of Shīʿism in Persia.

After his success in the struggle for power in Persia, Karīm Khān did not indulge overmuch in military ventures. His government was a thrifty one which tried to live within its means, and unnecessary warfare could be an expensive luxury. Indeed, he waged no campaigns outside his own territory except for an attack on southern Iraq in 1188–90/1775–6, which resulted in the siege and capture of the port of Baṣra. There seem to have been at least two motives for this unusual action on Karīm's part: worries over Persian access to the great Shīʿī shrines in Ottoman Iraq, and a wish if possible to divert trade away from Baṣra and towards ports in Persian hands.

Karīm Khān Zand's achievement, we may say, was modest but solid and worthwhile. He can most clearly be criticized over his failure to make clear and adequate provision for the succession. The other Zand princes were far from possessing Karīm's qualities as either man or ruler, and his death in 1193/1779 was followed by a further period of anarchy. Out of the turmoil of the next fifteen years the hegemony of the Qājārs emerged. Their leader, the able but brutal Āghā Muḥammad Khān, had the last Zand ruler, Luṭf ʿAlī Khān, tortured and killed in 1209/1794. In 1210/1796 he dealt similarly with Shāh Rukh, the Afshār ruler of Khurāsān. In the following year he himself was assassinated by two of his own servants, presumably to general relief. With the accession of his nephew Fatḥ ʿAlī Shāh, the Qājār dynasty had established itself in Persia.

If there is a dividing line between the "medieval" and the "modern" history of Persia, the most plausible point at which to place it is at the beginning of the Qājār dynasty. Some have seen the Ṣafawids as the founders of modern Persia, partly because of the great changes they did indeed bring about, especially the definition of the country's borders and the imposition of Shīʿism as the official form of Islam. But it may be suspected that Western historians have been too easily beguiled by a mere date: Shāh Ismāʿīl became ruler in 907/1501, and this coincides all too conveniently with the period conventionally seen as the beginning of modern European history. Yet there is no break in Persian history at this point to parallel the changes in European development symbolized by the Renaissance and the Reformation. Western categories and Western periodization cannot simply be transferred wholesale to the lands of Islam. There, the really momentous changes in society, associated as they were with "modernization" and the overwhelming impact of the West, came in the nineteenth century. That is when the modern history of Persia and the Middle East began. The period covered by this book – what might justly be called the history of medieval Persia – does, in its own terms, have a real unity and coherence.

EIGHTEENTH-CENTURY RELIGIOUS DEVELOPMENTS

Politically, the eighteenth century in Persia may have been a time of chaos, only partly alleviated by the period of Karīm Khān Zand's rule in Shīrāz. But for Twelver Shīʿī Islam, the official religion of Persia since the time of Shāh Ismāʿīl I, it was a time in which important foundations were laid and controversies decided. There were three developments of particular significance.

First, the century saw an increasing dissociation of Shīʿism from state control. Under the Ṣafawids, with their close involvement in Shīʿism, the faith had been in some sense almost a department of state, even though individual men of religion, such as Muḥammad Bāqir Majlisī, had become increasingly influential during the latter years of the dynasty. Its fall was followed by the rule of the Sunnī Afghans and the quasi-Sunnī Nādir Shāh. The close link with the state was broken, and despite the benevolent attitude of Karīm Khān towards Shīʿism, it was not subsequently to be repaired.

When the Qājārs became shāhs of Persia at the end of the century, making no claims to descent from the *imāms*, Shīʿism had learned to do without the state, to manage its affairs independently of the government. In these circumstances the basic Shīʿī suspicion of the legitimacy of secular government in the absence of the Twelfth Imām was able to come nearer the surface. Such a view had on occasion been propounded during the Ṣafawid period but had never been dominant, at least publicly. But under the Qājārs, relations between Shīʿism and the Persian state were to suffer from many more tensions than they had under the Ṣafawids. This is not to say that the radical practical conclusions about the legitimacy of secular government that were drawn by some in the later twentieth century had any place in the eighteenth or nineteenth. There was a context of accommodation and compromise over the political realities which was recognized by both sides. Neither was anxious for a fight to the death. But the potential for serious conflict between "church" and "state" was there.

The second development of importance arose out of a controversy within Shīʿism over what the precise character of the faith ought to be. The struggle was fought out mainly in the great Shīʿī shrine cities in Iraq, rather than inside Persia; and it is perhaps worth pointing out how useful the Shīʿī *ʿulamāʾ* subsequently found the fact that several of their most holy shrines, and therefore many of their most senior representatives, were situated in an area beyond the political control of the shāhs of Persia.

The two parties to the controversy were known as Akhbārīs and Uṣūlīs, and the argument was essentially over the question of whether or not it was legitimate for the *ʿulamāʾ* to exercise *ijtihād*, independent judgement. The Akhbārīs maintained that there could be no *ijtihād* in the absence of the Twelfth Imām. They considered that until his return his followers should confine themselves to the study and application of *ḥadīth*, the Traditions of the Prophet and also, in Shīʿī usage, of the *imāms*: hence the name by which they were known, for *akhbār* is another term for "Tradition". Such Traditions were stories of the Prophet's or the *imāms*' lives and actions, their authenticity warranted by a chain (*isnād*) of individuals leading back through time to an actual witness of the real or alleged incident. The Traditions were used, and in many cases fabricated, in order to lend authority to legal or doctrinal rulings. The Akhbārī view – not wholly dissimilar in its Shīʿī context from the orthodox Sunnī position – was, then, arguing for the authority of precedent over the risks involved in innovation on the part of an *ʿālim*, however learned in the sacred law he might be. It was a conservative theological and legal position, the acceptance of which would have limited the role and potential power of the *ʿulamāʾ*.

The Uṣūlīs held that the use of *ijtihād* was legitimate, indeed obligatory. In their view, a faithful Shīʿī should choose for himself an *ʿālim* who was recognized by his peers as fit to exercise *ijtihād* (and hence was known as a *mujtahid*), and should obey his rulings and follow his example in matters of the law. Although the standing of a *mujtahid* was dependent on the profundity of his learning – that is, of the legal knowledge of the past – it came to be the Uṣūlī belief that a ruling of a living *mujtahid* should always be preferred to a ruling derived from one who was dead. The acceptance of their position hence allowed scope for considerable innovation, and opened the door to the acquisition of greater influence on the part of the *ʿulamāʾ*. The possibility was also allowed for that there might be one or more *mujtahids* whose learning and authority would be so considerable that their rulings would take precedence over those of all of their contemporaries. Such men were given the title *Marjaʿ al-taqlīd* ("source of imitation").

The Akhbārīs were the dominant party during the first half of the eighteenth century, but thereafter the Uṣūlīs took the lead, especially under the leadership of the long-lived *mujtahid* Bihbihānī (1705–1803). Although the Akhbārī view was not totally suppressed, Uṣūlī Shīʿism became the established form of the faith in Persia during the Qājār period and after.

Lastly, it is worth noting that the eighteenth century saw the increasing popularity of *taʿzīya*, passion plays concerned particularly with the battle of Karbalā (61/680), where the third Shīʿī *imām* Ḥusayn, son of ʿAlī and grandson of the Prophet, was martyred at the hands of the forces of the Umayyad caliph Yazīd. The *taʿzīya* was distrusted by the *ʿulamāʾ*, for it was of popular origin and out of their control; but it was never successfully suppressed, and at moments of conflict between Shīʿism and the state it could serve as an eloquent paradigm, with a shāh who was seen as an oppressor, or whose actions were represented as anti-Islamic, on occasion being cast in the role of Yazīd.

Thus it was that the eighteenth century, a period whose political history was for the most part dismal and anarchic even by the exacting standards of the Persian past, was in other respects of great creative significance. The permanent importance of the changes within Shīʿism which took place hardly needs further emphasis. A knowledge of what happened in the eighteenth century, as well as in the earlier centuries of Islamic Persia, is an essential prerequisite for anyone who wishes to understand the evolution of Persia during our own day. That is not the only, or even necessarily the best, reason for studying the history of Persia; but it is a valid consideration.

NOTE

1. J. R. Perry, *Karim Khan Zand: a History of Iran, 1747–1779*, Chicago and London 1979, 216.

Bibliographical Survey

ABBREVIATIONS

BSOAS: Bulletin of the School of Oriental and African Studies
CAJ: Central Asiatic Journal
CHI: Cambridge History of Iran
EI²: Encyclopaedia of Islam (2nd edn)
EIr: Encyclopaedia Iranica
HJAS: Harvard Journal of Asiatic Studies
JAOS: Journal of the American Oriental Society
JESHO: Journal of the Economic and Social History of the Orient
JRAS: Journal of the Royal Asiatic Society
ZDMG: Zeitschrift der Deutschen Morgenländischen Gesellschaft

PRIMARY SOURCES

The two major categories of primary source material in the period with which this book is concerned are documents and chronicles of various kinds. These are supplemented, especially in the Ṣafawid period and after, by other types of source, notably the accounts of European travellers. Our period is so long that it will be possible here to mention only a selection of the most important items. Of these sources the chronicles in general provide the historian's basic evidence. This might not have been so had the state archives of Persia survived until the present day; but they have not. As is the case with the study of most Middle Eastern history before the Ottoman period, the historian has, for the most part, to do without the kind of systematic archival evidence that is so important an element in the reconstruction of much of the medieval European past.

This is not to say that no documents at all have survived. Many are to be found, albeit divorced from their original archival context, in chronicles and administrative handbooks and formularies: and for Persia there is at least one major surviving archive, that of the Ṣafawid shrine in Ardabīl, which preserves a mass of documents relating to the property and affairs of the Ṣafawid order, some of which date from substantially before the time of Shaykh Ṣafī al-Dīn. A number of the earliest documents are edited and discussed in M. Gronke, *Arabische und persische Privaturkunden des 12. und 13. Jahrhunderts aus Ardabil (Aserbeidschan)*, Berlin 1982. The interest of certain of the later Ardabīl documents is enhanced by their existence in dual-language versions – both Persian and Mongolian. Some of these have been edited: see for example G. Herrmann and G. Doerfer, "Ein persisch-mongolischer Erlass des Ǧalāyeriden Šeyḫ Oveys", *CAJ* xix, 1975, 1–84; and "Ein persisch-mongolischer Erlass aus dem Jahre 725/1325", *ZDMG* cxxv, 1975, 317–46.

B. Fragner, *Repertorium persischer Herrschaftsurkunden. Publizierte Originalurkunden (bis 1848)*, Freiburg 1980, is an invaluable handbook to the available original and "near-original" Persian documents; and a variety of collections exist, some (to be considered later) specifically concerned with a particular period, others of wider interest, such as L. Fekete, *Einführung in die persische Paläographie. 101 persische Dokumente*, Budapest 1977. A number of documentary collections have been published in Persia, such as S. ʿA. Mu'ayyid Thābitī, *Asnād wa nāmahā-yi tārīkhī az awwal-i dawra-i islāmī tā awākhir-i ʿahd-i Shāh Ismāʿīl Ṣafawī*, Tehran 1967, S. J. Qā'im-Maqāmī (ed.), *Yakṣad u panjāh sanad-i tārīkhī az Jalāyir tā Pahlawī*, Tehran 1970, and ʿA. Nawā'ī's series, *Asnād wa mukātabāt-i tārīkhī: Az Tīmūr tā Shāh Ismāʿīl*, Tehran 1963, *Shāh Ismāʿīl Ṣafawī*, Tehran 1969, *Shāh Ṭahmāsb Ṣafawī*, Tehran 1972, *Shāh ʿAbbās*, vol. I, Tehran 1974.

There are a number of articles on Persian historical writing in B. Lewis and P. M. Holt (eds), *Historians of the Middle East*, London 1962: see especially C. Cahen on the Saljūq period, A. K. S. Lambton on biographical literature, and B. Spuler's general account. A more detailed discussion by Spuler will be found in his "Die historische und geographische Literatur in persische Sprache", in Spuler (ed.), *Handbuch der Orientalistik*, Middle East section, vol. 4, *Iranistik*, part 2, *Literatur*, I, Leiden and Cologne 1968, 100–67. The standard, though incomplete, reference work on manuscripts and editions of Persian works is C. A. Storey, *Persian Literature*. The most relevant volume is vol. 1, part 1, London 1927–39 (reprinted 1970), part 2, London 1953. Those who can read Russian will find Y. Bregel's 3-volume revision of the sections on history, *Persidskaya Literatura*, Moscow 1972, much fuller and more up to date. What E. G. Browne has to say about historians in his *Literary History of Persia*, 4 vols, Cambridge 1928, is still worth reading. See also J. Rypka, *History of Iranian Literature*, Dordrecht 1968.

For the period when the Saljūq empire was at its height, up to the death of Malikshāh in 485/1092, there is a curious lack of surviving contemporary narrative sources, though we know of a number, now lost, which were used by later writers. Most of the more important chronicles are in Arabic rather than Persian. The Saljūq *wazīr* Anūshīrwān b. Khālid (who died in the 1130s) wrote memoirs in Persian which were incorporated (in Arabic) into the *Nuṣrat al-fatra* of ʿImād al-Dīn Iṣfahānī (died 597/1201). This is among the most significant of Saljūq sources: it is usually used in the slightly abridged version, the *Zubdat al-nuṣra*, of Bundārī, *Histoire des Seljoucides de l'Iraq*, ed. M. T. Houtsma, Leiden 1889. The most imposing Arabic work is Ibn al-Athīr's universal history, *Al-kāmil fi'l-ta'rīkh*, ed. C. J. Tornberg, 14 vols, Leiden 1851–76, the later volumes of which deal with the Saljūq, Khwārazm-shāh and early Mongol periods: see D. S. Richards, "Ibn al-Athīr and the later parts of the *Kāmil*: a study of aims and methods", in D. O. Morgan (ed.), *Medieval Historical Writing in the Christian and Islamic Worlds*, London 1982, 76–108. Ibn al-Jawzī, *Al-muntaẓam fī ta'rīkh al-mulūk wa'l-umam*, vols 5–10, Hyderabad 1938–40, is important. Mention should also be made of the *Akhbār al-dawlat al-saljūqiyya* (attributed to ʿAlī b. Nāṣir), ed. M. Iqbāl, Lahore 1933.

In Persian, Bayhaqī's Ghaznawid history, the *Ta'rīkh-i Masʿūdī*, ed. ʿA. Fayyāḍ, Mashhad 1971, has material on the beginning of the Saljūq period. There is an anonymous general history, the *Mujmal al-tawārīkh*, ed. M. Bahār, Tehran 1940, written in 520/1126, as well as Ẓahīr al-Dīn Nīshāpūrī's *Saljūq-nāma*, ed. G. Khāwar, Tehran 1954, much of the substance of which is also to be found in Rāwandīs *Rāḥat al-ṣudūr*, ed. M. Iqbāl, London 1921. There are some local histories of note, such as Ibn Funduq's *Ta'rīkh-i Bayhaq*, ed. A. Bahmanyār, Tehran 1930, and several works on Kirmān, of which the most interesting is perhaps Afḍal al-Dīn's *ʿIqd al-ʿulā*, ed. ʿA. Iqbāl, Tehran 1961. There is a remarkable travel account dating from the very beginning of the period, the *Safar-nāma* of Nāṣir Khusraw, ed. M. Dabīr-Siyāqī, 1957, 1976; ed. with French translation by C. Schefer, Paris 1881, repr. 1970; English translation by W. M. Thackston, Jr, *Nāṣer-e Khosraw's Book of Travels*, New York 1986, but not a great deal of the book is concerned with Persia. In many ways the most indispensable Persian source is Niẓām al-Mulk's *Siyāsat-nāma*, best MS. ed. H. Darke (as *Siyar al-mulūk*), 3rd.

edn, Tehran 1985; trans. H. Darke, *The Book of Government*, 2nd edn, London 1978: various other editions and translations. On this work see A. K. S. Lambton, "The dilemma of government in Islamic Persia: the *Siyāsat-nāma* of Niẓām al-Mulk", *Iran* xxii, 1984, 55–66.

Collections of documents and manuals containing documents from Saljūq times include H. Horst, *Die Staatsverwaltung der Grosselǧūqen und Ḫorazmšāhs (1038–1231). Untersuchung nach Urkundenformularen der Zeit*, Wiesbaden 1964; the anonymous *Al-mukhtārāt min al-rasāʾil*, ed. I. Afshār, Tehran 1976; al-Mayhanī, *Dastūr-i dabīrī*, ed. A. S. Erzi, Ankara 1962; and Muntajab al-Dīn Juwaynī, *ʿAtabat al-kataba*, ed. ʿA. Iqbāl, Tehran 1950. What may be made of such a source is shown by A. K. S. Lambton, "The administration of Sanjar's empire as illustrated in the *ʿAtabat al-kataba*", *BSOAS* xx, 1957, 367–88.

Aside from Ibn al-Athīr, the most important chronicle to treat the Khwārazm-shāhs in any detail is ʿAṭāʾ Malik Juwaynī's history of the Mongols, the *Taʾrīkh-i Jahān Gushā*, ed. M. Qazwīnī, 3 vols, Leiden and London 1912, 1916, 1937; trans. J. A. Boyle, *The History of the World Conqueror*, 2 vols, Manchester 1958. But before turning to the Mongol period proper, Nasawī's Arabic biography of his master, the last Khwārazm-shāh, should be mentioned. The standard edition is O. Houdas (ed. and trans.), *Histoire du Sultan Djelal ed-Din Mankobirti*, 2 vols, Paris 1891–5. An early Persian translation, *Sīrat-i Jalāl al-Dīn Mīngbirnī*, ed. M. Minovi, Tehran 1965, is worthy of attention.

The sources for the history of the Mongol Empire as a whole are most recently surveyed in D. O. Morgan, *The Mongols*, Oxford 1986, Chapter 1. The Persian sources are perhaps the most important single body of material within that mass of evidence, not merely for the history of Persia. For the early part of the period the major source, in addition to Nasawī and the last sections of Ibn al-Athīr, is Jūzjānī's *Ṭabaqāt-i Nāṣirī*, ed. ʿA. Ḥabībī, 2 vols, Kābul 1964–5, primarily a dynastic history of the Ghurids of Afghanistan, written about 658/1260 but the work of a contemporary of Chingiz Khān's invasion forty years before. It is especially valuable because it was written in India, outside the Mongol sphere of influence. At almost the same time Juwaynī, a much younger man than Jūzjānī, wrote his Mongol history, the fullest extant account of the early Mongol Empire in general and of early Mongol Persia in particular. The introductions by E. G. Browne to Qazwīnī's edition and by Boyle to his translation are useful discussions.

The greatest Persian historian of the Mongol period was Ghazan's *wazīr* Rashīd al-Dīn. His *Jāmiʿ al-tawārīkh* is an immensely, indeed uniquely wide-ranging work, entitling its author to be regarded, almost, as a "world-historian". There are a great many editions and translations of the various parts of the work. The best edition of the section on the Īlkhāns is that by A. A. Alizade, *Jāmiʿ al-tawārīkh*, vol. 3, Baku 1957. This includes a Russian translation. The same ground is covered, between them, by E. Quatremère, *Histoire des Mongols de la Perse*, Paris 1836, reprinted Amsterdam 1968; *Ta'rīḫ-i Mubārak-i Ġāzānī . . . Abāġā bis Gaiḫātū*, ed. K. Jahn, The Hague 1957, and *Geschichte Ġāzān-Ḫāns*, ed. K. Jahn, London 1940. Quatremère includes both a French translation of the section on Hülegü and the general introduction to the whole work, which is not otherwise available. A convenient account of the man and his work is to be found in Boyle's introduction to his translation of the section on *The Successors of Genghis Khan*, New York and London 1971. Many aspects are examined in the *Rashīd al-Dīn Commemoration Volume*, *CAJ* xiv, 1970. Jūzjānī, Juwaynī and Rashīd al-Dīn are discussed by D. O. Morgan, "Persian historians and the Mongols", in Morgan (ed.), *Medieval Historical Writing*, 109–24.

Also of very great importance is the history of a contemporary of Rashīd al-Dīn, the *Ta'rīkh-i Waṣṣāf*, ed. M. M. Iṣfahānī, Bombay 1852–3, reprinted Tehran 1960. Waṣṣāf wrote in an extremely convoluted Persian style, and even those well schooled in the language may find the modern Persian abridgement, *Taḥrīr-i ta'rīkh-i Waṣṣāf*, ed ʿA. Āyatī, Tehran 1968, a useful guide. Ḥamd Allāh Mustawfī Qazwīnī's *Ta'rīkh-i guzīda*, ed. ʿA. Nawā'ī, Tehran 1958–61, a general history to the end of the Ilkhanid period, is not very full, but the geographical part of his *Nuzhat al-qulūb*, ed. and trans. G. Le Strange, 2 vols, Leiden and London 1915–19, is of considerable value. For Öljeitü's reign there is Qāshānī, *Ta'rīkh-i Ūljāytū*, ed. M. Hambly, Tehran 1969. Extracts from a variety of Persian and other sources are provided in English translation in B. Spuler, *History of the Mongols*, London 1972.

There are many local histories dating from or dealing with the Mongol period. The most interesting is perhaps Sayfī's *Ta'rīkh-nāma-i Harāt*, ed. M. Z. al-Ṣiddīqī, Calcutta 1944. Of several chronicles of the different Caspian provinces, Awliyā Allāh Āmulī's *Ta'rīkh-i Rūyān*, ed. M. Sutūda, Tehran 1969, may be singled out. For the Jalayirid successor-state to the Ilkhanate, see Abū Bakr al-Quṭbī al-Aharī, *Ta'rīkh-i Shaikh Uwais*, ed. and trans. J. B. van Loon, The Hague 1954.

Non-Persian sources for Persia in the Mongol period should not be neglected. On the Arabic side, the Mamlūk chronicles offer some material, as does the relevant part of al-ʿUmarī's *Masālik al-abṣār*, ed. and trans. K. Lech, *Das mongolische Weltreich*, Wiesbaden 1968. Syriac sources of note include the last part of the *Chronography* of Bar Hebraeus, ed. and trans. E. A. Wallis Budge, 2 vols, London 1932, and the biography of the Nestorian prelate Yaballāhā III, trans. Budge as *The Monks of Ḳūblāi Khān, Emperor of China*, London 1928.

So far as documents are concerned, many of Ghazan's reforming edicts are reproduced, apparently in full, in Rashīd al-Dīn's *Jāmiʿ al-tawārīkh*. Rashīd al-Din's *waqf-nāma* has survived, in part in his own hand, ed. M. Minovi and I. Afshār, Tehran, facsimile 1972, printed text 1977–8, So has a collection of his letters, ed. M. Shafīʿ as *Mukātabāt-i Rashīdī*, Lahore 1945, ed. M. T. Dānishpazhūh as *Sawāniḥ al-afkār-i Rashīdī*, Tehran 1980–1; but these may well be spurious. There is an interesting financial memorandum written for Hülegü (or possibly Abaqa) by Naṣīr al-Dīn Ṭūsī, ed. M. Raḍawī in *Majmūʿa-i rasāʾil-i Khwāja Naṣīr al-Dīn*, Tehran 1957, trans. V. Minorsky, "Naṣīr al-Dīn Ṭūsī on finance", in his *Iranica*, Tehran 1964. There are important administrative and accounting manuals from the end of the period, such as those of ʿAlā-yi Tabrīzī, ed. and trans. M. Nabīpūr, *Die beiden persischen Leitfäden des Falak ʿAlā-ye Tabrīzī über das staatliche Rechnungswesen im 14. Jahrhundert*, Göttingen 1973, and Muḥammad b. Hindūshāh Nakhjawānī, *Dastūr al-kātib fī taʿyīn al-marātib*, ed. A. A. Alizade, 2 vols in 3, Moscow 1964, 1971, 1976. From the Jalayirid period comes Ibn Kiyā al-Māzandarānī's *Die Resālä-ye Falakiyyä*, ed. W. Hinz, Wiesbaden 1952.

For the fourteenth century the most important chronicler is the Timurid historian Ḥāfiẓ Abrū, who wrote a number of works, including a geography of which only small sections have been published. He composed a continuation of Rashīd al-Dīn, *Dhayl-i Jāmiʿ al-tawārīkh*, ed. K. Bayānī, 2nd edn, Tehran 1971, 1st edn trans. Bayānī as *Chronique des Rois Mongols en Iran*, Paris 1936. Also of note are five short works, *Cinq Opuscules de Ḥāfiẓ-i Abrū*, ed. F. Tauer, Prague 1959.

The two major chronicles of Temür are both called *Ẓafar-nāma*: one by Niẓām al-Dīn Shāmī, ed. F. Tauer, 2 vols, Prague 1937–56, the other by Sharaf al-Dīn ʿAlī Yazdī, ed. M. ʿAbbāsī, 2 vols, Tehran 1958: the facsimile edition by A. Urunbayev, Tashkent 1972, includes an interesting introductory section which is not otherwise published. These are both court chronicles: less friendly to Temür are Ibn ʿArabshāh, *Kitāb ʿAjāʾib al-maqdūr fī akhbār Tīmūr*, in Arabic, ed. ʿA. M. ʿUmar, Cairo 1979, trans. J. H. Sanders, *Tamerlane or Timur, the Great Amir*, London 1936; and Ibn Khaldūn's account of his meeting with the conqueror, W. J. Fischel (trans.), *Ibn Khaldūn and Tamerlane*, Berkeley and Los Angeles 1952. A fascinating Western account is Clavijo, *Embassy to Tamerlane 1403–1406*, trans. G. Le Strange, London 1928.

The writing of history flourished at the Timurid courts, especially that of Shāh Rukh. Later Timurid historians, in addition to Ḥāfiẓ Abrū, include ʿAbd al-Razzāq Samarqandī, *Maṭlaʿ al-saʿdayn*, ed. M. Shafīʿ, 2 vols, Lahore 1941–9; Mīrkhwānd, *Rawḍat al-ṣafāʾ*, ed. ʿA. Parwīz, 10 vols, Tehran 1960 (much of it a continuation for long after Mīrkhwānd's death: vols V and VI are the most relevant); Khwāndamīr, *Ḥabīb al-siyar*, ed. J. Humāʾī, 4 vols, Tehran 1955 (continues to the reign of Ismāʿīl I); and Muʿīn al-Dīn Naṭanzī, *Muntakhab al-tawārīkh-i Muʿīnī*, ed. J. Aubin, Tehran 1957. For Timurid administration see especially ʿAbd Allāh Marwārid, *Sharaf-nāma*, ed., with translation and commentary, H. R. Roemer, *Staatsschreiben der Timuridenzeit*, Wiesbaden 1952.

The most important source for the Türkmen dynasties is the Aq-Qoyunlu chronicle, Abū Bakr Ṭihrānī Iṣfahānī, *Kitāb-i Diyārbakriyya*, ed. N. Lugal and F. Sümer, 2 vols, Ankara 1962–4. For the later Türkmen period, see Khunjī's *Taʾrīkh-i ʿālam-ārā-yi Amīnī*, trans. in part by V. Minorsky, *Persia in A.D. 1478–1490*, London 1957. Examples of local histories written in the fifteenth century are those of Yazd, ed. I. Afshār: Jaʿfar b. Muḥammad Ḥasan Jaʿfarī, *Taʾrīkh-i Yazd*, 2nd edn, Tehran 1965, and Aḥmad b. Ḥusayn, *Taʾrīkh-i jadīd-i Yazd*, Tehran 1966.

The accounts of European ambassadors in this period and immediately after are in *A Narrative of Italian Travellers in Persia*, trans. C. Grey, and *Travels to Tana and Persia by Josafa Barbaro and Ambrogio Contarini*, trans. W. Thomas, ed. Lord Stanley of Alderley, Hakluyt Society, London 1873. The Italian texts of Barbaro and Contarini are in *I viaggi in Persia degli ambasciatori veneti Barbaro e Contarini*, ed. L. Lockhart *et al.*, Rome 1973. Two collections of documents are M. S. Keçik, *Briefe und Urkunden aus der Kanzlei Uzun Ḥasans*, Freiburg 1976, and Mudarrisī Ṭabāṭabāʾī (ed.), *Farmānhā-yi Turkumānān-i Qarā-Qūyūnlū wa Āq-Qūyūnlū*, Qum 1974. H. Busse, *Untersuchungen zum islamischen Kanzleiwesen an Hand turkmenischer und safawidischer Urkunden*, Cairo 1959, extending into the succeeding period, is of great value.

The essential source for the origins of the Ṣafawid movement is Ibn Bazzāz's biography of Shaykh Ṣafī al-Dīn, the *Ṣafwat al-ṣafāʾ*. The only full edition is of a sixteenth-century doctored version, ed. A. Tabrīzī, Bombay 1911: the original remains unedited. Much may yet be learned from the documents in the shrine at Ardabīl, which has been described as "the cupboard where the [Ṣafawid] skeletons were kept". Shāh Ismāʿīl's poetry (in Turkish) is edited by T. Gandjei, *Il Canzoniere di Šāh Ismāʿīl Ḫatāʾī*, Naples 1959: see also V. Minorsky, "The poetry of Shāh Ismāʿīl I', *BSOAS* X, 1942. An anonymous work partly ed. and trans. E. Denison Ross, "The early years of Shāh Ismāʿīl, founder of the Ṣafavī Dynasty", *JRAS* April 1896, has often been quoted as a near-contemporary source; but it is now known to have been written in the seventeenth century. Many of the most interesting Ṣafawid chroniclers were writing in the last quarter of the sixteenth century. These include Ḥasan Rūmlū, *Aḥsan al-tawārīkh*, vol. XI, (on the fifteenth century) ed. ʿA. Nawāʾī, Tehran 1970, vol XII, ed. and trans. C. N. Seddon, *A Chronicle of the Early Ṣafawīs*, 2 vols, Baroda 1931–4 (new edn ʿA. Nawāʾī, Tehran 1979); Qāḍī Aḥmad Qumī, *Khulāṣat al-tawārīkh*, ed. I. Ishrāqī, 2 vols, Tehran 1980, partial eds E. Glassen, *Die frühen Safawiden nach Qāżī Aḥmad Qumī*, Frieburg 1970, H. Müller, *Die Chronik Ḫulāṣat al-Tawāriḫ*, Wiesbaden 1964 (early part of ʿAbbās's reign); and Āfushtaʾī Naṭanzī, *Naqāwat al-āthār*, ed. I. Ishrāqī, Tehran 1971. The most important of all Ṣafawid chronicles is Iskandar Beg Munshī's *Taʾrīkh-i ʿālam-ārā-yi ʿAbbāsī*, ed. I. Afshār, 2 vols, Tehran 1956, trans. R. M. Savory, *The History of Shah ʿAbbas the Great*, 2 vols, Boulder 1978: continuation (*Dhayl*) ed. S. Khwānsārī, Tehran 1939.

The accounts of Ṣafawid Persia written by European travellers of various kinds are legion. For the early period, see M. Membrè, *Relazione di Persia*, ed. G. Scarcia, Naples 1968 (written in 1542), and Anthony Jenkinson, *Early Voyages and Travels in Russia and Persia*, ed. E. D. Morgan and C. H. Coote, 2 vols, Hakluyt Society, London 1866. Many travellers wrote about the Persia of Shāh ʿAbbās I. The Sherleys may be approached through E. D. Ross, *Sir Anthony Sherley and his Persian Adventure*, London 1933, and the study of the family as a whole by D. W. Davies, *Elizabethans Errant*, Ithaca 1967. Sir Thomas Herbert's account, *A Relation of Some Yeares Travaile*, London 1634, has been abridged by W. Foster, *Travels in Persia 1627–1629*, London 1928. Pietro della Valle's *Viaggi*, Rome 1658–63, remain rather inaccessible in various senses. There are several editions, e.g. G. Gancia (ed.), *I viaggi di Pietro della Valle, il Pellegrino*, Brighton 1843. On him see W. Blunt, *Pietro's Pilgrimage*, London 1953; and J. D. Gurney, "Pietro della Valle: the limits of perception", *BSOAS* XLIX/1, 1986, 103–16. From later in the seventeenth century come R. du Mans, *Estat de la Perse en 1660*, ed. C. Schefer, Paris 1890, repr. 1969, and J. Chardin, *Voyages . . . en Perse, et autres lieux de l'Orient*, ed. L. Langlès, 10 vols, Paris 1811 (partial English trans., ed. P. M. Sykes, London 1927). *A Chronicle of the Carmelites in Persia and the Papal Mission of the 17th and 18th Centuries*, ed. and trans. H. Chick, 2 vols, London 1939, was compiled from documents written over a long period. This is very far from exhausting the important travellers, but one who journeyed in the other direction should be mentioned: *Don Juan of Persia. A Shiʿa Catholic 1560–1604*, trans. G. Le Strange, London 1926.

There are two instructive administrative manuals from the end of the

Ṣafawid period: the *Tadhkirat al-Mulūk*, ed. and trans. (with invaluable commentary) V. Minorsky, London 1943, and the *Dastūr al-Mulūk*, made available by M. T. Dānishpazhūh, "Dastūr al-Mulūk-i Mīrzā Rafī'ā wa Tadhkirat al-Mulūk-i Mīrzā Samī'ā", *Majalla-i Dānishkada-i Adabiyyāt-i Tihrān* XV, 1968, 504–75; XVI, 1968–9, 62–93, 198–322, 416–40, 540–64. A useful guide to original Ṣafawid documentary evidence is R. Schimkoreit, *Regesten publizierter ṣafawidischer Herrscherurkunden. Erlasse und Staatsschreiben der frühen Neuzeit Irans*, Berlin 1982. For economic history and the history of trade, the archival evidence, such as the East India Company's *Gombroon Diary*, to be found in such repositories as the India Office in London is of considerable importance. On the documentary evidence for foreign affairs see Riazul Islam, *A Calendar of Documents on Indo–Persian Relations*, 2 vols, Tehran and Karachi 1979–82, on which much of his *Indo–Persian Relations: a Study of the Political and Diplomatic Relations between the Mughul Empire and Iran*, Tehran 1970, is based.

The most important of Nādir Shāh's chroniclers is Mīrzā Mihdī Astarābādī, *Ta'rīkh-i jahān gushā-yi Nādirī*, ed. S. 'A. Anwār, Tehran 1963; *Durra-i Nādira*, ed. S. J. Shahīdī, Tehran 1963. Two published Zand chronicles are Nāmī Iṣfahānī, *Ta'rīkh-i gītī gushā*, ed. S. Nafīsī, Tehran 1939, and Gulistāna, *Mujmal al-tawārīkh*, ed. M. Raḍawī, Tehran 1966. Also of relevance to eighteenth-century history is a curious anecdotal work: Muhammad Hāshim (Rustam al-Ḥukamā'), *Rustam al-tawārīkh*, ed. M. Mushīrī, 2nd edn, Tehran 1974, trans. B. Hoffmann, *Persische Geschichte 1694–1835 erlebt, erinnert und erfunden. Das* Rustam at- tawārīḫ *in deutscher Bearbeitung*, 2 vols, Bamberg 1986.

MODERN WORKS

General

The most important large-scale and up to date history of Persia is the *Cambridge History of Iran*. The volumes that cover the period discussed in this book are 4, *From the Arab Invasion to the Saljuqs*, ed. R. N. Frye, Cambridge 1975; 5, *The Saljuq and Mongol Periods*, ed. J. A. Boyle, Cambridge 1968; and 6, *The Timurid and Safavid Periods*, ed. P. Jackson and L. Lockhart, Cambridge 1986. Vol. 7, *The Eighteenth Century to the Present*, has not yet been published. Vol. 1, *The Land of Iran*, ed. W. B. Fisher, Cambridge 1968, should also be consulted. Like all co-operative works, the *Cambridge History* is uneven in quality, but at its best it is invaluable (as for example Lambton on "The internal structure of the Saljuq Empire" and Petrushevsky on "The socio-economic condition of Iran under the Īl-Khāns" in vol. 5, and Roemer's five chapters on political history in vol. 6). Many aspects of the first half of the period are discussed in an extremely important recent work, A. K. S. Lambton, *Continuity and Change in Medieval Persia: Aspects of Administrative, Economic and Social History, 11th–14th Century*, New York 1987.

Older general histories, such as Sir Percy Sykes's 2-volume *History of Persia*, are no longer of great value, but A. Bausani, *The Persians*, London 1971, is a stimulating short account of the whole of Persian history. A good deal may enjoyably be learnt about Persia from Sir Roger Stevens, *The Land of the Great Sophy*, 3rd edn, London 1979. W. Barthold, *An Historical Geography of Iran*, trans. S. Soucek and ed. C. E. Bosworth, Princeton 1984 (first published in Russian in 1903) is the work of one of the greatest Islamic historians, and though it is not perhaps among his best books it is well worth consulting. It may be used in conjunction with G. Le Strange, *The Lands of the Eastern Caliphate*, Cambridge 1905 (reprinted London 1966). Barthold's most celebrated book, *Turkestan down to the Mongol Invasion*, 3rd edn, London 1968, though not concerned primarily with Persia as such, remains indispensable. Two other classic studies which should not be missed are A. K. S. Lambton's *Landlord and Peasant in Persia*, London 1953, and her London University inaugural lecture, *Islamic Society in Persia*, London 1954 (reprinted in Lambton, *Theory and Practice in Medieval Persian Government*, London 1980).

There are relevant chapters in P. M. Holt, A. K. S. Lambton and B. Lewis (eds), *The Cambridge History of Islam*, 2 vols, Cambridge 1970, and in K. M. Setton (gen. ed.), *A History of the Crusades*, 5 volumes so far, Madison 1969– . Especially valuable are C. Cahen's chapter on "The Turkish invasion: the Selchükids" in vol. 1, and "The Mongols and the Near East" in vol. 2. M. G. S. Hodgson's *The Venture of Islam*, 3 vols, Chicago 1974, can be hard work but is worth the effort; and he is more interested in Persia than most writers of general histories of Islam.

The essential work of reference is *The Encyclopaedia of Islam*, 1st edn, Leiden 1918–38, 2nd edn, 1960– (it had reached letter M at the time of writing). A new *Encyclopaedia Iranica* has recently commenced publication (New York and London 1982–): it is still on letter A. As bibliographical guides three may be recommended. In general, see C. Cahen, *Jean Sauvaget's Introduction to the History of the Muslim East*, Berkeley and Los Angeles 1965 (this is not entirely superseded by Cahen's own *Introduction à l'histoire du monde musulman médiéval, VIIe–XVe siècle*, Paris 1982); specifically for Persia, there is L. P. Elwell-

Sutton (ed.), *Bibliographical Guide to Iran*, Brighton 1983. For articles, see J. D. Pearson, *Index Islamicus 1906–1955*, Cambridge 1958, with many later supplements. Historical atlases of Islam are not for the most part of outstanding quality. The best is W. C. Brice (ed.), *An Historical Atlas of Islam*, Leiden 1981.

The Early Islamic Centuries

Only a few works can be mentioned as further reading on the period briefly surveyed, by way of introduction, in Chapter 2. The period as a whole is covered in B. Spuler, *Iran in früh-islamischer Zeit*, Wiesbaden 1952; in *CHI* vol. 4; and in a shorter book, R. N. Frye's curiously titled *The Golden Age of Persia: the Arabs in the East*, London 1975. Much early Islamic Persian history is to be found in Hugh Kennedy's volume in this series, *The Prophet and the Age of the Caliphates*, London 1986. It has an especially valuable chapter on the Buyids. For the Sasanian prelude to Islamic Persia, see *CHI*, vol. 3, *The Seleucid, Parthian and Sasanian Periods*, ed. E. Yarshater, Cambridge 1983. The standard work has long been A. Christensen, *L'Iran sous les Sassanides*, 2nd edn, Copenhagen 1944.

The Saljūqs and after

The best introduction is Cahen's chapter in *A History of the Crusades* vol. 1, mentioned above. For a detailed narrative, see C. E. Bosworth, "The political and dynastic history of the Iranian world (A.D. 1000–1217)", in *CHI* vol. 5. There are many useful articles in D. S. Richards (ed.), *Islamic Civilisation 950–1150*, Oxford 1973, especially those by Bosworth, "Barbarian invasions: the coming of the Turks into the Islamic world", and Lambton, "Aspects of Saljūq-Ghuzz settlement in Persia" (also reprinted in Lambton, *Theory and Practice*). On Saljūq administration see Lambton, "The internal structure of the Saljuq empire", in *CHI* vol. 5 (also in *Theory and Practice*), and her more recent views in *Continuity and Change*. See also C. L. Klausner, *The Seljuk Vezirate*, Cambridge, Mass., 1973. There is interesting material on Niẓām al-Mulk and other subjects in E. Glassen, *Der mittlere Weg: Studien zur Religionspolitik und Religiosität der späteren Abbasiden-zeit*, Wiesbaden 1981. On the *iqṭāʿ* the two standard discussions are C. Cahen, "L'évolution de l'iqṭāʿ du IXᵉ au XIIIᵉ siècle", *Annales* 8, 1953, 25–52, and Lambton, "Reflections on the *iqṭāʿ*", *Arabic and Islamic Studies in Honor of Hamilton A. R. Gibb*, ed. G. Makdisi, Leiden 1965, 358–76 (also in *Theory and Practice*). The *EI*² article IḲṬĀʿ is by Cahen.

On the Ismāʿīlīs the best accounts are by M. G. S. Hodgson, *The Order of Assassins*, Leiden 1955, and "The Ismāʿīlī state" in *CHI* vol. 5. B. Lewis, *The Assassins: a Radical Sect in Islam*, London 1967, is an attractively written and stimulating short book. The Qara-Khitai and the Khwārazm-shāhs have not been much studied. On both, see Barthold, *Turkestan*, Chapter 3. On the Qara-Khitai, there is K. A. Wittfogel and C. Fêng, *History of Chinese Society: Liao 907–1125*, Philadelphia 1949, Appendix 5. On the Khwārazm-shāhs, see Bosworth in *CHI* vol. 5.

The Mongols

The most interesting introduction to the Mongol phenomenon as a whole is J. F. Fletcher, "The Mongols: ecological and social perspectives", *HJAS* 46/1, 1986, 11–50. The standard general account is J. J. Saunders, *The History of the Mongol Conquests*, London 1971. Similar in scope, but more recent, is D. O. Morgan, *The Mongols*, Oxford 1986. By far the best study of Chingiz Khān is P. Ratchnevsky, *Činggis-Khan: sein Leben und Wirken*, Wiesbaden 1983. There are many biographies in English, but the only one of real note is the partial study of H. D. Martin, *The Rise of Chingis Khan and his Conquest of North China*, Baltimore 1950. S. Jagchid and P. Hyer, *Mongolia's Culture and Society*, Boulder and Folkestone 1979, is a recommendable general book on the Mongols, and R. Grousset, *The Empire of the Steppes*, trans. N. Walford, New Brunswick, 1970, and G. Hambly (ed.), *Central Asia*, London 1969, are worth reading for the wider chronological context of Central Asian history.

The standard work on the Mongols in Persia is B. Spuler, *Die Mongolen in Iran*, 4th edn, Leiden 1985. In English, see the relevant chapters in *CHI* vol. 5, especially J. A. Boyle, "Dynastic and political history of the Īl-Khāns", and I. P. Petrushevsky, "The socio-economic condition of Iran under the Īl-Khāns", a summary of a major work in Russian. For the individual Īlkhāns whose names happen to begin with A (a high proportion), the best accounts are the articles by P. Jackson in *EIr*. Barthold, *Turkestan*, is particularly relevant for this period. The 1968 edition has very significant additional material not contained in earlier English editions. Lambton, *Continuity and Change*, is as important for this as for the Saljūq period.

Temür and the Timurids

At present the best study of Temür in English is H. Hookham, *Tamburlaine the Conqueror*, London 1962, but the standard work will be B. F.

Manz, *The Rise and Rule of Tamerlane*, when it is published. H. R. Roemer, "Tīmūr in Iran" and "The successors of Tīmūr", *CHI* 6, are excellent, as is his chapter on the immediately post-Ilkhanid period, "The Jalayirids, Muzaffarids and Sarbadārs". There is a very interesting book on the latter "dynasty": J. M. Smith, *The History of the Sarbadār Dynasty, 1336–1381 A.D., and its Sources*, The Hague and Paris, 1970. The nearest thing to a good book in English on the Timurids is W. Barthold, *Ulugh Beg (Four Studies on the History of Central Asia* vol. 2, trans. V. and T. Minorsky), Leiden 1958. There is a study of the most important of the later Timurids' capitals: T. Allen, *Timurid Herat*, Wiesbaden 1983. Much may be learned about the province of Kirmān in the Timurid period from J. Aubin, *Deux Sayyids de Bam au XVe siècle. Contribution à l'histoire de l'Iran timouride*, Wiesbaden 1956.

The Türkmen Dynasties and the Rise of the Ṣafawids

The two major books on Persia in the fifteenth century are W. Hinz, *Irans Aufstieg zum Nationalstaat im fünfzehnten Jahrhundert*, Berlin and Leipzig 1936, and J. E. Woods, *The Aqquyunlu: Clan, Confederation, Empire*, Minneapolis and Chicago 1976. There are many relevant articles by V. Minorsky, which will be found in his three collections: *Iranica*, Tehran 1964; *The Turks, Iran and the Caucasus in the Middle Ages*, London 1978; *Medieval Iran and its Neighbours*, London 1982. There is a study of Iṣfahān in this and the succeeding period: R. Quiring-Zoche, *Isfahan im 15. und 16. Jahrhundert*, Freiburg 1980. On the rise of the Ṣafawids, parts of M. M. Mazzaoui, *The Origins of the Ṣafawids: Šīʿism, Ṣūfism and the Ġulāt*, Wiesbaden 1972, are useful, but the book as a whole is not entirely satisfactory. The best account is found in the first twenty pages of Roemer, "The Safavid period", *CHI* vol. 6. J. Aubin, "La propriété foncière en Azerbaydjan sous les Mongols", *Le Monde Iranien et l'Islam* IV, 1976–7, 79–132, is interesting on the landholdings of the Ṣafawid *shaykhs*. On the career of Junayd, the forthcoming article by A. H. Morton, "Junayd of Ardabīl", is important.

The Ṣafawids

V. Minorsky's introduction and commentary to his facsimile edition and translation of the *Tadhkirat al-Mulūk*, London 1943, referred to above, remain fundamental to all study of the Ṣafawid period. The outstanding recent study is Roemer, "The Safavid period". The only attempt at a book-length history in English of Persia in the Ṣafawid period is R. M. Savory, *Iran under the Safavids*, Cambridge 1980. A useful summary account is H. Braun, "Irān under the Ṣafavids and in the 18th century", in F. R. C. Bagley (ed. and trans.), *The Muslim World: a Historical Survey. Part III: the Last Great Muslim Empires*, Leiden 1969, 181–218. Most of the best work in recent decades has been in languages other than English, especially German and French. Important examples are K. M. Röhrborn, *Provinzen und Zentralgewalt Persiens im 16. und 17. Jahrhundert*, Berlin 1966, and the numerous articles of J. Aubin, such as "Šāh Ismāʿīl et les notables de l'Iraq Persan", *JESHO* 2, 1959, 37–81, and "La politique religieuse des Ṣafavides", in *Le Shīʿisme imāmite*, Paris 1970.

An admirable general book on Twelver Shīʿism is M. Momen, *An Introduction to Shiʿi Islam*, New Haven and London 1985. There is important material on the imposition of Shīʿism in S. A. Arjomand, *The Shadow of God and the Hidden Imam*, Chicago and London 1984, though the author's manner of presentation does much to conceal the fact. See also A. H. Hourani, "From Jabal ʿĀmil to Persia", *BSOAS* XLIX/1, 1986, 133–40. On foreign affairs in the early Ṣafawid period see A. Allouche, *The Origins and Development of the Ottoman–Ṣafavid Conflict (906–962/1500–1555)*, Berlin 1983. On the Özbegs see J. F. Fletcher, "Western Turkestan: the emergence of the Uzbeks", forthcoming in the *Cambridge History of Inner Asia*, and M. B. Dickson, *Sháh Ṭahmásb and the Uzbeks (The Duel for Khurásán with ʿUbayd Khán: 930–946/1524–1540)*, Princeton 1958 – technically an unpublished dissertation, but in fact made available in book form by University Microfilms.

On economic history see R. W. Ferrier, "Trade from the mid-14th century to the end of the Safavid period", and B. Fragner, "Social and internal economic affairs", *CHI* vol. 6. There is a recent book in English: M. Keyvani, *Artisans and Guild Life in the Later Safavid Period*, Berlin 1982. N. Steensgaard, *The Asian Trade Revolution of the Seventeenth Century*, Chicago and London 1974, contains important ideas of relevance to Persia. There are many books on the art and achitecture of the period, such as A. Welch, *Shāh ʿAbbās and the Arts of Isfahan*, New York 1973. W. Blunt and W. Swaan, *Isfahan, Pearl of Persia*, London 1966, is attractive; see also the collection of papers, *Studies on Isfahan, Iranian Studies* VII, 2 parts, ed. R. Holod, 1974. R. Hillenbrand, "Safavid architecture", *CHI* vol. 6, is especially notable.

The end of the dynasty is studied in great detail by L. Lockhart, *The Fall of the Ṣafavī Dynasty and the Afghan Occupation of Persia*, Cambridge 1958. On this the review article by M. B. Dickson, "The fall of the Ṣafavī Dynasty", *JAOS* 82, 1962, 503–17, is important.

The Eighteenth Century

On the brief Afghan period see Lockhart, *The Fall*. L. Lockhart, *Nadir Shah*, London 1938, remains standard. The best book on the eighteenth century is J. R. Perry, *Karim Khan Zand: a History of Iran, 1747–1779*, Chicago and London 1979. On Shīʿism in the eighteenth century see Arjomand, *The Shadow of God*, H. Algar, "Shiʿism and Iran in the eighteenth century", in T. Naff and R. Owen (eds), *Studies in Eighteenth Century Islamic History*, Carbondale, etc., 1977, 288–302 and 400–3, and N. R. Keddie, "The roots of the ulama's power in modern Iran", in Keddie (ed.), *Scholars, Saints and Sufis: Muslim Religious Institutions in the Middle East since 1500*, Berkeley and Los Angeles 1972, 211–29. A. K. S. Lambton, "The tribal resurgence and the decline of the bureaucracy in the eighteenth century", in Naff and Owen, *op. cit.*, 108–29 and 377–82, is a useful discussion.

Glossary

It should be noted that the terms are defined according to their meaning at the time and place in which they appear in this volume. At other times and in other places, some were used in other senses.

Akhbārī Shīʿī theological school which held that the Traditions of the Prophet and the *imāms* provided the Muslim with sufficient guidance, and was opposed to the use of *ijtihād* (q.v.).
Amīr Military commander.
Amīr al-umarāʾ Commander-in-chief.
Anda Sworn brother, in Mongol society.
Atabeg "Father of the prince" (Turkish): originally the guardian of a Saljūq prince and the regent of his appanage; the rulers of some of the successor-states to the Saljūqs were *atabegs* or pseudo-*atabegs*.
Barāt Draft, especially on the revenue from taxation.
Bāṭin Esoteric interpretation of Islam.
Beg Tribal leader; also prince (Turkish).
Caliph (Ar. *khalīfa*) "Representative, successor": the legitimate, acknowledged head of the universal Sunnī Islamic community.
Catholicus Head of the Nestorian Christian church.
Chʿao Chinese paper currency.
Dār al-ḥarb "Abode of war": in Islamic law, all territories not under Muslim jurisdiction.
Dār al-Islām "Abode of Islam"; in Islamic law, all territories under Muslim jurisdiction.
Dargāh The court.
Dawla Dynasty, state.
Dihqān Landed proprietor, head of a village who held certain lands by hereditary right and was responsible for the collection and payment of the taxes (Sasanian and early Islamic periods); in modern Persian, a peasant.

Dīnār From *denarius* (Latin): unit of gold currency.
Dīwān Department of government.
Ghāzī Fighter for the Islamic faith.
Ghulām, see also *mamlūk* Slave soldier, imported or descended from individuals imported from outside Islamic territory.
Ḥadīth A tradition, especially of the Prophet or the Shīʿī *imāms*.
Hazāra "Thousand" (Persian): a military formation of the Mongol period, nominally 1,000 strong.
Ijtihād Independent judgement in matters of the Islamic faith.
Īlchī Envoy (Mongol period and after).
Īlkhān "Subject *khān*": the ruler of the Mongol kingdom in Persia and Iraq.
Imām A leader in communal prayer; the leader of the Islamic community; the caliph; in Shīʿī usage the term when used for the leader of the community is confined to the family of the Prophet.
Iqṭāʿ Assignment of land or its revenue; provincial government.
Ismāʿīlī Member of a Shīʿī sect, represented especially by the Fatimid caliphate and the Assassins.
Īwān A portico.
Jizya Poll-tax on the non-Muslim population.
Khān Title of a Mongol or Turkish ruler or tribal leader.
Kharāj Tax; tribute; land-tax.
Khāṣṣa In the Ṣafawid period, lands in the personal domain of the shāh.
Khuṭba Address given in the mosque in which the ruler's name is customarily mentioned; this mention is a prerogative of sovereignty.
Madhhab Doctrine; rite; a school of Islamic law.
Madrasa Islamic religious college.
Mamālik Kingdoms; provinces; in the Ṣafawid period, provinces granted to the Qizilbash (q.v.) and therefore ruled indirectly.
Mamlūk, see *ghulām*.
Marjaʿ al-taqlīd "Source of imitation": the highest rank attainable by a *mujtahid* (q.v.).
Masjid Mosque.
Mawlā (pl. *mawālī*) Client of an Arab tribe (usually a non-Arab).
Maẓālim Court exercising jurisdiction supplementary to that of the *qāḍī* (q.v.), to deal with the grievances and petitions of the subjects.
Miḥrāb Niche in a mosque indicating the direction of Mecca, and hence of prayer.
Mujtahid One qualified to exercise *ijtihād* (q.v.).
Mullā Member of the Islamic religious classes.
Mullā-bāshī Chief *mullā* (later Ṣafawid period).

Muqṭaʿ Holder of an *iqṭāʿ* (q.v.).
Mustawfī Revenue accountant.
Nawrūz Persian New Year festival (21 or 22 March); also a personal name.
Nizārī One who believed that at the time of the Fatimid dynastic crisis in 487/1094, Nizār was the rightful Ismāʿīlī *imām*.
Nöker Comrade, follower, in Mongol society.
Qāḍī Islamic judge.
Qalān Mongol tax of uncertain character.
Qanāt Underground water channel, usually for irrigation purposes.
Qiyāma The Resurrection.
Qizilbash "Red-heads": the Türkmen tribal followers of the Ṣafawid order.
Qūbchūr Mongol tax on flocks and herds; poll-tax.
Qullar Members of the Ṣafawid *ghulām* (q.v.) cavalry.
Qurchī Member of the small permanent military force of the early Ṣafawid shāhs.
Quriltai Mongol assembly of notables.
Raʿāyā Subjects, peasants.
Ramaḍān Ninth month of the Islamic year, during which Muslims fast from sunrise to sunset.
Ṣadr Head of the Shīʿī religious institution in the early Ṣafawid period.
Ṣāḥib-dīwān Minister of finance; title used for the chief minister during the Ilkhanid period.
Shahāda The Muslim profession of faith.
Shaḥna Military governor.
Shamanism Traditional religious beliefs of the steppe peoples.
Sharīʿa The Holy Law of Islam.
Shaykh Literally "old man": a Muslim, especially *ṣūfī*, religious leader.
Shīʿa Literally "party" (of ʿAlī, Muḥammad's cousin and son-in-law): those Muslims who believed that the headship of the Islamic community rightfully belonged to the Prophet's descendants.
Ṣūfī A Muslim mystic.
Sulṭān A title of Saljūq and subsequent rulers.
Sunnī The majority grouping in Islam: those who claimed to follow the tradition (*sunna*) of the Prophet.
Suyūrghāl Literally "favour", "reward" (Mongolian): a form of *iqṭāʿ* (q.v.).
Tāj "Crown": the twelve-gored cap worn by the Qizilbash (q.v.) followers of the Ṣafawids.
Tamghā Mongol tax on commercial transactions.

Taqiyya Tactical dissimulation in matters of Islamic belief, especially among Shīʿīs.
Taʿzīya Shīʿī passion play.
Tiyūl A form of *iqṭāʿ* (q.v.).
Tümen Ten thousand; a Mongol military formation, nominally 10,000 strong.
Tūpchī Artilleryman.
Twelvers Shīʿīs who accept a line of twelve infallible *imāms*, beginning with ʿAlī and ending with Muḥammad al-Mahdī, who disappeared *c.* 264/878 but is expected to return.
ʿUlamāʾ (sing. *ʿālim*) Scholars in the Islamic religious sciences.
ʿUrf Customary law.
Uṣūlī Shīʿī theological school which favoured the use of *ijtihād* (q.v.).
Wakīl Deputy, especially of the shāh during the early Ṣafawid period; title assumed by Karīm Khān Zand.
Wālī Governor.
Waqf Islamic endowment, usually for a religious or charitable purpose.
Wazīr Chief minister.
Yām Mongol postal-courier system.
Yarghuchi Mongol judge.
Yarlīgh Edict (Ilkhanid period).
Yāsā Mongol decree, law, custom.

Genealogical Tables

Medieval Persia 1040–1797

1 The Great Saljūqs

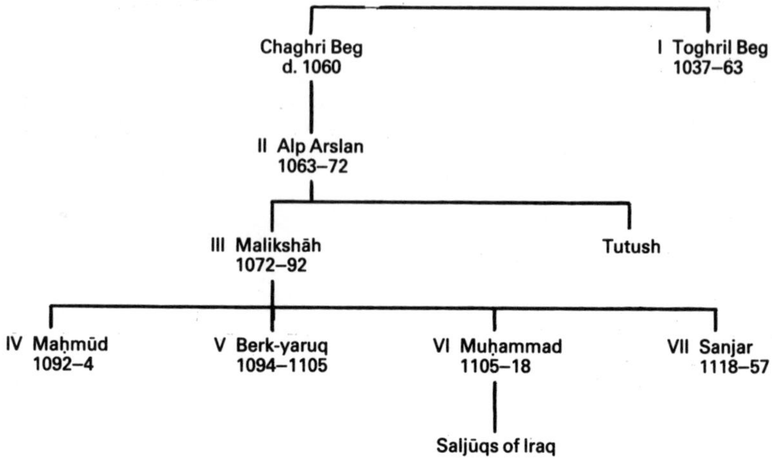

2 The Īlkhāns

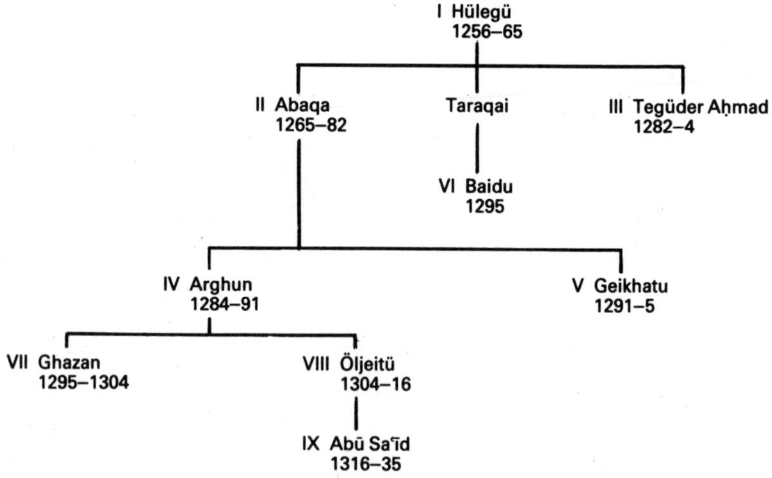

3 The Timurids

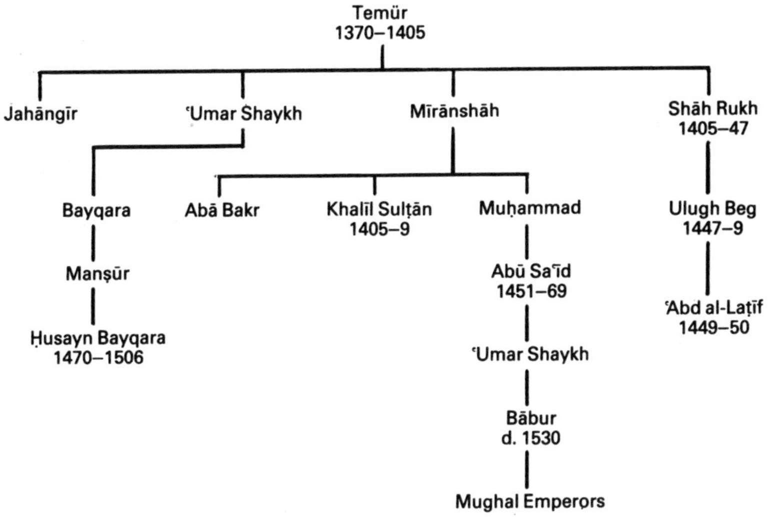
Temür
1370–1405
Jahāngīr
ʿUmar Shaykh
Mīrānshāh
Shāh Rukh
1405–47
Bayqara
Abā Bakr
Khalīl Sulṭān
1405–9
Muḥammad
Ulugh Beg
1447–9
Manṣūr
Abū Saʿīd
1451–69
ʿAbd al-Laṭīf
1449–50
Ḥusayn Bayqara
1470–1506
ʿUmar Shaykh
Bābur
d. 1530
Mughal Emperors

4 The Ṣafawids

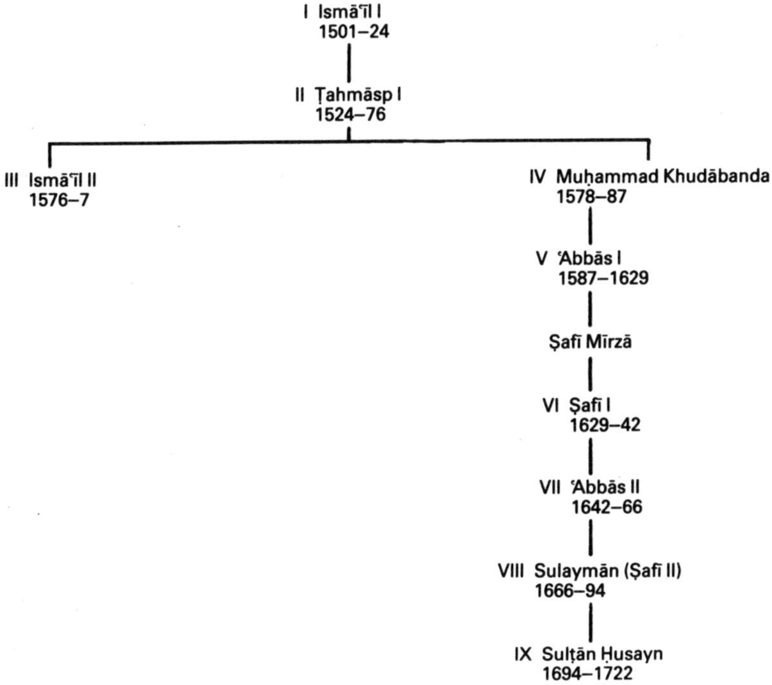
I Ismāʿīl I
1501–24
II Ṭahmāsp I
1524–76
III Ismāʿīl II
1576–7
IV Muḥammad Khudābanda
1578–87
V ʿAbbās I
1587–1629
Ṣafī Mīrzā
VI Ṣafī I
1629–42
VII ʿAbbās II
1642–66
VIII Sulaymān (Ṣafī II)
1666–94
IX Sulṭān Ḥusayn
1694–1722

Map

General map of the region

ARAL SEA
U S S R
WĀRAZM
FARGHĀNA
R. Oxus (Āmū Dar yā)
R. Zarafshān
Bukhārā
Samarqand
CHINA
TRANSOXANIA
R. Panj (Oxus, Āmū Daryā)
Tirmiz
Marv
R. Murghāb
Balkh
Mazār-i Sharīf
shhad
TUKHĀRISTĀN
HINDU KUSH
āpūr
BACTRIA
Harāt
Kābul
Harī Rūd
AFGHANISTAN
Ghazna
Farah
R. Hilmand
SĪSTĀN
Qandahār
Zaranj
PAKISTAN
R. Indus
BALŪCHISTĀN
RĀN
ULF OF OMAN

Index

Cairo, 42, 44, 60, 68
calendar, Mongol, 54
caliphate, theory and practice of, 16, 17, 18, 23, 27, 43, 50
calligraphy, 95, 99
Capuchins, 140
Carmelites, 140
Caspian Sea, 4, 21, 23, 34, 44, 57, 77, 95, 107, 113, 136
cataphracts, 12
Cathars, 10
Cathay, 47
Caucasus, Caucasians, 60, 109, 110, 117, 129, 134, 135, 146, 148, 150
cavalry, 6, 12, 23, 28, 48, 54–5, 87, 92, 116, 117, 135
Central Asia, 2, 5, 10, 12, 19, 21, 25, 26, 29, 33, 34, 38, 42, 47, 48, 51, 56, 59, 60, 63, 67, 74, 85, 90, 93, 95, 97, 139, 146
Chaghatai, 59, 85
Chaghatai Turkish language, 98, 100
Chaghatais, Chaghatai Khāns, khanate, 63, 74, 85, 86, 87, 92, 114
Chaghri Beg, 26, 28
Chahār Bāgh, Iṣfahān, 138
Chāldirān, battle of, 116–17, 118, 122, 125
cha'o (paper currency), 70
Chardin, Sir John, 140, 147, 148
Charles I of England, 140
chess, 93, 94
Chihil Sutūn, Iṣfahān, 148
Chin Dynasty, 47, 52, 56
China, 12, 47, 52, 53, 55, 56, 59, 60, 62, 63, 65, 70, 81, 88, 91, 119
Chinese Central Asia, 47
Chinese language, 48
Chingiz Khān, 48, 49, 51, 52, 54–8, 59, 66, 73, 79, 80, 83, 85, 86, 88, 89, 90, 91, 92, 93, 95, 99, 100, 101, 102, 151
Chopan, 78
Chopanids, 78, 83
Christianity, 10, 14, 15, 45, 47, 69, 72, 73, 77, 147, 149
  Armenian, 139, 140
  Greek Orthodox, 14
  Jacobite, 65
  Nestorian, 53, 56, 64–5
  Roman Catholic, 53
Chūha Sulṭān Takkalū, 124, 125
Circassians, 129, 130, 134
cities in Persia, 4–5, 57
Clavijo, 4
climate, Persian, 4
coinage, 20, 23, 24, 48, 70, 75, 103
Colbert, 140
Constantinople, 13, 14, 91, 116, 154
conversion
  to Buddhism, 53, 56, 65
  to Christianity, 53, 64, 65, 73
  to Islam, 15, 22, 53, 61, 64, 65, 68, 72–4, 81, 107, 129
  to Shīʿism, 16, 120–2, 150
Coptic language, 14
Cossacks, 113, 148
Cotton, Sir Dodmore, 140
crusaders, crusader states, 42, 43, 45, 60, 64
Ctesiphon, 9, 13, 17
Cyrus the Great, 6, 7, 8

Damascus, 16, 17, 42, 60, 91
Dāmghān, 114
Dandānqān, battle of, 22, 26
Dār al-Islām, 25, 26, 43, 47, 52, 53, 58
Dārā (Darius III), 8
Dargāh, 35–6
Darī language, 2
Darius the Great, 7, 8
darughas, 93
Dasht-i Kavīr, 4
Dasht-i Lūṭ, 4
Daylam, Daylamites, 23
Delhi, 90, 100, 154
Delhi sultanate, 18, 48, 90
della Valle, Pietro, 135, 140
deserts, 3–4
Deutschland, 1
dihqāns, 12, 16, 19
Diocletian, 12
Dīwān, 36–7
Dīwān al-inshāʾ waʾl-ṭughrā, 37
Dīwān al-zamām waʾl-istīfāʾ, 37
Dīwān-i ʿarḍ, 37
Dīwān-i ishrāf-i mamālik, 37
Dīwān-i mamālik, 136
Diyārbakr, 104, 112, 133
drafts, see *barāt*
du Mans, Raphael, 140
Durrānī empire, 155

East India Company
  Dutch, 139
  English, 139
Edessa, 43
Egypt, 7, 13, 14, 15, 18, 19, 23, 43, 44, 60, 63, 68, 69, 73, 74, 91, 104, 116
England, 96, 140
Englestan, 2
English, 1, 133, 139, 140
English language, 2

Mosul, 43
Mubāriz al-Dīn, 83
Mughal Empire, Mughals, 100, 127, 133, 144, 146, 154
Mūghān, 153
Mughulistān, Mughuls, 85, 86, 89, 90, 114
Muḥammad (Prophet of Islam), 2, 13, 16, 147, 159
Muḥammad (Saljūq sulṭān), 41
Muḥammad al-Mahdī, 120
Muḥammad Ḥasan Khān Qājār, 156
Muḥammad Khudābanda, 130–1, 141
Muḥammad Shaybānī, 113, 114, 115, 125
mujtahids, 147, 148, 149, 160
mullā-bāshī, 149
mullās, 140
muqṭaʿ, 38–40
al-Muqtafī, caliph, 43
Murād Aq-Qoyunlu, 106, 112
Murshid Qulī Khān Ustajlū, 131, 134
Mushaʿshaʿ, 113
mushrif-i mamālik, 37
al-Mustaʿlī, caliph, 44
al-Muʿtaṣim, caliph, 18
mustawfī, 37, 76
mustawfī al-mamālik, 37
Muzaffarids, 83–4, 89

Nādir Shāh, 122, 152–5, 156, 157, 158
Naimans, 56
Naqsh-i Rustam, 9, 10
Naqshbandī order, 97
al-Nāṣir, caliph, 43, 49
al-Nāṣir, Yūsuf, 60
Naṣīr al-Dīn Ṭūsī, 65
Naṣr, 21
nationalism, 6, 7, 20
Nawrūz (*amīr*), 72
Nawrūz (New Year), 10, 24
nerge, 55
New Julfā, 138
New Persian, *see* Persian language
Nicholas IV, pope, 65
Nihāwand, battle of, 14
Nīshāpūr, 5, 26, 34, 57
Niẓām al-Dīn Shāmī, 99
Niẓām al-Mulk, 11, 29–32, 35, 36–7, 41, 44
Nizār, 44
Nizārīs, *see* Ismāʿīlīs
nöker, 53, 54, 56, 86
nomadism, nomads, 6, 11, 26, 28, 30, 33, 34, 35, 51, 52, 55, 63, 67, 68, 73, 81, 85, 86, 87, 89, 90, 91, 101, 102, 116, 119, 128, 156
North Africa, 19, 91

Ögedei, 59, 63, 119
Oghuz, *see* Ghuzz
Oirat Mongols, 72, 114
Old Testament, 8
Öljeitü, 65, 68, 73, 76, 77–8, 138
Orkhon river, 52
Ottoman Empire, Ottomans, 31, 75, 91, 100, 102, 105, 106, 109, 110, 112, 115, 116–18, 119, 120, 124, 125, 127, 130, 132, 133, 134, 139, 144, 149, 153, 154, 157
Oxus river, 26, 48, 98, 115, 154
Özbeg Khān, 113
Özbegs, 97, 98, 99, 100, 113–14, 115, 120, 124, 125, 126, 127, 130, 131, 132, 133, 134, 144, 146, 149, 154

Pahlavi dynasty, 24
Pahlavī language, 2, 24
painting
  Chinese, 82
  Persian, 82, 98, 99, 129
Pakistan, 9
Palestine, 42, 60
Pānīpat, battle of, 100
Parī Khān Khānum, 130
Parsa, 1
Parsees, 10
Parthians, 8, 9
Pashto language, 2
Peacock Throne, 154
peasants, Persian, 5, 6, 12, 50, 67, 74, 80, 81, 135
Peking, 56
"People of the Book", 15
Persepolis, 9
Persian Gulf, 4, 23, 133, 137, 139, 150
Persian language, 1, 2–3, 14, 15, 21, 48, 140
Persis, 1
Peshawar, 154
Petrushevsky, I. P., 84
Pīr Muḥammad, 95
poetry
  Persian, 2, 21, 22, 98, 99, 103
  Turkish, 110
polo, 138
popes, 27, 65, 74
population of Persia, 3, 32–3
Portuguese, 125, 133, 139
prayer, Muslim, 10, 23
Prester John, 47

Qābūs-nāma, 11
Qāḍī ʿĪsā, 106, 107
qāḍīs, 36, 75, 121